D0116360

ROME, at HOME

Also by

SUZANNE DUNAWAY
. . . .

NO NEED TO KNEAD:
Handmade Italian Breads
in Ninety Minutes

ROME, at HOME

. . . .

THE SPIRIT OF *LA CUCINA ROMANA*
IN YOUR OWN KITCHEN

Written and Illustrated by

SUZANNE DUNAWAY

CONTRA COSTA COUNTY LIBRARY

Broadway Books

3 1901 03509 9029

BROADWAY

ROME, AT HOME. Copyright © 2004 by Suzanne
Dunaway. All rights reserved. No part of this book may be
reproduced or transmitted in any form or by any means,
electronic or mechanical, including photocopying,
recording, or by any information storage and retrieval
system, without written permission from the publisher. For
information, address Broadway Books, a division of
Random House, Inc.

PRINTED IN CHINA

BROADWAY BOOKS and its logo, a letter B bisected on
the diagonal, are trademarks of Random House, Inc.

Visit our website at www.broadwaybooks.com

First edition published 2004

Book design by Stark Design
Illustrated by Suzanne Dunaway

Library of Congress Cataloging-in-Publication Data

Dunaway, Suzanne
    Rome, at home : the spirit of *la cucina romana* in your
own kitchen / written and illustrated by Suzanne
Dunaway.—1st ed.
      p.   cm.
    Includes bibliographical references and index.
    I. Cookery, Italian.   2. Cookery—Italy—Rome
(Province)   I. Title.
TX723.D85 2003
641.5945'632s—dc21   2003052130

ISBN 0-7679-1377-9

CONTRA COSTA COUNTY LIBRARY

10 9 8 7 6 5 4 3 2 1

for Nicole and Simon
and their father, my life's sustenance

Contents

Contorni

Pane, Focaccia, e Pizza

Dolci

ACKNOWLEDGMENTS

Grazie to:

Betsy Amster, fastest agent in the West, for opening doors

Jennifer Josephy, *una redattrice bravissima*

Christine Benton, copyeditor, for her superb attention to detail

Allyson Giard, for her steady calm

Elizabeth Rendfleisch and Jean Traina, for a design as inviting as *la cucina romana*

Gabriella Piga, for an unexpected and nourishing friendship through which we share our love of Rome and *la cucina romana*

Maria Teresa Bolacchi, for *sostegno* and moonshine

Nicole Dunaway, for taming the dread double consonants, for a pinch of sugar, and for four more reasons to cook good food

Julian, David, Lisa, and Oli, for letting me eat off their plates

Simon and Ciallo, for good palates

Manuel Spatafora, a *buona forchetta,* a sage friend in food, and more

Beatrice, Giovanni, and Gerardo Panichi, for a quarter of a century of hospitality and knowledge at their table

Paola Gallenga, for a memorable Roman feast

Annalisa Angelini, for sending Frate Barbanera just in time

Everyone at Buona Forchetta for keeping the office running, the dough rising, and the customers happy

Anabel and Graham Baker, for space to spread out in Suffolk, and a still life of figs

All who sit at our table and share the MOL

My husband, as supportive as the stones of the Pantheon

In memoriam: Sandy Graham, Igi Polidoro, Felix Landau

AUTHOR'S NOTE

La cucina romana is based on one premise: *simple is better.* To master Roman cooking, buy the freshest, tastiest ingredients possible and then get out of the way. This book is about my love for Rome and Romans and how a city and its memorable food went straight to my heart and stayed for more than thirty years.

I started cooking at the age of five, when my mother gave me a lasting gift: scraps of her buttery pie dough to keep me out of her hair. With those small pieces of dough I discovered that cooking for me was as natural as breathing, and I went on to start Buona Forchetta Hand Made Breads in my home kitchen, a business I ran with my husband for almost ten years. As a cooking teacher with students on every level, I can assure you that simple Roman cooking is easily accessible to any cook and will bring great joy into your life.

If you are used to cooking from books with complicated recipes that could have been simpler, if you cry when exotic dishes fail, feel frustrated about the time it takes to prepare dinner for eight, and still have a passion for cooking, read on. Your luck is about to change.

Do not be seduced or intimidated by trendy foods. Get out a pasta pot, a skillet, a few basic ingredients, and a bottle of wine. *La cucina romana* will brighten your kitchen and your spirits, and cooking will never be the same.

a love
affair
....
with Rome

Roma, mai in una vita.—In a lifetime, one could not know Rome.

If one must see Venice and die, then one sees Rome and lives. Each time I leave Rome, a piece of my heart stays at Canova, my corner café near the Piazza del Popolo, or refuses to leave the outdoor markets at Campo dei Fiori, Ponte Milvio, and Testaccio. I am as smitten with Rome as any Italian teenager with his first *amore,* and my love grows deeper with each bite of fresh mozzarella and each whiff of autumn's white truffles. My good fortune is to have met and married a man who lived and worked in Rome for ten years and whose passion for the city and *la cucina romana* merged with mine so completely. My appetite for Rome was nourished over almost three decades, as I saw the city's eternal beauty through his eyes and those of his ex-wife and two Roman children.

The powerful sense of belonging that draws me to Rome began on a graduation trip to Europe that started in Copenhagen, where, as I stepped for the first time on European soil, I was suddenly, unquestionably, home, almost fainting from the emotion. I knew very little of Europe, but it was as clear as grappa to me that somewhere on this suddenly familiar continent I would find my heart's desire. Subsequent events in my life would certainly lead me closer to Rome, even if with a few detours.

Just after college, a girlfriend and I, carefree and adventurous, picked up a lavender Fiat roadster (christened "The Grape") in Florence, then headed south to Viareggio, where we, by chance, encountered two very compelling reasons to stay: a pair of handsome brothers we met on the beach that day. It was our great luck to rent a newly vacant apartment belonging to a Milanese doctor whose Roman wife became our landlady and my instant role model. She was of a certain age, dressed in a pale cappuccino-colored designer suit, the top button of which was open just enough to allow a glimpse of exquisite lingerie and ample bosom. Signora Domenici was not like anyone I had known in Houston. Lifting one perfectly shaped eyebrow, she coolly appraised our scandalous miniskirts, long straight hair, and white patent leather boots for a full two minutes. She then took the rent in cash and clicked off on her three-inch Italian heels. We never met again, but if she was a Roman, then Rome would be my city.

I had learned to cook as a child, with my mother's expert teaching followed by years spent plowing through *Gourmet*'s cookbooks Volume I and II, but in Viareggio my Italian food education was begun. Our inexperience was evident—we almost gave away a whole prosciutto sent us by my parents for Christmas because we thought it too big and salty! The handsome brothers introduced us to prosciutto's affinity for mozzarella, melons, and figs, which of course kept the jewel of Parma securely in our own larder.

From all this bounty we gained a few much-needed pounds and were followed by men on the street, whispering "bona," a word in *romanesco* (Roman slang) meaning "voluptuous and sexy." We even began letting our underwear peek out of our blouses.

A year and half later we bid farewell to our outdoor market, our butcher, and what would become the bittersweet nostalgia of youth and returned, each to her own reality and the brothers to theirs. With a longing that still recurs with each departure from Italy, I headed home.

I took back to my kitchen my newfound knowledge of prosciutto and a yearning to return that spanned too many years. I never dreamed that I would be taking daily morning walks to a high terrace over the Piazza del Popolo, gazing whenever I wished over the sumptuous feast spread out before me in all seasons. I could not know then that the fountains of Rome would become sweet voices, murmuring to me to return again and again, and that I would begin hundreds of Roman mornings at my favorite bar, Scapi, and be greeted year after year by the exuberant owner and the *barista* with his broad smile.

Now, before I step through the door, he pushes the button for my usual tiny cup of *caffè macchiato,* meaning "spotted" or "stained" with milk, forming a little heart of coffee on the foam. The lovely *caffè* one finds only in Rome is drunk, almost always standing up at the bar, from cups or glasses, *macchiato* or *ristretto,* meaning concentrated almost to a syrup. For reasons I am still trying to figure out, women do not order *caffè al vetro* (in a glass), but I defy the rule, loving to watch the hot foam swirling through the deep chocolate brown of the coffee. The first moments of a Roman day, of course, begin with beauty.

As I eavesdrop on shop girls having their cappuccino and *cornetto*—the Italian croissant, staple of all brief Roman breakfasts—I follow the custom of never drinking cappuccino after about 10:00 A.M. and never, never at lunch or dinner. A Roman cannot understand this heresy, for who would wish to down a large cup of milk and coffee after savory antipasto, pasta, meat, salad, and fruit? The word *espresso* is not used in Italy, simply because it means only one thing, *caffè*—order "*caffè*" as the Romans do if you'd rather not stand out like pink plaid Bermuda shorts. The sliver of lemon peel is an American invention and finds a better home in the Torta di Ricotta (page 273), where it is needed, instead of tainting a creamy, intense elixir of freshly ground beans with citrus oil. *Caffè corretto* ("corrected" with booze) is another matter. A little shot of grappa in the *caffè* every now and then can't hurt you and only livens up the cup, especially in winter. I pour the last of my red wine into my after-dinner *caffè,* a habit, I must admit, I learned from a Neapolitan but which tastes just as good in Rome.

The sexy exchange between the beauties and the *barista* is Rome's daily language, spoken by all. Flirting, to Romans, is just another necessary form of nourishment. The other *barista* continues his morning chores, rhythmically slicing, with a long flat knife, a tray of fresh *michette,* the hollow, crusty little rosettes of bread made only in Rome, to be filled for lunch with prosciutto and mozzarella. Their only competition are Rome's tantalizing *tramezzini,* the famous triangular sandwiches made on thin slices of soft white bread trimmed of crust and filled with such delectable combinations as mozzarella and tomato, tuna and artichokes, hard-boiled eggs and tomatoes, or any whimsical pairing the *barista* might invent. These addictive temptations are stacked as carefully and artfully in their glass cases as the bricks in a Roman arch, then draped for longevity with a spotless damp white towel in the same way southern matrons preserve their famous tomato sandwiches. *Tramezzini* are impossible to resist, even if just after a *cornetto.* I take my leave just as my talented *barista,* delicately and attentively, whips up a fresh batch of mayonnaise in a blender for the day's *tramezzini* and panini. I wonder what he whips up in his own kitchen.

Rome's famous rosette (or michette)
with prosciutto and mozzarella

The same artistry and care are given to even the smallest event. In the open market my flower vendor will take ten minutes to gift-wrap a 5-euro bunch of tulips as if it were going to Sophia Loren or the pope, weaving ribbons and lengths of straw through perfectly formed folds in hand-printed paper, creating one of his many daily masterpieces. The time spent by Roman merchants on choosing the right paper design, the right ribbon color, the intricate details of wrapping anything from paper clips to panettone, is awe-inspiring. I once received the gift of a small picture frame encased so beautifully that, for a few days, it hung on the wall in all its finery.

On my hundreds of walks down via della Croce to the open market, I must always stop to say *"buon giorno"* and give a coin to the same grizzled-bearded old homeless man who, along with other elderly or unfortunate inhabitants, is supported and nurtured by the neighborhood. From my first day in Rome, he has been on the corner near my bar, engaging everyone in lively if not completely comprehensible conversation or quietly studying the world as it passes by. A large piece of my day will be missing when he is gone.

I linger over greetings to now-familiar shopkeepers as they clean their windows with an alcohol smelling of grappa—I keep a bottle in L.A. to remind me of my lovely Roman mornings. Along with that pungent smell, fragrant smoke from wood-burning pizza ovens turns every corner with me along with the ever-tempting scent of ground coffee wafting out from such famous coffee roasters *(torrefazione)* as Caffé Colombiano and Sant'Eustachio.

Even fortified with a *tramezzino* against the danger of shopping while hungry, I can still go completely *pazza* in Rome's magnificent outdoor markets. I love my daily shopping ritual, which takes place right around the corner from our apartment and which is inspiration for new dishes.

My beef butcher and pork market are just down the street from the chicken purveyor, and although I might have to hit the big *supermercato* for larger quantities of staples and paper goods, even those may be found in the compact little neighborhood shops called *alimentari,* which carry everything from bread, pasta, and cans and jars of necessities such as capers and tuna to Digerseltz, Italy's favorite antacid.

Although I am fortunate to have the Santa Monica Farmers' Market, bountiful and beautiful, I still dream of another of my favorite markets—a seemingly endless stretch of booths along the Tiber at the Milvian Bridge, where Constantine dispatched Maxentius, paving the way for Christianity. Clothing, scarves, and embroidered linens hang from booth struts like colored banners among the *salumi* and prosciutti, and wondrous bargains abound if you take time to browse.

The Roman housewives and I have our favorite stalls at which we have shopped for decades and will continue to do so. One does not abandon tradition and friendship without considering consequences, and a change in loyalty, an indiscretion that might take months or a lifetime to repair, does not go unobserved. I avoid the whole dilemma by happily patronizing all.

Over the years, market vendors have been my best teachers, passing out such tidbits as how to air-dry meats in the proper way, how long to stir polenta, the best days to buy fish and mozzarella, where the best fruits or vegetables are grown (near Rome), and philosophic comments about the world of Italian soccer (this often heated dialogue can last most of the day if I'm not careful), Rome's place in the universe (number one), and where politics are headed (down the drain).

Rome's feast continues at the vast covered market in via Guido Reni, where our truffle purveyor presides over his heady, earthy wares of *tartufi bianchi* and porcini. The sweet and sharp smell of pepper-studded pecorino and the creamy dairy smells of *caciotta*, a delicate cheese from nearby farms, hang heavy in the air. The intoxicating perfume of broad-leafed basil, oregano, arugula, and *mentuccia*, the Roman mint, are almost more seductive than *caffè* and window cleaner.

Although most vendors prefer not to have their wares handled, my repeated visits and a friendly chat with each eventually made me one of the cognoscenti, left alone to sniff melons, gently press peaches, and bag my treasures at will. I learned quickly that a casual *"Sto guardando"* ("I'm just looking") or *"Posso scegliere?"* ("May I choose my own?") would help me move at my own speed through markets without offending. A perceptive merchant will see that you are purposeful and serious about food and will not stand in the way of your pleasure at planning the most important times of the day. After all, his demeanor will say, you and I share the same pursuit of good tastes and what makes life worth living.

Testaccio, one of Rome's oldest neighborhoods, named after a mountain of broken shards from amphorae (a kilometer in circumference, 150 feet high) that arrived for three centuries on ships at the nearby port on the Tiber, is the site of a market that covers more than a city block and can take several hours to visit thoroughly. Standing sentry behind her booth, the tomato seller with cheeks like her wares offers me suggestions on what to do with more than twenty shapes and sizes of the mainstay of *la cucina romana:* tiny deep red Sicilian cherry tomatoes called *pomodori di Pachino;* rich, meaty, dense globes the size of small grapefruit called *cuore di drago* (dragon hearts); tomatoes with the name costoluto genovese that look like little Cinderella coach pumpkins; and plump plum tomatoes for a perfect pasta sauce.

Near the market, on the via Mastro Giorgio, is da Felice, a legendary trattoria where actors such as Italy's beloved Roberto Benigni *(Life Is Beautiful)* often have lunch. The crotchety owner, who can be even more contrary if you stop at two courses, serves huge bowls of Bucatini alla Gricia (page 120), mostly to regulars.

At the open market in Campo dei Fiori, the heart of one of Rome's most raucous, lively neighborhoods, I visit a particular mushroom vendor for intensely flavored porcini, found and dried in Calabria by his wife, who, without fail, adds an extra handful to my already generous kilo. Next to her stand are sensual, curvy little eggplants for Caponata (page 40); dark green and purple artichokes destined to be steamed with mint or deep-fried (Carciofi alla Giudia, page 42); and dried red peppers, no bigger than teardrops, with the taste of sweet pimientos lurking under their heat. These tiny fireballs add the "angry" to Penne all'Arrabbiata (page 117) and the zing to Spaghetti all'Aglio, Olio, e Peperoncino (page 115), but it is the lively camaraderie among so many with the same purpose that adds the real spice to my day.

I return again and again to my familiar tiny neighborhood market in the via Bocca di Leone at the corner of via della Croce near the Piazza di Spagna, which occupies a space no bigger than two parked Ferraris and yet contains everything a cook could want. It is also close to home, and I have ninety-two steps to climb! My husband buys salmon-colored pepper-scented Sonya roses, 8 euros an armload, to place on the table in the middle of our apartment, celebrating yet another return. In summer the vendor's enormous buckets are filled with plate-sized sunflowers, even more roses, and of course daily, in all seasons, chrysanthemums for the graves of dearly departed, never for gifts or inside the house, as one might end up in the same place.

As I stand awestruck yet again, unable to decide among this particular morning's riches, the tiny lady who has been my morning connection to the evening's menu for so long at once sees my consternation and begins to offer her own suggestions.

"Ah, signora," she greets me, "what are you cooking today? Just look at the sweet red onions and giant Sicilian lemons to make an antipasto, and don't forget *un bel melone* for your prosciutto." I am made to feel that her wares are arranged just for me, an honored guest among her humble boxes and crates. She mixes three kinds of tiny lettuce leaves in a bag, then reminds me that one can embellish a salad with a fennel bulb and some arugula. I buy the peppery wild arugula with skinny leaves and will eat it by itself with only dark, pungent oil and a sprinkle of salt. My love for this spicy green is perhaps exceeded only by my passion for fresh truffles or drinking from the fountains of Rome. Our transaction ends with my purchase of several flawless red and yellow bell peppers for Peperoni con Fagioli e Tonno (page 52), and when I tell her that I have a *tartufo* (truffle) at home for my fettuccine, *fatte in casa,* she throws both hands in the air and exclaims how honored she is to have her wares accompany such a treasure.

For my fresh anchovies, I visit the fishmonger who sells out of the back of his truck, having put up a simple white table upon which boxes of the daily catch are set at angles for better viewing.

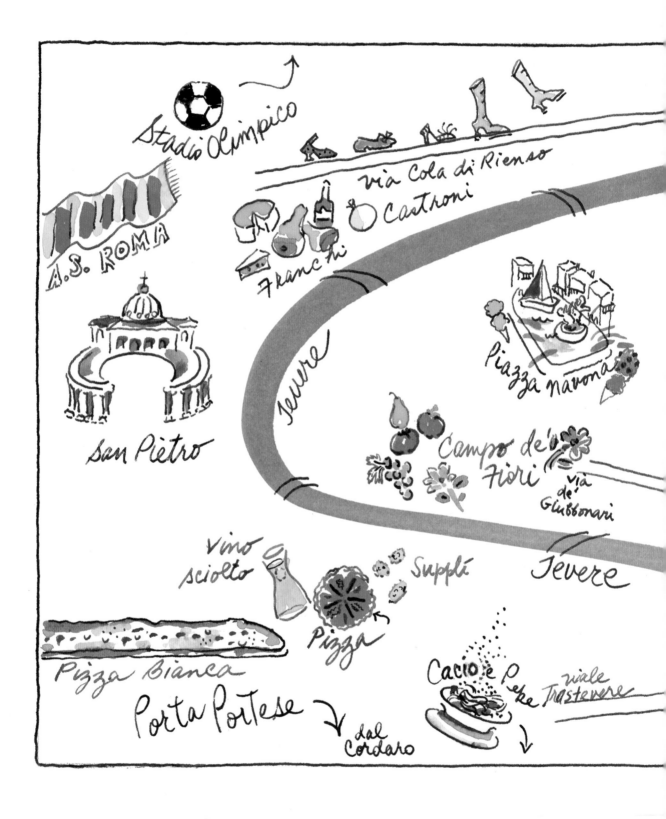

Tiny little octopi and minuscule shrimp smelling of the sea make me wish I had a pot of smoking olive oil and could make a Fritto Misto (page 159) right there in the street, no doubt drawing a crowd.

The larger, whole fish such as salmon and *branzino* are laid out, gleaming and bright-eyed, on cutting boards, and the eels are curled in silver bracelets, their tails neatly tucked into their mouths. Fresh anchovies are my downfall, however, and I buy a half kilo, thinking we will never be able to eat them all. I dip them in an olive oil batter (Pastella I or II, page 30), fry them crisp, eat them in minutes, and wish for more to marinate in oil and lemon.

In my zeal to be back in Rome's streets, I cannot resist via Cola di Rienzo, which leads all the way from the Tiber to the Vatican City. Here I visit two of Rome's largest and most exciting shops for *buone forchette,* those who love to eat, but not until I have worked my way through endless boutiques, visited corner street vendors and, my passion, the fifteen to twenty or so shoe shops scattered among the others. Castroni, my favorite gourmet food source, is a wonderland of coffees, confections, delicacies from every country, smoked salmon, caviar, truffle oils, chocolates—you name it. And if Castroni does not have it, Franchi, just up the street, will. I stop here to eat a perfect mozzarella at one of the little tables, trying not to be tempted by shelves of wine, cases of cheese from all over Italy, local *salumi* and prosciutti, fresh pasta, and some of the best take-out food in Rome.

I have, with much willpower, stopped taking Italy back home—coffee, truffle oil, wine, 20-pound pasta machines, guanciale—because of the many resources here in the States. It is much more fun to arrange your own little Rome, at home, with whatever is in your city, and it is certainly easier on your back.

It is my strong opinion that nowhere in Italy can one eat so consistently well as in Rome. Roman cooking stands apart because of the simplicity with which perfect ingredients are prepared: grilled, braised, fried, or eaten raw with a few drops of peppery olive oil and lemon. The Romans have a saying, *"Parla come mangi,"* romanesco for "Speak as you eat," which means "Speak as plainly as you would eat." This directness is at the heart and soul of the Rome experience and especially *la cucina romana.*

There are no "executive chefs" in Rome, only real cooks in the kitchen every day making real food, cooks who have been trained from childhood to appreciate simple flavors and textures and possessing the skill to make food emerge clean and pure, on a plain white plate, with no frills. Italians simply do not eat huge portions or eat between meals, with the occasional exception of the famous thin Pizza Bianca (page 231), topped only with olive oil and coarse salt, or a quick gelato in the late afternoon. "Appetite is the best sauce," as the Romans say, and it would be a sacrilege and counterproductive to dull a sharp one. In Rome, snacks are not prevalent.

It will be as simple for you to prepare almost any recipe from *la cucina romana* in your own kitchen as it is for a Roman cook. The only thing missing might be a glimpse of St. Peter's out the window or a high terrace from which to gaze at rooftops and the dramatic skyline of the famous pines of

Rome. But a table lit by candles or sun, surrounded by friends, small glasses of Frascati, or even a cat on a windowsill should not be difficult to arrange.

To embrace *la cucina romana* is to free your spirit from restrictions that are simply not relevant to such a clean, healthy cuisine. Romans are bemused by our obsession with diets, and the conclusion of most is that moderation in all things will take one into a grand old age. Italians live longer than we do, according to many surveys, despite their smog, cigarettes, infamous driving habits, and daily consumption of pasta and bread. The foods of *la cucina romana* will bring health and joy to your kitchen and delighted guests to your table. You might even find yourself oblivious to trendy diets and the latest food fads by which we are so assailed.

In Rome, I learn a little more on each visit how to live life with awareness of each moment, how to stroll, instead of rush, through my life. I have felt, from my first serendipitous visit to Italy, a deep and enduring accord with Romans, both ancient and modern, who speak as they eat, directly from their generous hearts.

Ne ammazza più la gola che la spada.—Gluttony kills more than the sword • Excellent ingredients are the foundation on which to build good cooking, and how fortunate we are in America to have such bounty! In most large cities there are small or large Italian markets full of De Cecco pasta (or other good brands made from hard wheat semolina), dried porcini, hot peppers, jars of capers, tuna packed in olive oil, sweet canned plum tomatoes, and bottles of pungent extra virgin olive oil. You don't need much more than these and a little fresh basil, a few vegetables, ripe fruit, and inexpensive wine to bring the flavors and smells of

the Roman kitchen

Rome to your kitchen every day. We eat very simply at our house. After years of perfecting beurre blanc, reducing huge quantities of stock to concentrates, and creating sixteen-layer chocolate tortes, I discovered Italy. Simplicity. Ease. More time spent at the table instead of in the kitchen. • I remember almost every meal I have had in Italy—a plain bowl of pasta and sugo enhanced by the soft shadows of a fragrant wisteria vine next to my table; a waiter's quick smile and suggestions; the delight of the cook when he saw that I was "making the little shoe" (*fare la scarpetta*), cleaning my plate with a little crust of bread. For me, long, complex dinners of intricately prepared delicacies at three-star restaurants pale beside a dish of perfect fresh pasta under its aromatic blanket of shaved truffles, or milk-fed lamb chops grilled over vine cuttings and seasoned only with salt and pepper. Am I lazy? Jaded? Or have I found at last that simplicity suits me best?

I believe you can cook world-class food at home without exhausting procedures and techniques, even though it is very pleasurable, now and then, to study more complex cuisines out of curiosity or simply to polish skills. *La cucina romana* is the kind of basic, rational cooking from the heart that follows Einstein's dictate: "Make things as simple as possible, but not simpler."

You will easily find the ingredients you need for most of the dishes in this book at any decent supermarket or, better yet, in your own backyard. I strongly advocate a pot or two of fresh herbs on every deck or terrace or, if possible, a small garden of tomatoes, arugula, parsley, basil, and such. After all, 30 pounds of tomatoes can be grown in a two-by-two-foot container! (See Sources and Seeds.) The main thing to remember is that fresh, healthful produce and the best meat, poultry, and fish that you can find will almost always produce good results when combined with discretion.

I sauté over medium heat and simmer over low heat. High heat is used only for heating oil for frying or to caramelize or reduce a sauce. Most recipes begin with extra virgin olive oil and few ingredients. Almost any good vegetable can be turned into a sauce or grilled and sprinkled with lemon juice and Parmesan or dipped in good olive oil. I use vegetables such as fresh cauliflower, zucchini (flowers attached), celery root, and beet slices, brushed with olive oil and roasted at 400°F for about 30 minutes, until caramelized, to accompany fish or chicken. Guests who say they detest beets end up eating the whole dish, and those who cringe at cauliflower always take second helpings. In trattorie, meat, poultry, and fish are served grilled or roasted with a few potatoes or other *contorni,* and desserts may be made easily, without fuss, in anyone's kitchen. Those resistant to stirring ice crystals during the freezing of ice cream (see Gelati and Sorbetti, pages 256 and 258) may want to indulge in La Glacière by Braun, a small, efficient ice cream maker that takes exactly 20 minutes to produce a perfectly smooth gelato, sorbetto, or granita.

Good olive oil, fresh vegetables, fruit, eggs, a few cans or jars of certain staple items, dry pasta or your own fresh noodles (Pasta all'Uovo, page 88), Parmigiano-Reggiano, and enough wine to start the conversation are ingredients enough for any simple but memorable meal. I keep all of the juices strained from steamed vegetables in a closed container in the refrigerator. At any one time, this magic potion might contain the elixir (and nutrients) from potatoes, spinach, carrots, broccoli, or sweet green peas, but keep in mind that when you use it you will have to adjust the salt in the recipe since the vegetable broth contains salt from its first go-around. I keep meat, chicken, and fish broth separately in small containers, savory springboards for my next menu. Any not used within a week may be frozen for the future. These concentrated reductions taste so much better than commercial ones and add a new dimension to something as simple as a good soup, pasta sauce, or even boiled potatoes, but their main purpose is to inspire you to create your own simple and direct combinations.

I always have a large package of salad greens in the fridge and an equally large bowl filled with beautiful seasonal fruit in my kitchen, even if only winter pears and apples are to be had. I would love to see children here reach for an apple, a pear, or some grapes, as do Roman kids, instead of high-fat, low-quality salty and sugary snacks. A bowl of nuts and a nutcracker are also found on most coffee tables in Roman houses, keeping company with many silver-framed photographs of the family. There is something so amiable and civilized about sitting around the table at the end of meal, cracking nuts and chatting over a last glass of wine, that I wonder why the practice never caught on here. Dinners used to be served from soup to nuts, remember? And most children love to crack nuts—at the very least, it will occupy them, like making grissini, for a good half hour!

Sugo in Italy means only one thing: tomato sauce, with or without meat. Although sugo is very good on the day it is to be eaten, it is also delicious made ahead of time and kept in the fridge for up to one week. I make my sugo, along with pesto (during basil season), mayonnaise (inspired by

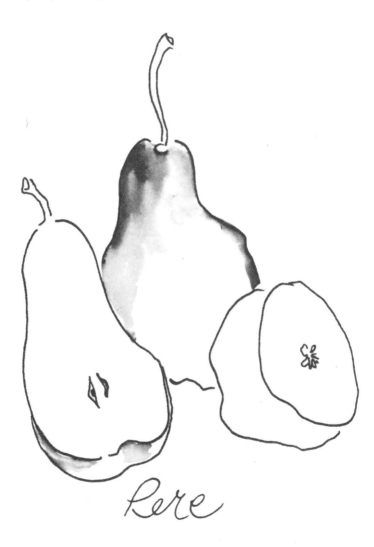

Pere

my mother, whose mayonnaise spoiled me for any other), and any stocks I might need, once every week or so. This gives me flexibility when entertaining or whipping up a quick dinner for two at the end of a twelve-hour workday. Just as I could not paint without basic colors, I could not possibly cook as well without these basic sauces on hand. A spoon of pesto in a soup lifts it from plain to ethereal, and a homemade tomato sauce may be used on pasta with a little cheese, in *penne all'arrabbiata,* and as an addition to many soups, stews, and sauces. Nothing that comes in a jar will be equal to your own, and with a food processor or blender in the kitchen you need devote only about 15 minutes to any one of these endeavors! That includes stocks, which, after the onion, carrot, and celery are chopped (a food processor does all the work), practically make themselves. All you have to do is skim a couple of times, strain, and freeze.

Any fear you might have of not being prepared for an onslaught of family or guests will disappear if you follow my suggestions for having sauces on hand and stocking your pantry and refrigerator with basics. Get out a box of pasta, put the water on to boil, chop some pancetta and onion, add your delicious fresh tomato sauce, pour the wine, and place bowls of Bucatini all' Amatriciana (page 120) before your astonished guests. Most of my pasta sauces may be made before the pasta water boils, which will give you plenty of time to cut up some fruit for dessert or even make gelato.

Roman Ingredients

ANCHOVIES *(Alici or Acciughe)*
Flat anchovies under olive oil, found in most supermarkets and Italian markets, are best, since the ones packed in salt tend to be larger and stiff and require boning. Anchovies are delicious for lunch on toast with butter, served with a few slices of fresh tomato and sweet onion. Fresh ones are used in *fritto misto* (sometimes called *frittura di paranza*).

ARTICHOKES *(Carciofi)*
Many farmers' markets sell fresh artichokes, but frozen hearts are surprisingly tasty. I keep a couple of boxes in my freezer for a quick pasta sauce or to throw into the pan with roast lamb when artichokes are not in season. I do not care for commercial marinated, flavored, or processed artichokes and do not use them in any recipe.

BACON *(Pancetta)*
Bacon comes plain or smoked, but I prefer plain since smoked meat can overpower a dish. Any Italian market will have pancetta, plain or with pepper, which is very zingy. Many parts of the country specialize in local cured meats, and a thick-sliced naturally cured bacon will do very nicely. Keep $^{1}/_{2}$ pound in the freezer for pasta sauces, stews, beans, and such.

BASIL (*Basilico*)

Almost all supermarkets now sell fresh herbs in packets. To grow your own in spring through summer, plant a few seeds in a pot and place in a sunny window (see Sources and Seeds).

BAY LEAF (*Alloro*)

Pick fresh if possible; otherwise buy dried. I am aghast at food writers who say to use two or three bay leaves in a recipe, especially a fish dish! They can ruin a meal just as effectively as lousy bread. But they can also impart imperceptible, subtle flavor, when used in *very* small amounts. The Italian laurel is not half as strong as ours, but even so, I suggest tiny pieces for any dish calling for bay leaf, about $1/2$ inch. Trust me. You want the ingredients to shine through, not the strong taste of bay leaf. If you can taste it, you've used too much.

BEANS, DRIED OR FRESH (*Fagioli Secchi o Freschi*)

I keep a pound or two of dried white Great Northern beans and brown pinto beans on hand, because I love them in place of meat and for their versatility. In summer you will find fresh shelling beans similar to cannellini or borlotto at farmers' markets. Buy a few pounds, call up a friend, and spend a sweet afternoon shelling and chatting. Freeze fresh beans in resealable plastic bags for winter dishes such as *pasta e fagioli* and hearty soups. You will find that beans and rosemary are a steady couple in Roman cooking, so be sure to have a rosemary plant on hand, too. I prefer white beans to the brown borlotto. Fresh beans will cook in less than an hour. Dried beans require precooking or soaking and more time.

BELL PEPPERS (*Peperoni*)

I simply do not use green bell peppers in anything, although I love the long green Italian peppers occasionally found here. Red, yellow, orange, and brown all are acceptable, but green bell peppers have little flavor and become soggy when roasted. When roasting peppers, keep in mind that those at the peak of the summer have a high sugar content. Sugar holds moisture, so that after the peppers are blackened, the skins separate easily from the flesh because of the steam that has been created between flesh and skin. Older peppers, or peppers out of season, are dry and tasteless because their sugar is depleted.

BROCCOLI (*Brocco*)

Italian broccoli are either broccoletti, small flowers on thin stems, or broccoli like ours with heavy stems and large heads. Both are cooked until very tender (no crisp broccoli in Rome) with olive oil, garlic, and hot peppers.

BUTTER (*Burro*)

The butter in my recipes is salted. I love Plugra, but any good sweet cream butter will do. If you prefer unsalted, adjust the salt in recipes ever so slightly upward. If you have access to great cream, just put it in your food processor and let it rip until it separates and becomes butter. Pour off the liquid, or whey, use it in breads or soups, and pack the remaining solids in a dish, adding a little salt if you like.

CAPERS *(Capperi)*
Used in many dishes. I buy large jars as they stay fresh in the fridge for weeks and are far more economical.

CHEESE *(Formaggi)*
Only Parmigiano-Reggiano is used in recipes and always grated except in Rotelle alla Romana (page 116). Buy center cuts if possible. A chunk of Parmesan and a firm Comice or Bosc pear is one of the world's most loving couples. Parmesan is the most important cheese in your larder, so buy only the best Parmigiano-Reggiano and have at least a cup on hand for recipes for four.

I often serve cheese and fruit in place of dessert, and I like to have at least three on hand. My first choice is mozzarella di bufala, if available, but this cheese, if you can find a good one, must be eaten quickly in its prime. In Rome, the best mozzarella is from a small food shop called Carilli on via di Torre Argentina, but it arrives from Caserta, the heart of mozzarella country, only on Monday, Wednesday, and Friday. Volpetti, on via della Scrofa, and Franchi, on via Cola di Rienzo, also sell wonderful mozzarella. In Lazio, the region of Italy around Rome, and several other areas of Italy, you will find a fresh cheese called *caciotta* with a delicate, sensual, buttery flavor and thin rind. It is the cheese we always take on picnics and then back to Los Angeles for a nostalgic dinner upon arrival. The famous pecorino Romano made from ewe's milk is very good with apples and pears, and a soft Taleggio, fontina, Gorgonzola, or goat cheese is on hand at most trattorie. If not, there is always a piece of very good Parmesan or ricotta salata.

CHOCOLATE *(Cioccolato)*
Use only the best dark chocolate, 65 percent or more cocoa. I love Valrhona. Inferior chocolate will always be tasted in a dessert.

FLOUR *(Farina)*
I am a baker, and naturally my pantry is full of various flours, but you will need only a good all-purpose unbleached white and one high-gluten flour, plus a small bag of rye and whole wheat if you intend to make some of my easy breads, and a small bag of semolina flour for pasta, although it is optional. Spelt flour is the most nutritious and may be added to focaccia dough very successfully. I mill my own from spelt grains, but that may be taking it a little too far for most cooks. Most health food stores have a vast array of good flours, among them Arrowhead, King Arthur, and Bob's Red Mill.

garlic peeling made easy!

GARLIC *(Aglio)*

Buy fresh—*never* dried, in powder, or in salts. Sweet, pure garlic is best eaten in spring until late summer. Period. Then, along with most things in nature, it gets the urge to procreate and starts sprouting little green shoots inside each clove, which can give off a strong acid taste and smell when cooked and especially when used raw. Before using, check for a sharp, acrid smell. Garlic should smell crisp and pure, even in winter, even with sprouts. Trim out the sprout with a paring knife and use only the firm white outside part of the garlic clove, or try to find the lovely red- or purple-streaked garlic in supermarkets that often comes from countries where the season is longer or opposite from ours, such as Mexico or Chile. Offset the effects of garlic with a sprinkling of parsley over the dish or a mouthful of parsley after the meal. A shot of milk helps, too, but nothing will help your dish if you use garlic that is ready for the compost pile. To peel garlic, treat yourself to one of the best inventions on the market, the Selandia peeler (see Sources and Seeds), which is nothing but a rubber tube into which you put unpeeled cloves and then roll up and down on a hard surface until you don't hear anything. Out come the peeled garlic cloves, just like rolling dice! To clean fingers of garlic odor, rub them against anything made of stainless steel, under water. The smell will disappear instantly.

FENNEL *(Finocchio)*

Often used in salads. This vegetable does not get enough attention in our country. Its feathers, as I call the green fronds, are delightful sprinkled on fish dishes or potatoes, and the bulb itself, braised in broth with onion and potatoes, or eaten raw with olive oil, adds variety to a menu. Fennel seed is known to be excellent for digestion; imagine what the whole plant can do!

HOT PEPPERS *(Peperoncini)*

I use only one small hot dried pepper in any dish for four to eight people. Remember to wash your hands thoroughly after crumbling a pepper into a dish. If you grind these peppers to sprinkle on pizza, one light sprinkle is enough. There are other tiny peppers, often from Mexico, slightly longer and with far less heat, which work as well, but I love the flavor of the Italian ones.

LEMONS (*Limoni*)

I am never without great piles of lemons or limes. A few drops of lemon juice will turn almost any dish with a pretty good flavor into an excellent one. Lemon juice enables you to use less salt, because it intensifies the existing salt in meat, fish, chicken, and vegetables. When you wonder why your soup is bland, even though you have been working on it for hours, try adding a squeeze of lemon juice. Lemon also removes fish smells and other odors from your hands and whitens nails.

LETTUCE (*Insalata*)

I think Romans would give up their window shopping rather than give up salad after a meal. Romans love their salad greens, especially *rughetta*, the Roman word for arugula. A salad after a meal cleanses the palate, soothes the stomach, and refreshes the spirit, not to mention the fact that a salad is a lovely vehicle for good olive oil and "making the little shoe." I combine medium-quality extra virgin olive oil and my 150-year-old vinegar made from a "mother" given to me by a man whose Sicilian grandmother started the whole thing when she was a young housewife. To make a salad you need four people: A spendthrift for the oil; a miser for the vinegar; a wise man for the salt; and a crazy man, a *pazzo*, to toss it. Keep that in mind when making salad and you'll always make a good one.

I first found my favorite salad green, arugula, growing wild in the ruins of Paestum, but barring a ruin in your neighborhood, both domestic and wild may be grown from seeds (see Sources and Seeds). Romaine, or Roman lettuce, is picked young and crisp and is one of the ingredients in Vignarola (page 219), a springtime dish of fava beans, peas, and lettuce.

NUTMEG (*Noce Moscata*)

Buy whole nutmeg, which is often used, grated, in ricotta fillings for pasta, on top of custards, and added to some meat dishes. I strongly suggest buying a nutmeg grater or using one of the new Microplane graters in various sizes.

NUTS (*Noci*)

Buy fresh in season, shelled or unshelled, fall and winter. Being a Texan, I keep Texas pecans in my freezer for desserts, but Romans use hazelnuts, walnuts, and pinoli. Hazelnuts are seasonal, so when you find them, buy a few packages and freeze them, as they tend to disappear from markets during the year. I serve nuts in the shell after dinner with cheese and fruit.

OLIVE OIL AND COOKING OILS

Buy the best extra virgin oil you can find for bruschette, soups, and salads. Buy a less expensive extra virgin olive oil for cooking, such as Montolivo (sold at our local Costco), Colavita, or Bertolli, found at most supermarkets across the country. Taste various brands at your market or specialty food shops and look for a peppery or sweet finish, whichever you prefer. I love the after-burn and distinct flavor of olives in a strong, cold-pressed oil. Olive oil does not go bad unless exposed to direct light or heat over time, but mine never sees the light of day long enough for that to happen. My favorites: Albereto, grown on Lorenza de Medici's estate, and any dark, green, peppery, first cold pressing from small growers in Umbria or Tuscany, but many other parts of Italy also produce excellent oil. The best way to taste olive oil is to go out in the country near Rome and visit a farm during the fall harvest and olive pressing. Take a loaf of *pane casereccio* (Rome's rustic bread baked in a wood oven) with you and dip into the vats of new oil right there on the spot.

Many trattorie and home cooks use sunflower oil for frying. I keep a bottle on hand, but I almost always end up using my less expensive olive oil just because I like the taste. Both are fine to use, but olive oil burns at a lower temperature, and there are some who feel that when burned olive oil is not good for your health. The debate goes on.

ONIONS *(Cipolle)*

One of the basic elements of a good stock, onions, like garlic, are seasonal. They, too, start procreating in autumn, and this can bring tears to your eyes. Onions become harsh in flavor and are less digestible than new spring bulbs. Take out the green, sprouting center, peel off the outer two layers, and use the rest. I have found, in choosing onions, that flat ones are tastier than round, except the large globes from Vidalia, Georgia, Maui, or Texas, all of which may be eaten like apples when first harvested. In autumn and winter, onions, like tulips, stay fresher in the refrigerator.

OREGANO *(Origano)*

Preferably grown fresh in a pot or your yard. I do not use oregano much at all, preferring fresh basil, lemon thyme, and parsley, but a true *pizza napoletana* has, in addition to anchovies, a few leaves of fresh oregano. I taste oregano (overused in many recipes) and immediately think of Italo-American food, not a bad thing in itself, but it is not authentic Italian food. In any case, I am staunchly against using dried herbs in cooking or salads, and I urge you to plant your own or scour your supermarkets for fresh ones.

PARSLEY *(Prezzemolo)*

I use the flat-leaf Italian parsley since I find it has a sweetness not found in curly parsley. In Roman cooking it is always used in dishes such as *spaghetti alle vongole, salsa verde,* and many soups and stews.

PASTA *(Pasta Asciutta)*

My pantry contains more pasta than most small grocery stores. My husband and I eat pasta almost every day for lunch, dried or fresh. I like De Cecco best but often buy certain shapes from Barilla and occasionally try out new brands. Still, De Cecco is my staple, and for specific sauces, I make my own fresh pasta (you will, too!). There are many kinds of handmade dry pastas, such as Latini, from companies that cater to the gourmet. I buy two or three boxes each of spaghetti, rotelle (wheels), farfalle (butterflies), penne, and ditalini (little fingers, short tubes) at any one time, but it disappears before you can say "sugo."

PINE NUTS *(Pinoli)*

Traditionally used in pesto (although I use *pistacchi* in mine), and when toasted, may be sprinkled over grilled eggplant or caponata. Pinoli may be used in pasta sauces calling for nuts, but because they are expensive, I tend to use other nuts instead. They are used frequently in desserts. Toast pinoli in a teaspoon of olive oil in a skillet over low heat, stirring constantly so as not to burn the nuts. They are ready when golden brown.

RICE *(Riso)*

Use arborio, carnaroli, or Roma (round-grain rice) for risotto. Risotto requires grains with a thick starch coating and slow absorption, able to stand up under simmering broth and much stirring, which form the creamy texture of a perfect risotto.

SALT *(Sale)*

Buy boxes of coarse sea salt for your pasta water and plain fine sea salt for everything else. I love the sound of coarse salt being ground over a bruschetta—or anything for that matter—so I keep a grinder on the table. Salt is now a gourmet item, and I seem to be acquiring a collection from France, Hawaii, Italy, and elsewhere, but I use a coarse Italian or La Baleine fine French sea salt for daily cooking. Expensive *fleur de sel,* the best French salt, I save for bruschette.

SALT PORK *(Cotenne di Prosciutto)*

Keep frozen or in small pieces for individual dishes. I love cooking with salt pork, especially in winter or when shelling beans are fresh in summer. A tiny bit goes a long way, and you must adjust the seasoning accordingly. Occasionally you will find authentic *guanciale* or pork cheek at an Italian market for use in many Roman pasta sauces or stews, but salt pork will be fine in its place. The other trick is to talk your local Italian market into selling you the very last bit of a whole prosciutto, the skinny leg end, to be used in Bucatini all'Amatriciana (page 120), Agnolotti di Carne (page 110), or to liven up any *sugo.*

SPELT *(Farro)*

The Roman army's power food. I am in love with this nutty, chewy grain. I grind it in a flour mill (one of the best gifts I have ever received!) and add it to my focaccia and bread dough. You can also use spelt flour for *pastella,* the batter used in fried dishes, or add a little to your fresh pasta dough. At Central Market in Texas, a whole rack is devoted to spelt bread products, and dried pasta containing spelt is sometimes available at Italian markets. Use farro in place of rotelle in Rotelle alla Romana (page 116) for a change from pasta.

TOMATOES *(Pomodori)*

Buy fresh and in cans. One day I shall write an article entitled "Peeled, Seeded, and Tasteless." I never peel or seed my tomatoes. What's the point, other than making the texture of a sauce smooth and refined, which is nice when you're trying to impress someone, but at what cost to nutrients, texture, and flavor? Peeling a banana I understand, but a tomato, never. The tomatoes I buy are grown organically, and much of their taste is in the skin. I am almost overwhelmed by the variety of tomatoes that has appeared in markets over the last five years. Heirloom tomatoes have made a comeback, perhaps knocking out some of the old beefsteaks, but I find that every tomato worth its salt comes from growers at farmers' markets, including those who have gone into hydroponic production. In winter you just have to take your chances with those from a hothouse. The trick is to buy as many as you can in summer, cut out the stem parts, whiz them up in a food processor or blender, add about $1/2$ teaspoon salt for 4 cups, a tiny pinch of vitamin C (ascorbic acid) crystals to preserve color (optional), and fill up as many containers as your freezer will hold for the winter. Canned plum tomatoes (often grown from San Marzano seeds, Italy's best), tomatoes already diced and ready for sauces, and any crushed tomato (no herbs, just plain) are my choices. Many sauces demand canned tomatoes and cannot be made as successfully with fresh ones. I buy canned tomatoes in cases of twelve; many supermarkets will give you a discount if you ask.

TUNA (Tonno)

Buy the best Italian tuna packed in olive oil in cans or jars in Italian markets. If you can't get Italian canned tuna packed in olive oil, use tuna packed in water (the ones packed in vegetable oil taste of the oil), adding flavor by pouring out the water, covering the tuna with olive oil, and letting it sit in the fridge for a day or so before using. The better the tuna, the better the dish, but beware. Once you have eaten imported tuna in olive oil, you'll have difficulty going back to everyday brands.

VINEGAR (Aceto)

Buy the best or make your own. I wish I could send to every cook little bottles of my Sicilian vinegar "mother." The taste is nutty, intense, and lasting, so that only a few drops are needed on salad. The grandmother of the man who gave it to me used to drink a shot of it each morning, which I tried once, and once only! Vinegar is easy to make, beginning with a mother (a rubbery mass that often forms on the surface of old wine) ordered from www.vinegarman.com. Put it in a large glass container such as a magnum wine bottle, pour in any leftover red wine you might have (that's the hard part), and wait three weeks. Vinegar will happen. Pour off what you need, reserving some of the vinegar mother for the next round. (See Sources and Seeds.)

WINE (Vino)

I love Italian wines (along with those of France's Rhône valley). Golden, fruity Vermentino, slightly drier Pinot Grigio, and the unpretentious wine of Frascati, created two thousand years ago to drink with Roman dishes, are some of the dry white wines we keep on hand for sipping and cooking. Morellino di Scansano and Montepulciano d'Abruzzo make up part of our cellar,

although many of these are becoming too expensive for daily drinking. Lazio growers are improving both their red and white wines each year, but the wine of Rome from casks, called *vino sciolto* or loose wine, is the wine I love. I often drink one of the least expensive Frascati wines found here, Fontana Candida, because its flavor, even if not exactly like the fresh, young wines in a Roman trattoria, whisks me away to a summer lunch under bougainvillea vines in my beloved city.

YOGURT *(Yogurt)*

It is getting more difficult to find a good whole-milk yogurt, but my favorite for cooking and eating is called Mountain High. Yogurt (and crème fraîche) is easy to make at home: Put a quart of milk in a glass jar and stir in a spoon or two of high-quality (*not* low-fat) plain yogurt. Set the jar, covered, in a warm place (85°F to 100°F), and wait. Yogurt will happen. Of course there are all sorts of kits and such, but you don't need to spend all that money and time. You may also set a very heavy metal pan full of water over a pilot light, then place your jar in the pan away from the direct flame of the pilot, and you will have yogurt overnight. For those who cannot eat a lot of fat, yogurt is a perfect substitute for cream in most recipes.

ZUCCHINI *(Zucchine)*

I use every kind of squash imaginable in my cooking, mainly because my garden reproduces them like rabbits and I have to use them up somehow (neighbors will take only so many). My favorite is called Rampicante (see Sources and Seeds), a long, firm-textured squash that is delicious raw in salads, grilled, or steamed for pasta sauces or fillings. I also love the little round pattypans and turban or butternut for pasta fillings and risotto. Any squash (and many other vegetables), if cut up into small chunks or thin slices, brushed with olive oil, and baked in a hot (400°F) oven for 20 to 30 minutes, makes a very quick vegetable course for any meal. Sprinkle with Parmesan and lemon juice, and serve.

Basic Techniques

La cucina romana requires no sleight of hand. Food is sautéed, grilled, fried, or steamed, and pasta is boiled. Most of the recipes in this book are enough for four people, which makes the math simple, but there will be leftovers with some recipes. These are your building blocks to make the next day's quick lunch or to satisfy a particularly hungry guest. You will see how quickly an extra portion of Pomodori al Riso (page 56) disappears! I figure it's easier to double the recipe for a dinner party of eight and perhaps have a little left over, than to make recipes for six and either have to cut them in awkward thirds for fewer people or enlarge them by various fractions for a larger group.

It is my firm belief that any food will benefit from having more surface area in contact with a pan or flame, which is why I cut vegetables, fruits, and many meats into small shapes. I prefer to cut meat into relatively thin slices, then sauté, grill, roast, or broil quickly to ensure a good crust and moist interior. The exception is a good steak, which must be cut thick to remain rare (*al sangue*). I love baked potatoes, but I cut all others into medium dice or slices. I sauté each ingredient separately before assembling a casserole, stew, or soup so that each ingredient retains its own integrity and flavor in the final dish.

In Italian, *quanto basta* is a wonderful phrase used often in recipes. It means "use enough to suffice." This applies often to the use of spices and salt and pepper (or bay leaf!). Salt and pepper seasoning is really up to you. Generally I salt as I go, meaning that when I am sautéing each ingredient separately, I add very little salt to each one, then put all ingredients together. This technique will always produce well-seasoned results. I use salt *quanto basta* and feel that certain vegetables, such as tomatoes, radishes, and cucumbers, always benefit from a little extra. You will find your own *quanto basta* as you begin cooking these recipes.

I don't use measuring cups or spoons when I cook, and I suggest that you learn how to gauge amounts by eyeballing, if only for convenience. Your hand, the best tool of all, is always with you and works just as well as any container. A good handful of a dry ingredient like flour or bread crumbs is about $1/2$ to $2/3$ cup, and it is also the size of a bunch (as in a bunch of parsley). If you scrunch up your hand into a little cup, holding all the fingers together tightly against the thumb, the very bottom of your hand where all the crinkles are may be filled with salt or sugar or any dry ingredient and will equal about one teaspoon. Open your hand a fraction, fill up the bottom, and that will be equal to a tablespoon.

I measure olive oil by counting as I pour from a container with a very small spout. "One olive, two olive, three olive, four olive, five olive" will yield about 5 teaspoons of olive oil if I pour in a steady, thin stream. You will figure out your own intuitive ways to measure and have much more fun cooking. A little more or less of anything in any dish is not really a disaster, except for salt or hot peppers. Be prudent with these.

Reduce simply means cooking a sauce or dish for a few minutes over relatively high heat to evaporate excess liquid and intensify flavor. It will also intensify the saltiness, so begin with less salt if the recipe calls for a reduction.

To cover with water or liquid means to cover the ingredients completely but only barely above the solids. It does not mean drown the ingredient in gallons of liquid.

I never peel or seed vegetables or fruits, with the exception of bananas, avocados, mangoes, and others with inedible skins or large stones, and the occasional apple for a tart, nor do I rub off the skins of almonds or hazelnuts for sauces or desserts. Nut skins are pulverized anyway in all my recipes and add nutrition and flavor to the dish.

A chicken breast in recipes means one half of a full double breast, not the whole thing.

To keep my nostalgia for Rome at bay between visits, I stock my kitchen with the same simple ingredients found in Rome's open markets and invite friends and family to share *la cucina romana*. In this way I can easily have a great deal of what I love in Rome, at home.

A tavola, non si invecchia.—One will not grow old at the table. • Almost every Roman restaurant offers lean, rich prosciutto, dazzling melon, mozzarella only hours out of its bath of whey, and any number of temptations that often double as a first or main course. At your own table a good antipasto can accommodate unforeseen guests or be assembled quickly as a meal after a long workday: mozzarella, prosciutto and melon (if in season), one of the many antipasto recipes that follow, a green salad, and some fruit. • Olive oil and vinegar or lemon can transform the lowliest anchovy into a morsel for the gods, and practically any leftover (a cook's most effective muse) may be bound with eggs and sprinkled with

antipasti

bread crumbs and Parmesan or pecorino and turned into a golden frittata. Vegetables, fish, cold meats, and egg dishes adorn the tables of Toto in via delle Carrozze, one of my favorite antipasto restaurants in Rome. One day there might be artichokes powerfully infused with olive oil, garlic, and mint. Another day a plate of delicate, rosemary-scented beans with tuna packed in olive oil, and the little egg-shaped mozzarella, *ovoline,* might frame a plate of salami, prosciutto, and sausages. In summer, grilled peppers and plump tomatoes stuffed with arborio rice, basil, and cubes of potato are enough for a quick light lunch.

Alici o Latterini Fritti

· ·

FRIED ANCHOVIES OR WHITEBAIT

Serves 4

Fresh, silvery anchovies (whitebait will do just fine) take a dip in seasoned batter or flour, salt, and pepper, just like southern chicken-fried steak, and then sizzle in olive oil until crisp. These tiny fish disappear in a couple of bites, so make plenty. Alici may be mixed with tiny fried seppie (sometimes called *moscardini*), shrimp, or rings of calamari or whole calamaretti for a spectacular Fritto Misto di Mare (page 59).

The two batters, Pastella I and II, are all-purpose, even for fruit, but used most often as the coating for the ingredients of a fritto misto, baccalà, or small fry. Pastella II contains an egg white, which lightens the batter, but foods fried with this pastella should be eaten quickly after frying or they will collapse.

PASTELLA I
1 cup flour
1 cup water
1 tablespoon extra virgin olive oil
$^1/_4$ teaspoon salt
$^1/_4$ teaspoon freshly ground pepper

PASTELLA II
1 cup flour
1 cup water
1 tablespoon extra virgin olive oil
$^1/_4$ teaspoon salt
$^1/_4$ teaspoon freshly ground pepper
1 egg white

1 $^1/_2$ pounds fresh anchovies or whitebait, cleaned
Olive or sunflower oil for frying
Lemon wedges for serving

PASTELLA I

Combine all the ingredients in a bowl, whisking until well blended.

PASTELLA II

Combine the first 5 ingredients in a bowl, whisking until well blended. Beat the egg white until it holds stiff peaks but is not dry and fold it into the batter.

TO FRY THE FISH:

Add the fish to either batter and toss to coat. Heat a deep, 10- to 12-inch frying pan over high heat for 30 seconds. Pour in about 1$\frac{1}{2}$ inches of olive oil and heat to smoking. Slip the fish from the batter into the hot oil, taking care that they do not touch. Lower the heat to medium-high. Cook until the fish are nicely browned and crisp, 2 to 3 minutes, and transfer them to a paper towel on a plate to drain—or use large brown grocery bags on which to drain fried foods as I do. Continue adding the fish until all are cooked. If they stick to each other during frying, simply cut apart with your trusty kitchen scissors.

Serve with lemon wedges.

Variation:

For an alternative coating, mix 1 cup flour, 1 teaspoon salt, and $\frac{1}{2}$ teaspoon each fresh ground pepper and paprika in a small brown grocery bag. Rinse the fish, then shake them in this mixture and proceed with frying.

. . . .

Pastella I or II batter may be enlivened with more ground pepper, some grated Parmesan, a small amount of minced garlic, or a few drops of truffle oil when used to fry vegetables, but not for fish.

Bresaola con la Rughetta

. . . .

THIN CURED BEEF WITH ARUGULA

Serves 4 to 6

Bresaola, from the word *brasare,* "to braise," is not cooked at all, and you'll be surprised how easy it is to make your own air-dried beef at home. When presenting this marvel to guests, you might well be perceived as the kind of person who chews reindeer hide to stitch your own shoes. Homemade bresaola is well worth the time, however, even if the imported kind is available.

A lean cut of beef is marinated, wrapped in cheesecloth, and left to air-dry for several weeks. You will immediately taste the difference between yours and the commercial variety, and there is great satisfaction in knowing how to cure one's meats (or make shoes) in an emergency.

I bottle good red wine

I $^1/_2$ cups coarse sea salt

I large onion, sliced thin

2 carrots, sliced thin

4 garlic cloves, crushed

2 tablespoons freshly ground pepper

$^1/_4$ cup juniper berries, crushed

2 bay leaves

I very small bunch fresh thyme

6 pounds lean beef, such as a tritip or brisket

Arugula, olive oil, and lemon juice for serving

Parmigiano-Reggiano for garnish (optional)

Mix all the marinade ingredients and place the meat and marinade in a container large enough to hold the meat but small enough to allow the marinade to cover the beef. Cover the dish and let the meat sit in the refrigerator for 1 week, until the beef feels firm to the touch, turning it once after 3 to 4 days.

Remove the meat, dry, and wrap it in cheesecloth. Hang the meat in a cool place with good circulation, such as a cellar, utility area, or screened back porch. Let it hang for 2 to 3 weeks (depending on the ventilation), until it feels quite firm, like a salame. Remove the cheesecloth to see if any white mold has formed on the bresaola. This is normal and happens to the best of *salumi* and hard sausages. You may brush it off or wipe the meat with lemon juice or wine vinegar to kill the mold and then store the bresaola, wrapped in new cheesecloth, in the refrigerator. If the bresaola smells bad or there is pink or black mold on the outside, discard it immediately. Preserved correctly, bresaola will be smooth, with a rich, dark color from the wine marinade.

TO SERVE
Cut very thin slices of bresaola to cover a plate, slightly overlapping. Sprinkle a handful of arugula over the meat, dress with olive oil and lemon juice, and serve. I like it, too, served like carpaccio, strewn with thin slices of Parmigiano-Reggiano.

Bruschette

· ·

GRILLED BREAD WITH VARIOUS TOPPINGS

Serves 4

Remember that *ch* in *bruschetta* sounds like *k,* as in "brusketta," just as in Buona Forchetta (the bakery I founded in Los Angeles), architect, or Chianti, which, by the way, goes well with bruschette.

Every cook in Rome has a favorite bruschetta, but the classic one is only a generous slice of Pane Casereccio (page 242) grilled over a fire, brushed with extra virgin olive oil, and sprinkled with salt. I love to serve bruschette as a light supper late at night after a long evening when I have pushed my dinner hour a little too far. Almost anything in the refrigerator or garden may be put on toasted bread with a little good olive oil to bathe it in glory. My favorite is still the classic— grilled bread, oil, and salt—although I rub my own slice generously with a cut garlic clove.

A bruschetta's summer garb, however, is chopped ripe tomatoes, a little garlic, and basil.

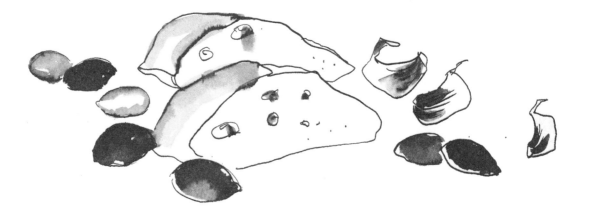

Six $^1/_2$-inch-thick slices rustic bread
I garlic clove, cut in half (optional)
3 ripe tomatoes, chopped and drained
6 tablespoons extra virgin olive oil
$^1/_4$ cup fresh basil, chopped fine
I teaspoon balsamic vinegar
Salt and freshly ground pepper

Grill or toast the bread until nicely browned on both sides. Rub with the cut garlic if desired.

Combine the tomatoes, olive oil, basil, and vinegar in a small bowl. Toss gently and season with salt and pepper to taste. Spoon the mixture onto the grilled bread and serve immediately.

Bruschette Toppings (dressed always with olive oil):
Imported Italian tuna, capers, and arugula
Thin slices of sweet summer onions, raw or grilled
Thin slices of grilled eggplant
Thin slices of young artichoke, sautéed in olive oil and sprinkled with lemon
Thin slices of fresh Parmigiano-Reggiano, arugula, and a few drops of lemon
2 cups pitted Kalamata or pimiento-stuffed green olives, I small garlic clove, and the juice of a
    lemon puréed in the bowl of a food processor
4 or 5 anchovies mashed with 2 tablespoons butter

Insalata di Mare

· ·

SEAFOOD SALAD

Serves 4

A seafood salad—in fact all salads—must be kept simple, in this case dressed only with good oil, lemon, and salt. (Some cooks use vinegar, but I prefer lemon, which complements, without overwhelming, the flavors of the sea.) Most are built around calamari (tender young squid), lovely sweet clams called *tartufi di mare* (truffles of the sea), tiny clams called *vongole* that are used mainly for *spaghetti alle vongole,* little triangular mollusks called *telline,* cuttlefish called *moscardini* that look like tiny lightbulbs with tentacles, *gamberetti* or tiny pink shrimp, and mussels of all shapes and sizes. A particularly good one is served at Orsetto, which is just outside the walls of the center on via Flaminia, and at Arancio d'Oro, near the Trevi fountain.

I ^{1}/$_4$ cups extra virgin olive oil
I pound squid, cleaned (see page 37)
2 pounds fresh clams, scrubbed
I pound mussels, scrubbed
I garlic clove, chopped
^{1}/$_2$ cup thinly sliced celery
^{1}/$_2$ pound small or medium raw shrimp
^{1}/$_2$ pound rock shrimp (optional)
Juice of 2 lemons, plus a little grated zest
Salt
2 tablespoons minced fresh flat-leaf parsley

Heat $^1/_2$ cup of the olive oil in a large, shallow skillet with a lid over medium-high heat. Add the squid, clams, and mussels and cover, lowering the heat to medium. After 3 minutes, add the garlic and cover again, steaming just until the clams and mussels are opened, about 3 more minutes. Reserve the juice for Risotto alla Pescatora (page 142) and remove the clams and mussels from the shells.

In the same skillet, heat 2 tablespoons of the remaining olive oil over medium heat, add the celery, and cook until translucent, 3 to 4 minutes. Add the shrimp, and rock shrimp, if using, chopped if medium, left whole if tiny, and cook 3 to 4 minutes just until pink and tender. Put everything into a large bowl and toss with the remaining olive oil and the lemon juice and zest. Add salt to taste, let sit for half an hour, and serve at room temperature, sprinkled with parsley.

. . . .

To clean squid: Using scissors, cut each squid down the middle between the flippers on each side. Open and snip out the tiny silver sac of ink, reserving it for Risotto al Nero di Seppie (page 138). Pull out all of the guts, including the transparent "bone," and discard. Peel off the outer speckled skin and discard. Cut off the tentacles close to the body in one piece and take out the little hard round beak and discard. Cut the body across into $^1/_2$-inch pieces.

Use a few poached sea scallops (see Zuppa di Pesce, page 80) to make the insalata more substantial.

Cannellini al Olio, Aglio, e Prezzemolo

....

FRESH WHITE BEANS WITH OLIVE OIL, GARLIC, AND PARSLEY

Serves 4

In late spring and summer, the open markets of Rome are filled with fresh white beans called *cannellini,* which are tender, sweet, and nutty at the same time, completely different from the dried version in texture, although either may be used in this recipe. I add a little wine (or beer) to my bean water, which gives depth to its flavor. Dried beans will require more cooking time.

The fresh ones need shelling, and what a good excuse to invite a friend over, share recipes, and catch up on the latest gossip. In Rome, you may, for a price, buy them already shelled, but you'll miss the precious time with your friend.

3 cups shelled fresh cannellini (about 4 pounds in the pod) or 1 pound dried cannellini (If using
    dried beans, follow the instructions for cooking beans in Pasta e Fagioli, page 78)
4 tablespoons extra virgin olive oil
1 small onion, chopped fine
3 garlic cloves, minced
$^1/_2$ cup dry white wine
1 fresh rosemary sprig
1 teaspoon salt
2 tablespoons minced fresh flat-leaf parsley
Freshly ground pepper

Heat 2 tablespoons of the olive oil in a medium skillet and sauté the onion over medium heat until translucent and a little brown around the edges, about 5 minutes. Add all but a teaspoon of the garlic and cook for a minute more.

Put the fresh or precooked dried beans in a large pot and add cold water to cover. Bring to a simmer, skim off any foam from the surface, and simmer for 30 to 45 minutes for fresh beans, 30 minutes for precooked beans, or until the beans are tender, adding water or wine as needed. Add the cooked onion and garlic, the wine, rosemary, and salt. The liquid should cook down nicely toward the end and be slightly thickened. Let cool.

Mix the cooked beans with the reserved garlic, parsley, the rest of the olive oil, and fresh ground pepper, and serve in pasta bowls with more olive oil on the side.

Variation:
Purée the cooled bean mixture in a food processor with a few leaves of sage, sautéed until crisp in 1 tablespoon of extra virgin olive oil. Add a few drops of lemon and serve as a spread for bruschette.

. . . .

Regardless of their reputation for being gastrointestinal troublemakers, beans, according to my guru, Harold McGee (On Food and Cooking), *were honored by four ancient Roman families whose names were derived from beans: Fabius from the fava, Piso from the pea, Lentulus from the lentil, and Cicero from the chickpea, or ceci. Even the famous Tuscan zolfino was cultivated first by the Romans.*

Caponata

·························

SWEET AND SOUR BRAISED VEGETABLES

Serves 4 to 6

My caponata can be made in very little time and will surely find its way from antipasto to bruschetta to fettuccine, depending on your mood.

Every cook has an opinion about caponata, and I am no exception. Does a true caponata contain peppers? Olives? Zucchini? Not mine. I consider this recipe to be about as authentic as it can get (except for the optional fennel, which I feel works beautifully with sweet and sour flavors), but you are certainly welcome to add anything else that tickles your palate. My opinion, however, is that zucchini are for ratatouille (and green olives are for martinis).

Caponata will keep for up to 3 weeks in the refrigerator, but always serve it at room temperature.

1 large eggplant, cut into $^1/_2$-inch dice (the French fry attachment on a food processor works beautifully; cut the eggplant lengthwise into 1 $^1/_2$-inch pieces or chunks and push them through as you would potatoes)

2 teaspoons salt

$^3/_4$ cup extra virgin olive oil

2 large onions, chopped fine

3 stalks of celery, chopped fine

1 small fennel bulb, chopped fine, fronds reserved for garnish (optional)

4 garlic cloves, chopped fine

1 tablespoon sugar

1 $^1/_2$ to 2 cups tomato sauce from Pasta al Pomodoro o al Sugo (page 100)

$^1/_4$ cup capers

2 tablespoons red wine vinegar

2 teaspoons balsamic vinegar

$^1/_4$ cup toasted pine nuts

Fresh basil leaves, shredded

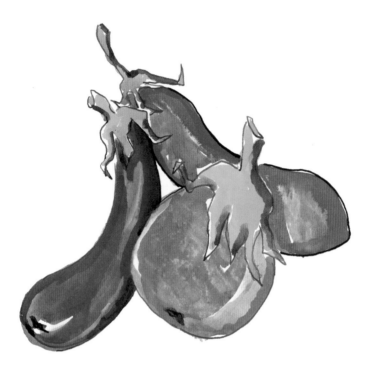

Place the eggplant in a colander and sprinkle with the salt. While it drains, chop the other vegetables. Blot the eggplant with paper towels after 15 minutes.

Heat half the olive oil in a large skillet and sauté the eggplant over medium-high heat until very brown and crispy around the edges. Transfer to a plate. Add a little more olive oil to the pan and add the onions and celery (and the fennel, if using). Cook over medium heat until nicely golden, then add the garlic and cook for 2 minutes more.

Put the eggplant back in the pan, sprinkle with the sugar, and add the tomato sauce, capers, and vinegars. Simmer together until some of the liquid is reduced and the mixture is fairly thick and shiny, 15 to 20 minutes.

Let cool and serve, garnished with toasted pine nuts, shredded basil, and fennel fronds, if using.

Carciofi alla Giudia

. . . .

ARTICHOKES FRIED IN THE JEWISH MANNER

Serves 4

The Jewish ghetto, one of the oldest in Europe, birthplace of exquisite fried artichokes, houses some of the most eclectic trattorie in Rome. Since artichokes are relatively expensive to serve in small trattorie, you really must seek out a slightly larger establishment in or out of the ghetto. Gigetto al Portico d'Ottavia and Piperno in the ghetto, La Campana near piazza della Fontanella Borghese, Girarosto Toscano in Prati, and Paris in Trastevere (Roman cuisine with Jewish overtones) all serve this addictive vegetable.

It is very easy to make these at home, but the prep takes a little time. Begin to fry about 15 to 20 minutes before you serve.

6 medium globe or 16 baby artichokes
Salt
1 quart extra virgin olive oil
Lemon wedges for serving

Trim the artichoke stems to 1 inch and, with a vegetable peeler, peel off the outer layer. Snap off the outer, darker leaves, down to the yellow ones, and save them for another use (steamed quickly and served with olive oil and lemon, melted butter, or cooled, with mayonnaise) unless the artichokes are very small—discard those outer leaves. Steam or parboil the artichokes in salted water for 10 minutes or longer, depending on their size. Drain and cool.

Turn each artichoke upside down and tap it lightly on a flat surface until the leaves spread slightly outward like flower petals or gently separate the leaves with your fingers, taking care not to break them.

Heat the oil until smoking in a deep, wide saucepan and put the artichokes in, bottoms down. Lower the heat to medium and fry until deep golden brown. The small artichokes normally turn over of their own accord, but if they don't, turn them over, raise the heat slightly, and continue frying until the leaves are brown and crispy, 6 to 8 minutes. Drain on a paper towel, salt, and serve with lemon wedges.

Note: I often cut my cleaned artichokes into 4 wedges if large or in half if small, to get more surface area and a crisper texture. They may not be as authentic as the whole ones, but they are just as beautiful.

Be sure to cool, strain, and use the oil again for frying artichokes or other vegetables.

. . . .

Sometimes the larger Roman artichoke is more manageable when making a flower shape before frying, because the smaller ones, when young, have brittle leaves that tend to break off.

Many trattorie parcook artichokes in season and then freeze them to serve during the rest of the year. They must first be steamed in salted water, brushed with lemon juice to preserve the color, and then dried well and frozen quickly so as not to become mushy.

Carciofi alla Romana

. . . .

ARTICHOKES WITH GARLIC AND MINT

Serves 4 to 6

I share with Caterina de' Medici a passion for artichokes, which are said to be right up there with oysters and caviar as an aphrodisiac. But it's really the taste that drives me mad.

Legend has it that an Arab farmer's beautiful daughter observed her donkey eating strange thistles. She tried them herself, first raw, then grilled, and finally she stewed them with herbs (most likely wild mint and garlic) and sold them at her local market. A prince got wind of the new delicacy, met the cook, and they lived happily ever after, no doubt enjoying their newfound love potion.

Historically, wealthy Romans, to protect their precious supply of carciofi, forbade the masses to buy or eat them. The Roman naturalist Pliny pointed out in his disdainful discourses on the Roman class system that "artichokes were discovered by asses and are still being consumed by them."

If you rarely have artichokes in your markets, you may substitute frozen ones, but the results will not be quite the same. Still, they will be tasty and most certainly whet your appetite for an excursion through the silvery fields south of Rome. The medium-sized artichoke with the name *romanesco* is used for this dish, but use whatever artichokes you can find.

Some of the best artichokes in Rome are served at Nino, just off the Piazza d'Espagna on via Borgognona, and Trattoria 31 on via delle Carrozze. Sometimes Carciofi alla Romana are a bit too salty, but quaffing a little more vino sciolto, the lovely low-alcohol white wine from Frascati, will take care of that.

$^1/_2$ cup extra virgin olive oil

6 medium globe or 20 baby artichokes, leaves trimmed down to the yellow part, stems peeled, and greenish tops cut off to the yellow part

6 garlic cloves, chopped

4 fresh mint sprigs, leaves only

$^1/_2$ teaspoon salt

$^1/_2$ cup dry white wine or water

1 large lemon

Heat the olive oil in a large pot with a lid over medium heat, then add the artichokes, cutting each in half if you like to create more surface area to be browned. Cook for a few minutes, until golden, turning once, then add the garlic, mint leaves, and salt. Cover and simmer for 6 to 7 minutes, then add the wine or water, lower the heat, cover, and continue cooking for 15 to 20 minutes, until the artichokes are very tender. Squeeze the lemon juice over the artichokes and serve at room temperature in the oil.

Variation:

Puree the mixture in a food processor with 2 cups Brodo di Pollo or Brodo di Verdure (page 69 or 71) and a dash of cayenne and toss with any short pasta such as penne or ziti.

. . . .

Refrigerate fresh artichokes before peeling and the outer leaves will snap off easily. Once you've pared and trimmed them, toss them with lemon juice and store in a resealable plastic bag in the refrigerator. They will stay green and fresh for 2 to 3 days. Any discoloration disappears in cooking.

Carpaccio con Salsa di Mostarda o la Rughetta

THIN SLICED BEEF WITH MUSTARD SAUCE OR ARUGULA

Serves 6 to 8

According to the *Grande Enciclopedia Illustrata della Gastronomia,* many years ago in Venice there was a major art exhibit of Vittore Carpaccio's work and much discussion of his magnificent reds and yellows. Giuseppe Cipriani, another kind of artist (founder of Harry's Bar in Venice), created his own work of art for a client (a contessa whose doctor insisted she eat raw meat) and at the same time to honor the painter by approximating Carpaccio's rich colors of sepia and dun with raw prime beef and mustard.

Carpaccio, now considered the signature dish of Harry's Bar, has found its way into trattorie all over Italy, and it is often on summer menus along with Vitello Tonnato (page 198) as both are cool and light. Carpaccio may be dressed with the traditional senape (mustard) sauce (one of the few times mustard is used in anything) or simply with olive oil. Garnish with shaved Parmesan and fresh arugula leaves.

3 egg yolks
1 tablespoon Colman's dry mustard
$^1/_2$ teaspoon salt
1 to 1 $^1/_2$ cups extra virgin olive oil
Juice of 1 lemon, or more as desired
A few drops Worcestershire sauce, or more as desired
1 tablespoon red wine vinegar
2 $^1/_2$ pounds beef tenderloin, trimmed of all fat and any sinews removed
1 bunch arugula, cut into thin strips
Shaved Parmigiano-Reggiano

Using a food processor or a glass bowl and a whisk, combine the egg yolks with the mustard and salt. Start adding the oil, drop by drop, making sure the sauce starts to thicken before increasing the stream of oil. When the sauce is as thick as mayonnaise, add the lemon juice and Worcestershire sauce to thin it. Then continue adding oil, adding enough to make the mayonnaise creamy but not stiff. Now add the vinegar, which will thin the sauce out again. If you wish to make an even thinner sauce, add a little more Worcestershire or lemon juice.

Place 6 serving plates in the refrigerator. Rub the outside of the beef with salt and wrap it in butcher paper or wax paper. Put it in the freezer for 1 to 2 hours. Remove the beef from the freezer just before serving and, using a very sharp knife, carve it into very thin slices, arranging the slices in an overlapping design on the plates. Drip the mustard sauce over the carpaccio, creating a Jackson Pollock design, and strew the chopped arugula and shaved Parmigiano-Reggiano on top.

Fiori di Zucca

· ·

FRIED STUFFED ZUCCHINI FLOWERS

Serves 4

Every summer I plant a climbing *zucchina* called Rampicante, a rampaging, leafy climber that pushes its way through the garden and onto fences, then forms long, brilliant yellow-green squash in curving, fantasy shapes—one year there was even my initial, *S*, peeking out from the lush leaves.

The flowers are huge, perfect for stuffing, and the firm, almost seedless flesh may be eaten raw or cooked. Domestic *zucchine* or other squash flowers from your garden or market will do just as well.

Seeds for the rambunctious Rampicante are available from Shepherd's Garden Seeds (see Sources and Seeds).

12 zucchini flowers
12 anchovy fillets
1 pound fresh mozzarella, cut into 12 pieces
Extra virgin olive oil
Pastella I or II from Alici o Latterini Fritti (page 30)
4 lemon wedges

Open each zucchini flower gently and push an anchovy and a piece of mozzarella down into the center, closing the petals firmly around the filling. When all are ready, heat a thin layer of olive oil in a wide, shallow skillet over medium heat until smoking.

Dip each zucchini flower in batter, coating it well, and carefully place each in the hot oil, keeping them separated, if possible. Brown on each side for 2 to 3 minutes or until crispy and the cheese is melted. If they stick to one another, carefully cut them apart with scissors before turning. Drain on absorbent paper and serve with lemon wedges.

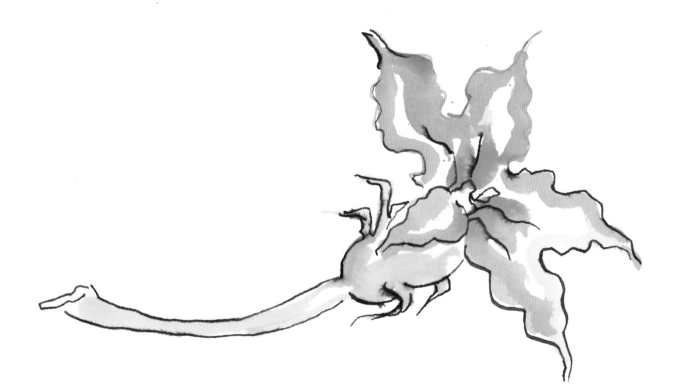

Crostini di Fegato

. . . .

CHICKEN LIVER PÂTÉ ON TOAST

Serves 4

Crostini are thin slices of toast spread with chopped chicken or goose liver and other toppings. They are also often made from livers of rabbit, pheasant, or woodcock and served along with the roast animal or bird. For more formal dinner parties, Romans use a fine-textured bread called *pane in cassetta* (thin sandwich bread), cut into pretty shapes before toasting. It is best to make the liver mixture as you need it, although the leftovers may be packed into a crock with a bit more butter and served again as a pâté.

2 tablespoons extra virgin olive oil
I tablespoon butter
I pound chicken livers, cleaned of all sinew and fat
2 tablespoons onion, chopped fine
A few drops Cognac
$^1/_4$ cup dry white wine
2 tablespoons capers, plus a few for garnish
4 anchovy fillets
2 fresh flat-leaf parsley sprigs
Freshly ground pepper
Pinch of salt
8 thin slices bread, cut into rounds or triangles, toasted

Heat the olive oil and butter in a medium skillet until bubbling, add the chicken livers, and sauté over medium heat until nicely browned on all sides, about 4 minutes. Add the onion and cook until translucent, about 3 minutes. Add the Cognac and white wine and simmer for 5 minutes or until the livers are cooked but still slightly pink inside. Put the liver mixture in the bowl of a food processor along with the rest of the pâté ingredients except salt and pepper. Pulse quickly just until the mixture is of rough spreading consistency but not puréed. Add salt and pepper to taste and spread on toast rounds. Garnish with a caper or two.

. . . .

Freeze all the livers that are hiding in roasting chickens, ducks, or geese for future crostini or supplì (page 144).

Melanzane al Basilico e Pinoli

. . . .

EGGPLANT WITH BASIL AND PINE NUTS

Serves 4

My sage mother often made this dish for us as children, knowing that my brother and I detested eggplant but would hardly know we were eating it after she had worked her magic. Everyone loves this, even die-hard eggplant haters.

I medium eggplant, cut into $^1/_2$-inch-thick slices, cut in half or into thirds, lengthwise
Salt
$^1/_2$ cup extra virgin olive oil
I cup flour, seasoned with I teaspoon salt, $^1/_2$ teaspoon freshly ground pepper, and I teaspoon paprika
Juice of I lemon
Leaves from 3 to 4 fresh basil sprigs, shredded
$^1/_2$ cup toasted pine nuts
$^1/_2$ cup grated Parmigiano-Reggiano

Lay the eggplant strips on a large plate or flat surface and sprinkle with salt. When droplets of water appear, after about 5 to 10 minutes, blot the strips and turn them over, repeating the process. Heat the olive oil in a large skillet, dip the blotted eggplant strips in the flour mixture, and sauté over medium heat until golden brown on each side, about 3 to 4 minutes per side. Sprinkle with lemon juice and add the basil leaves and pine nuts. Cook together for a few minutes more and serve sprinkled with Parmigiano-Reggiano.

Peperoni con Fagioli e Tonno

. . . .

SWEET BELL PEPPERS WITH BEANS AND TUNA

Serves 4

I sauté summer's red or yellow peppers (no green peppers, please!) and serve them alongside or on top of simmered or baked beans, both adorned with Italian tuna packed in olive oil. You can use the meaty brown beans called *borlotto,* found at most Italian markets, but I am not a fan of these mealy, heavy beans and prefer dried pinto beans, fresh cannellini, or any nice white fresh shelling bean such as cranberry. If using dried beans, skim off the foam that rises to the top during cooking. Use the quick-soaking method described here, which my Italian sister-in-law insists does in fact help suppress any of the disreputable side effects of dried legumes, as many other cookbooks also claim. Fresh beans do not require this step, but you will have to skim off the foam all the same.

Beans will split and toughen if the salt is added too soon. You can use half water, half wine or been for the cooking liquid for a richer flavor. I always roast, then sauté my peppers, because I feel they taste boiled when cooked only once.

1 pound dried cannellini, pinto beans or 1 $^{1}/_{2}$ pounds fresh, shelled cranberry beans

1 small onion, chopped fine

1 small fresh rosemary sprig

1 cup white wine or beer

$^{1}/_{2}$ teaspoon salt

$^{1}/_{2}$ cup extra virgin olive oil

A few fresh sage leaves

1 small sweet onion, chopped fine

2 garlic cloves, minced

1 small dried hot red pepper, crushed

3 red or yellow bell peppers

2 tablespoons minced fresh flat-leaf parsley

$^{1}/_{2}$ teaspoon freshly ground pepper

12 ounces tuna packed in olive oil, drained

Peppers
(Peperoni)

Cover dried beans with cold water and bring to a boil. Immediately turn off the heat and let them cool. Throw out the water, add the first onion and rosemary to the beans, cover them again with cold water and the wine, and bring to a boil. Cover fresh beans with cold water and continue.

Simmer dried beans for 1 to 1^1/$_2$ hours, fresh beans for 30 to 45 minutes, until tender, adding a cup or two of white wine, beer, or water as needed. Add the salt about halfway through the cooking time.

When the beans are tender, heat ^{1}/$_4$ cup of the olive oil in a small pan, add the sage leaves, and cook until crisp. Remove them, add the second onion to the olive oil, and cook over medium heat until translucent, 3 or 4 minutes. Add the garlic and hot pepper and cook for a minute or two longer. Add the contents of the pan along with the sage leaves to the beans and stir well.

Cut the peppers in half and remove all seeds and white membranes. Flatten, and grill them under a broiler or roast them over a gas flame on the stove or on a barbecue grill. When the skin is charred, transfer them to a plate and throw a damp dish towel over them to make them sweat a little, then slip off the blackened skin. They are now ready for any recipe calling for roast peppers.

Cut the peppers into ^{3}/$_4$-inch strips. Heat the remaining ^{1}/$_4$ cup olive oil in a skillet and sauté the peppers over medium heat for 6 to 7 minutes until crisp around the edges. Serve the beans and peppers side by side in a wide, flat dish, sprinkled with parsley and pepper and topped with chunks of tuna.

Scamorza ai Ferri

. . . .

GRILLED SMOKED CHEESE

Serves 6

Scamorza is an autumn dish found on all menus in Rome. When fresh, this cow's milk cheese—found at most Italian markets here—has the texture of mozzarella, but when smoked its texture becomes firm enough to put on the grill quickly, just enough to begin to melt the interior.

Use a fine grill, brushed with oil or nonstick spray, placed over low coals so that the cheese does not fall through when cooking. The rind of Parmesan may also be grilled in this manner, hard side down, and left just until the interior layer starts to melt.

Or cheat, like Jessica Guidi, whose father's company sells tons of Parmigiano-Reggiano and scamorza to most of the best Italian restaurants in L.A.: pop the rind into a miracle microwave for a few seconds and scrape off the melted part. Serve scamorza or Parmesan with boiled potatoes, slices of steamed and sautéed cauliflower, or thick slices of grilled rustic bread.

Pomodori al Riso

. . . .

TOMATOES STUFFED WITH RICE

Serves 4 to 6

This is my favorite summer dish in Rome next to Rotelle alla Romana (page 116). Some of the best stuffed tomatoes are found at the famous La Campana and a sweet little *tavola calda* with no name on via del Babuino toward the Piazza del Popolo, just down from Bar Notegen. Every good trattoria makes a version of stuffed tomatoes, but some tuck a few bites of cooked potato down into the rice, which makes for a lovely combination of textures. I go a bit further sometimes by pushing a cube of fresh mozzarella or Parmesan inside the tomatoes about 5 minutes before they are ready.

The tomatoes may be made well ahead of time for a dinner party since they are served at room temperature.

2 large Yukon Gold or other waxy potatoes
$^{1}/_{2}$ cup extra virgin olive oil, plus a little more to brush on the tops
Salt
6 medium ripe tomatoes
1 small bunch fresh basil leaves
Freshly ground pepper
6 heaping tablespoons arborio rice
Six $^{1}/_{2}$-inch cubes Parmigiano-Reggiano or 3 ounces fresh mozzarella cut into little cubes

Preheat the oven to 400°F. Cut the potatoes into medium dice, toss with 2 tablespoons olive oil and $^{1}/_{2}$ teaspoon salt, and roast in a single layer in a shallow baking pan for 20 minutes or until golden. They will finish cooking with the tomatoes. Meanwhile, oil a baking pan in which the tomatoes will fit snugly together along with the potatoes. Lower the oven temperature to 350°F.

Cut the tops off the tomatoes and set aside. With a serrated grapefruit spoon, scoop out the tomatoes, taking care not to break through the bottoms. Salt the cavities of the tomatoes. Put the pulp into the bowl of a food processor along with the basil, half the remaining olive oil, and salt and pepper to taste. Pulse several times to chop the pulp but not completely purée it. Add the rice and pulse once or twice to blend. Spoon the mixture into the hollowed-out tomatoes. Let whatever is left spill over into the baking dish. Put on the tops (mine never match), brush the rest of the olive oil over the tomatoes, and cover the dish loosely with foil.

Bake for 30 minutes. Remove the foil. With a large spoon or turkey baster, baste the tomatoes with the mixture in the bottom of the pan. Add the potatoes to the pan, and cook for 30 to 40 minutes longer. The tops of the tomatoes should be browned around the edges and the rice tender but al dente. Push a piece of fresh mozzarella or Parmigiano-Reggiano into each hot tomato. Serve at room temperature.

Frittata con Cipolle e Zucchine

. . . .

ONION AND SQUASH FRITTATA

Serves 4

This is a late-summer frittata made with the sweet, flat onions of August or September rather than winter onions, which can be a bit strong. I suggest using Maui, Vidalia, Texas browns, Walla Walla, or any sweet onion grown in your area, along with zucchini, pattypan, or yellow crookneck squash. You can also use the small, flat onions called *cipolline,* if available. The addition of a soft cheese such as Taleggio or fontina makes a richer frittata, but if you cannot find it, use jack or mild Cheddar.

$^{1}/_{4}$ cup extra virgin olive oil

2 large sweet onions or 8 cipolline, sliced thin

2 cups sliced or diced summer squash

1 small dried hot red pepper, crushed

3 cups cooked short pasta such as ditalini or penne

6 eggs

$^{1}/_{2}$ cup grated Parmigiano-Reggiano

Salt and fresh ground pepper

1 tablespoon butter

3 ounces fontina or other cheese, sliced, diced, or grated (optional)

A few drops lemon juice

Preheat the broiler.

Heat the olive oil in an omelet pan, add the onions and squash, and cook over medium heat until nicely browned, about 6 to 7 minutes. Add the pepper and pasta and mix well for a few seconds. Beat the eggs with a spoonful of the Parmesan and season to taste. Add the butter to the pan, and when it bubbles, pour the eggs over the onion mixture to cover. Dot the frittata with the cheese, if using, sprinkle with a little more Parmesan and the lemon juice, and place under the broiler until golden brown, about 2 minutes. Serve with more Parmesan.

Variation:
Add 1 cup fresh corn, 1 potato, sliced thin, 4 slices cooked diced bacon or guanciale, or 1 cup leftover rice.

Frittata con Pancetta e Uovo

. . . .

PANCETTA AND EGG FRITTATA

Serves 4

When you make the classic Italian bacon and egg pasta, Spaghetti alla Carbonara (page 123), make another $^1/_2$ recipe and use the leftovers for this frittata. Or make it from scratch with pancetta, guanciale, prosciutto, or American or Canadian bacon. If the bacon is very fatty, cook it first and drain off the fat.

I love serving big fresh tomato slices with this frittata, a kind of BLT in a pie.

$^1/_4$ cup extra virgin olive oil
I pound pancetta, sliced thin and then cut into $^1/_4$-inch strips or diced
I small dried hot red pepper, crushed
I small onion, sliced or chopped
2 cups cooked short pasta such as ditalini or penne
6 eggs
$^1/_2$ cup grated Parmigiano-Reggiano

Preheat the broiler.

Heat the olive oil in an omelet pan, add the pancetta and pepper, and cook over medium heat until the pancetta is barely crisp, about 5 minutes. Add the onion, cook until translucent, 3 to 4 minutes, and then add the pasta and mix well. Beat the eggs with a spoonful of the Parmesan and pour them over the pancetta mixture. Sprinkle with another spoonful of the Parmesan, cook just until set, about 3 minutes, then place under the broiler until golden brown, 2 to 3 minutes. Serve with the remaining Parmesan.

Variation:

Add $^1/_2$ cup cooked red, yellow, or orange peppers, thin slices of sautéed zucchini, thin slices of potato in place of pasta, or drained diced fresh tomatoes. Any melting cheese, sprinkled on top before broiling, may be used in place of Parmesan.

Asparagi all'Uovo con Parmigiano

. . . .

ASPARAGUS WITH EGGS AND PARMESAN

Serves 4

When the first magnificent asparagus arrives in spring, thick as twigs and meaty, this dish is served in trattorie as a main course, or at least a first course, like pasta. I love it for an easy Sunday night supper in place of our regular pizza.

2 pounds asparagus
$^1/_4$ cup extra virgin olive oil
I small onion, chopped fine
$^1/_4$ cup wine or Brodo di Verdure (page 71)
2 tablespoons butter
4 eggs
$^2/_3$ cup grated Parmigiano-Reggiano, plus more for serving

Preheat the broiler.

Break off the white ends of the asparagus to the tender green part and trim. Heat the oil in a nonstick skillet or omelet pan, add the onion, and cook over medium heat until translucent, 3 to 4 minutes. Add the asparagus spears and cook for 5 minutes or so, until they begin to brown. Add the wine or broth, cover, lower the heat, and cook for 3 to 4 minutes, until the asparagus is tender.

Make 4 spaces in the asparagus for the eggs by pushing some of the asparagus to the side of the pan and leaving some in the middle. Melt the butter in the spaces until sizzling, then carefully break an egg into each space. Sprinkle with Parmesan, add a spoonful of water, cover, and steam the eggs over medium heat just until set but not cooked through, about 2 to 3 minutes. Place the skillet under the broiler for I minute to brown the cheese and finish cooking the eggs.

Carefully lift out an egg with some of the asparagus and transfer to each of 4 warmed plates. Serve with more grated Parmigiano-Reggiano.

This dish is also called Asparagi alla Bismarck (topped with an egg) on many menus, the name Bismarck referring to the time of the Triple Alliance in the nineteenth century when this legendary chancellor of Germany was a symbol of power and energy to the world. Who knows when a cook first popped a poached egg on top of beefsteak, asparagus, pizza, and so on, but it certainly gives energy and opulence to the dish, just as he gave to his country.

Frittata di Carciofi

. . . .

ARTICHOKE FRITTATA

Serves 4

I remember watching a very old lady at the open market peeling and trimming artichokes with lightning speed, tossing them into a bucket of water filled with lemon wedges to keep them green, and could not believe my luck. The luxury of prepared artichokes (second only to having someone cut up all the fruit for a *macedonia* or shell fava beans) makes the cooking time for this dish about 15 minutes, start to finish. I often use leftover Carciofi alla Romana (page 44) for the subtle mint flavor they impart to the eggs, a spirited combination.

$^1/_4$ cup extra virgin olive oil

2 pounds baby artichokes, leaves snapped off to the yellow centers, trimmed, and sliced thin,
    or 2 cups sliced cooked artichoke hearts

2 tablespoons minced onion

2 garlic cloves, chopped fine

6 eggs

$^1/_2$ cup grated Parmigiano-Reggiano

Salt and freshly ground pepper

2 tablespoons butter

A few drops lemon juice

Preheat the broiler.

Heat the olive oil in a seasoned skillet or omelet pan (the frittata will come out more easily) and cook the artichoke slices over medium-high heat until crisp and golden brown around the edges, lowering heat to medium and covering the pan for a few minutes to cook them through, about 10 minutes. Add the onion and garlic and cook until translucent, about 3 to 4 minutes. Beat the eggs with a spoonful of the Parmigiano-Reggiano and season to taste. Add the butter to the pan, and when it bubbles, pour the eggs over the artichokes, shaking the pan to cover. Cook over medium heat for a few minutes to set the eggs, then sprinkle with a little more Parmigiano-Reggiano and the lemon juice and place under the broiler until golden brown, 2 to 3 minutes. Serve with additional Parmigiano-Reggiano.

Primi

1st courses

O mangi la minestra o salti dalla finestra.— Eat the soup or jump out the window! • The wiry little vegetable vendor at the open market near our apartment allows me, after having proved myself to be an obsessive cook even if foreign, to pick out my own fruits and vegetables. Then, of course, she asks if I want "un po' per il brodo," a few things for a soup. I thank her for reminding me, and we chat about the recipe as she tucks a few carrots, the heart of a celery bunch, and some parsley into my shopping bag. These necessities are free with a purchase, for no self-respecting cook would ever leave the market without

minestre

ingredients for the minestra, especially in winter, when golden bowls of broth are the cure for any affliction that comes with a change of seasons. My husband once came down with one of those knocks-you-flat flu bugs that seem to hit only when traveling, and of course, the first thing to do was make chicken soup. To go from the poultry shop for a hen (with eggs still attached!) to the vegetable vendor where we commiserate about winter maladies (her daughter had the same thing), and to the wine seller where a good, strong Amarone is suggested for influenza, is to feel intimately and deeply connected with the human race. Romans pamper and love, and even a flu creates camaraderie.

Healing smells from a golden stock warmed our chilly villa, the final minestra infused with each shopkeeper's caring contribution to my husband's health. I took a container of my potion to the little vegetable lady for her daughter. After all, today she had given me the heart of the celery.

TO CLARIFY STOCKS—Add 2 egg whites, 1 leek chopped fine, and $^1/_2$ pound ground veal or beef (or chicken, for chicken stock). Stir into the simmering stock and cook for 30 minutes. Strain the stock well and discard the solids, cool, remove the fat, and store in convenient amounts in the refrigerator or freezer.

SOFFRITTO (MIREPOIX)—Almost every Italian soup or stew begins with three things: onion, carrot, and celery, the trio called *mirepoix* in French cooking. Parsley should be added at the end, as it acquires bitterness when cooked over time, and recipes will vary in the use of thyme or bay laurel as part of the soffritto. The choice of herbs in a soffritto is very personal, but if I use anything at all, I use very small amounts, especially where bay leaves are concerned (see page 18).

Stocks

Soups play an important role in Roman cooking, especially on winter menus and for those wishing a lighter meal. You may even borrow a habit from the Tuscans and add bread cubes to a minestrone or broth to stretch its life a bit, but the most useful ingredient with which to begin a soup is a good stock.

Many Roman cooks use bouillon cubes, and quite frankly, there are some very good ones on the market, but I prefer to make my own stock, similar to consommé, for soups such as Cappelletti o Tortellini in Brodo (page 72) or any pasta or rice recipe calling for a good, rich bouillon. I reduce small amounts of the stock by half to make concentrates for other dishes. I think your own homemade soup stock puts a signature on a recipe, just as a chef's stock at a particular ristorante gives his personal touch to his creations. To tell the truth, I just love the process of chopping vegetables, simmering and skimming, and watching the magic as a golden or rich brown broth emerges from a few mundane ingredients.

A proper bouillon can be as stimulating as coffee, according to Larousse, and is considered one of the "nervine" foods, which calm nervous excitement and deliver a soothing sense of well-being, even in small quantities. Which is, of course, why it is a universal prescription for winter's maladies.

Begin with lean, meaty bones, add vegetables, and either roast them in the oven for an hour or so, adding water as needed, or simply simmer everything in a big pot on low heat for the same time to get the best results. You will have a very decent stock after spending very little time on preparation. The chopping will take 5 minutes, the skimming another 2 or 3, and then you can get on with other things, stopping back every now and then to add some liquid.

I urge all home cooks to make their stocks, simply because what goes into a dish initially comes out in the finished product. And if you begin with rich meat or vegetable stocks, you will be surprised at how much more flavor is in the final dish.

Any stock may be kept, under fat, for a week or so, then frozen for later use.

Brodo di Carne

· ·

MEAT STOCK

Makes 2 quarts

6 or 7 pounds meaty veal or beef bones or a mixture
2 onions, sliced
4 carrots, sliced
4 celery ribs, sliced
3 parsnips, sliced (optional)
I small garlic clove, minced
Salt and freshly ground pepper to taste (use sparingly)

Preheat the oven to 400°F. Cut as much of the meat off the bones as you can and chop it into small pieces. Put the bones, meat, and the rest of the ingredients in a large shallow pan and roast in the oven for 20 minutes. You may, at this point, add water to cover the meat and vegetables and continue cooking your stock in the oven or transfer the contents of the pan to a large stockpot, add cold water to reach the top of the ingredients, bring to a boil, lower the heat to a simmer, and every now and then skim off the foam that rises to the top until there is no more.

Simmer the stock for about I to I^{1}/$_{2}$ hours, add salt and pepper, strain through a fine strainer, and cool. Place in the refrigerator overnight and remove the top layer of congealed fat in the morning. The stock should be relatively clear. Freeze in small containers for up to 3 months.

Brodo di Pollo

. . . .

CHICKEN STOCK

Makes 2 quarts

You will see the difference in your chicken stock when you use only breast bones.

Use the same amount of onions, carrots, and celery as for Brodo di Carne (page 68) and add about 10 pounds of chicken breast bones, which your friendly butcher will save for you free upon request, since he throws them out. Put everything in a large, tall pot, barely cover with cold water, and bring to a simmer.

Skim off the foam that rises to the top and keep skimming until the broth is fairly clear and no more foam appears, about four or five passes with the skimmer. Simmer the broth for 40 minutes. Add salt to taste, strain the broth, discarding the solids, and let cool. I don't use pepper in chicken and fish stock because I like them to be neutral in many recipes. Beef stock is used in recipes that usually call for pepper.

Refrigerate overnight and skim off any fat that solidifies, or leave the fat to protect the stock and simply scoop out stock when you need it from under the fat. This is about the most pure, unadulterated, and low-fat chicken stock you can create, and the taste is the essence of chicken without the sometimes heavy, oily taste of stock made from backs, necks, and darker meat bones.

Brodo di Pesce

· ·

FISH STOCK

Makes 2 quarts

This easy stock is perfect for soups or for use in seafood risotti.

4 pounds chowder pieces with bones in, or a mixture of salmon collars, halibut, whitefish, sea bass,
    shark, swordfish, or whatever your fish market offers
1 cup white wine
1 large onion, sliced
4 carrots, sliced
2 celery ribs, sliced
3 fresh tomatoes, chopped fine, or 1 cup canned tomatoes, puréed
Pinch of saffron threads
Juice of 1 lemon

Put all the ingredients in a large soup pot and cover with cold water. Don't be afraid of fatty fish, since they give a fish soup body and depth, and your heart, healthful omega-3 acids. Do remove and discard the skin as soon as it loosens, about 3 minutes into the cooking time. Bring to a boil, lower the heat, and simmer for 30 to 40 minutes. Add salt to taste and strain, pressing down on the solids to extract all juices. Let cool, then refrigerate overnight. In the morning, remove and discard the thin layer of fat on the stock.

Brodo di Verdure

· ·

VEGETABLE STOCK

Makes 2 quarts

I save all the water in which I steam or boil vegetables, creating an instant, extremely useful broth that can be used to thin sauces, steam vegetables, or make risotto. It begins with water from boiled potatoes and may include water from broccoli, carrots, green peas, fava beans, thin green beans (fagiolini) or Romano beans, cauliflower, or sugar snap peas. Or you may start completely from scratch with the following:

2 onions, sliced
4 carrots, sliced
4 celery ribs, sliced
1 small fennel bulb (if you like fennel)
2 or 3 small potatoes, cubed
Juice of 1 lemon
Salt and freshly ground pepper to taste

Put everything in a large stockpot and cover with cold water (or use up the vegetable juices you have lurking in the fridge), bring to a simmer, and cook for 30 minutes or until the stock is flavorful enough for your purposes. Reduce for a few minutes over high heat for more intense flavor.

Cappelletti o Tortellini in Brodo

LITTLE "HATS" OR CIRCLES OF PASTA IN STOCK

Serves 4 to 6

Cappelletti are squares of stuffed pasta, folded over into a triangle, pinched into the shape of a pope's hat, and poached in broth or served with meat sauce. Ricotta and stracchino are the cheeses most often used, but the cappelletti may also be stuffed with ground veal, turkey, sausage, or butternut or other winter squash. Some cooks make their "hats" from circles and some from squares, folded over into half-moons or triangles, wrapped around the finger, and sealed to give the hat a nice curve or point.

The same filling may be used for tortellini, although the traditional filling is made with veal, turkey, or capon and a little prosciutto and mortadella. Once again, my view is that there are many good leftover things to put in either, so if you have excess roast chicken or an odd pork or veal chop, you might add the leftover meat to your filling.

Cappelletti or tortellini alla panna, another favorite on menus, are simply bathed in cream and sprinkled with Parmesan. For appetizers with drinks, tortellini may be deep-fried in olive oil until crisp, then sprinkled with Parmesan.

Normally, about 8 to 10 pieces are served in the soup bowl. At more elaborate dinners I sometimes make them bigger and put only 2 or 3 in the bowl so guests will have room for more courses.

$^{1}/_{2}$ **pound lean ground pork or veal**
$^{1}/_{2}$ **pound ground chicken or turkey breast**
3 ounces prosciutto, fat removed
2 ounces mortadella or prosciutto cotto (cooked ham)
3 tablespoons grated Parmigiano-Reggiano
2 egg yolks
Pinch of fresh grated nutmeg
Salt and freshly ground pepper to taste
1 recipe Pasta all'Uovo (page 88)
1 recipe Brodo di Carne, Brodo di Pollo, or Brodo di Verdure (page 68, 69, or 71)
Grated Parmigiano-Reggiano

FOLD

FILLING

PRESS TO SEAL

PRESS TO SEAL

Place a Teaspoon
of filling off-center.

Fold into
triangle,
sealing edges
well.

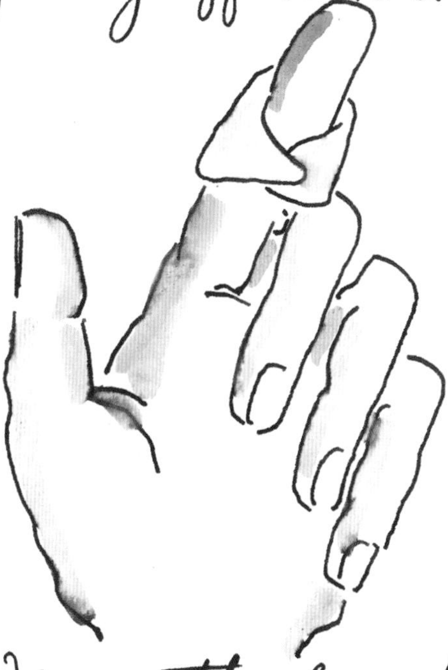

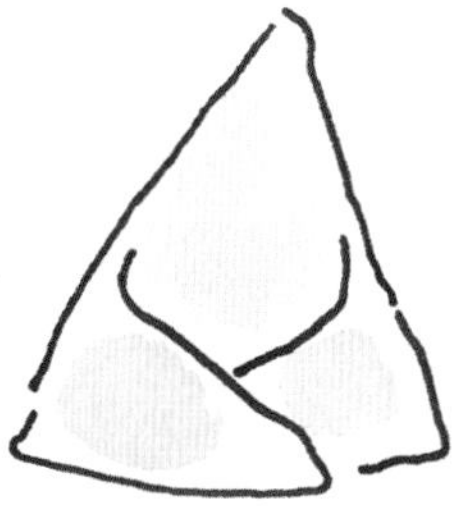

Wrap the dough
around your
finger...

...to make
a hat-shaped
pasta.

Put everything (except the pasta and stock) in the bowl of a food processor and pulse until the mixture is almost smooth but not puréed. You may add a spoonful of stock or white wine if the mixture seems too dry.

Cut pasta squares for cappelletti or circles for tortellini, slightly smaller for mini-tortellini and larger, about 3-inch squares, for cappelloni or tortelloni. Put a large pot of salted water on to boil while you form the cappelletti or tortellini.

Moisten the edges of the rounds or squares and place about 1 teaspoon filling off-center on each. Fold the rounds into half-moons or the squares into triangles, sealing the edges well. Holding one end of the half-moon or the end of the long side of the triangle, wrap the dough around your finger, bringing the other end over the first and pinching firmly to seal (see illustration, page 73). You will now have a little hat-shaped pasta. Repeat until all the filling is used.

The pasta can be made and formed a couple of hours before serving. Place on a tray and cover with a towel until ready to use. When the water is boiling, drop the hats into the water and cook for 2 to 3 minutes, until al dente. Remove and drain well.

Bring meat, chicken, or vegetable stock to a simmer, add the cooked pasta, and let simmer for a minute or two to heat through. Serve in pasta bowls with more Parmigiano-Reggiano.

Minestrone

. . . .

MIXED VEGETABLE SOUP

Serves 4 to 6

Why is the word *minestra* so much more tantalizing than *soup?* Without even knowing it, my mother made beautiful minestre, which we were given religiously the minute a Texas blue norther hit town, denuding the trees. Those relentless, freezing winters were, no doubt, preparing me for Italy in February.

At a delightful house on the estate of the Villa Ruffo (part of Villa Borghese), where we were fortunate to stay one winter, I spent many cold days cooking. Where else but next to the stove can you be really warm and toasty in a lovely but unheated villa? A comforting soup kept our spirits and body temperature up.

Chatting with women (there are hardly ever men!) at the butcher shop one morning, I was told that in a true minestra a spoon must stand up straight, and the soup must always contain beans. The Roman minestre vary from trattoria to trattoria, but one thing is sure: there is hardly a menu without one. A waiter, just like a good mother, will always offer you a minestra if you are not feeling well.

$^{1}/_{2}$ cup extra virgin olive oil

2 large onions, chopped

3 celery ribs, sliced thin

4 large carrots, sliced or chopped

2 medium zucchini, chopped fine

2 garlic cloves, minced

4 ripe tomatoes, whirred in a blender or food processor until not quite puréed

1 cup fresh beans or cooked dried beans

1 potato, chopped

A few fresh basil leaves or a spoonful of pesto

Juice of 1 lemon

1 $^{1}/_{2}$ quarts heated Brodo di Verdure, Brodo di Pollo, or Brodo di Carne (page 71, 69, or 68)

2 cups cooked pasta or rice

2 tablespoons minced fresh flat-leaf parsley

$^{1}/_{2}$ cup grated Parmigiano-Reggiano

Heat the olive oil in a large soup pot, add the onions, celery, carrots, and zucchini, and cook over medium heat until golden, 5 to 6 minutes. Add the garlic and cook for a minute. Add the tomatoes, beans, potato, basil or pesto, lemon juice, and stock and simmer for 30 to 40 minutes or until the vegetables are soft. Add the cooked pasta or rice and simmer for an additional 2 to 3 minutes to heat through. Serve each bowl sprinkled with parsley and Parmigiano-Reggiano.

Pasta e Fagioli o Ceci

· ·

PASTA WITH FRESH SHELLING OR GARBANZO BEANS

Serves 4 to 6

Discarding maps and simply following good smells, we followed our noses one day at lunchtime to a small, inexpensive trattoria near Piazza del Parlamento, da Gino, where we now always feel as welcome as Gino's new grandchild. Gino holds the honor of *Cavaliere del Lavoro,* similar to a knighthood in England, and I am sure it is for his *pasta e fagioli* and *saltimbocca.* Both are memorable, especially in crisp weather after a long walk with stomachs growling. This tiny trattoria is the essence of Rome.

The famous white zolfino bean, a tender, pale green marvel with a very thin skin, makes this dish sing, but at home you may substitute fresh cranberry beans.

I sometimes add a cup or so of white wine, even if it is not authentic, along with my stored vegetable or chicken stock to deepen the flavor.

1^{1}/$_{2}$ pounds shelled fresh white cannellini, zolfini, cranberry, or garbanzo beans or 1 pound dried
    cannellini or garbanzo beans (chickpeas)
5 cups Brodo di Verdure or Brodo di Pollo (page 71 or 69)
1 small onion, chopped fine
^{1}/$_{4}$ cup extra virgin olive oil
1 slice pancetta, about ^{1}/$_{2}$ inch thick, chopped fine (optional)
1 celery rib, chopped fine
2 garlic cloves, chopped fine
1 small dried hot red pepper, crushed
3 anchovy fillets
1 cup canned tomatoes, crushed
^{1}/$_{2}$ teaspoon salt
^{1}/$_{2}$ pound ditalini, bombolotti, or any very short pasta
^{1}/$_{2}$ cup grated Parmigiano-Reggiano

IF USING FRESH BEANS:

Cover the beans with stock and add the onion. Bring to a boil and simmer for 30 minutes, covered.

IF USING DRIED BEANS:

Cover the beans with cold water and bring to a boil. Turn off the heat and let cool. Discard the soaking water, add the stock and onion, and bring to a boil. Lower the heat and simmer for 1 to $1^1/_2$ hours or until tender, adding stock, wine or a little water as needed to keep the beans moist. Garbanzos may need to cook a bit longer. I sometimes use a cup of beer for a different flavor.

TO FINISH THE SOUP:

Heat the olive oil in a small skillet, sauté the pancetta and celery over medium heat for a few minutes, then add the garlic and pepper and cook until the garlic is golden, about 2 minutes. Add this mixture to the bean pot along with the tomatoes, anchovies, and salt. Cook for 30 minutes more, until the beans are tender. Meanwhile, put a large pot of salted water on to boil.

Take out half the beans to use for another dish, such as Peperoni con Fagioli e Tonno (page 52). Take out and purée a ladle of beans and return them to the pot.

Cook the pasta in the boiling salted water until just a minute under al dente. Drain and mix with the beans. Heat through and serve with Parmigiano-Reggiano.

. . . .

I am not a dried borlotto fan. They are tough, mealy, and bear no resemblance to summer's fresh cranberry beans, so use the dried white cannellini found in Italian markets, Great Northern, or pinto beans instead.

Almost any soup or casserole (such as ossobuco) benefits from puréeing a little of the vegetables and stock and adding it back to the pot, a technique used by cooks across Rome.

Broken bits of dried pasta may be used in place of short pasta. After all, this was a working man's dish, and cooks used whatever was at hand. Leftover cooked, plain pasta may be used instead of fresh-cooked.

If you have no stock, use water, wine, or beer.

Zuppa di Pesce

FISH SOUP

Serves 4 to 6

For years I have visited Rome's fish markets in search of the best sea creatures for soup. The Mediterranean offers *triglie,* with its hundreds of needlelike bones, or branzino (sometimes called *spigola, ragno,* or *pesce lupo,* "wolf fish"), a firm, tasty sea bass that needs only olive oil, lemon, and salt when grilled. Salmon is often eaten as carpaccio, although I prefer my salmon cooked medium pink and moist rather than raw (unless a sushi master is preparing it). Mullet abound, as do members of the tentacled family: octopus in every size, shape, and color; calamari, big and small; seppie (those adorable tiny creatures that look like little rubber thumb-covers with legs); and of course large and small shrimp; clams (sometimes called *arselle* or *tartufi*); crab; and scampi, or langoustines, to sweeten the pot.

A good fish soup is a triumph, no matter what is in it, but I always use some very basic techniques. Always start with olive oil and vegetables, stock made from chowder fish, the parts cut off when fish are filleted, more fish, and serve with good rustic bread. I promise you success every time and rave reviews.

Any fish you have in your part of the country will do just fine, even if in a pinch you have to use frozen, but fresh fish is always preferred.

granchio

^{1}/2 cup extra virgin olive oil

1 large onion, chopped fine

2 leeks, white parts only, sliced fine

2 celery ribs, chopped fine

1 small fennel bulb, chopped fine

3 garlic cloves, minced

1 small dried hot red pepper, crushed

2 pounds assorted boneless fish (halibut, sea bass, whitefish, salmon, swordfish, shark, monkfish, flounder, sole), cut into 1-1 ^{1}/2-inch pieces

1 ^{1}/2 cups white wine

2 large tomatoes, chopped fine or puréed in a food processor or blender

One ^{1}/2-inch sliver orange zest

5 to 6 cups Brodo di Pesce (page 70)

Juice of 1 lemon

Pinch of saffron threads

^{1}/2 pound medium shrimp, peeled and chopped coarse

1 pound clams, washed well

1 ^{1}/2 pounds mussels, cleaned

Rustic bread, toasted

1 garlic clove, cut in half

Heat the olive oil in a large soup pot. Add the onion, leeks, celery, fennel, and minced garlic and cook over medium heat until translucent, about 5 minutes. Add the red pepper and fish, turning the fish to coat with oil. Cook for another few minutes to seal all surfaces of the fish, then add the wine, tomatoes, orange zest, stock, lemon juice, and saffron, and simmer for 20 minutes over low heat. Add the shrimp, clams, and mussels and continue cooking, covered, until the clams and mussels open, about 10 minutes. Taste for seasoning and serve over toasted slices of rustic bread rubbed with a garlic clove.

Variation:

For a very different taste, serve fish soup with toasted bread spread with pesto (page 113) or salsa verde (page 178). Crab, shrimp, or lobster can also be added to any fish soup.

. . . .

Slice 1^1/2 pounds sea scallops horizontally into 2 to 3 pieces, depending on size. Poach them for 2 minutes in the strained stock, then remove and use in Insalata di Mare (page 36) or serve tossed with olive oil, lemon juice, and parsley. Their sweetness will enrich your stock.

Pappa al Pomodoro

. . . .

THICK TOMATO AND BREAD SOUP

Serves 4

The Italians make many dishes that are soothing to the soul, and this is one of the best. Bring me your tired and weary, your lovelorn, your cranky little ones or ailing *nonna,* and I shall set before them an instant cure: olive oil, fresh tomatoes, and bread, the most agreeable and effective triumvirate of the kitchen.

Some cooks add a cup of vegetable or chicken broth to make a thinner soup.

4 slices Pane Casereccio (page 242), or rustic bread, with or without crusts, toasted

2 garlic cloves, minced, plus 1 clove for the bread

2 tablespoons extra virgin olive oil, plus a little more for serving

6 medium tomatoes, puréed in a food processor or blender

A few fresh basil leaves, chopped fine

$^1/_2$ teaspoon salt

Rub the toasted bread with a cut garlic clove and tear into bite-sized pieces. Heat the olive oil in a skillet, add the minced garlic, and cook over medium heat just until golden, about 1 minute. Add the bread, tomatoes, and basil and cook for about 10 minutes. Serve in bowls with a splash of olive oil.

Variation:

For a delicious cold summer soup, put the olive oil, tomatoes, basil, and a tiny piece of the garlic in the bowl of a food processor and pulse for a few seconds. Serve chilled with a splash of extra virgin olive oil and more bread.

Stracciatella alla Romana

. . . .

CONSOMMÉ WITH EGG

Serves 4

Nothing could be easier than this soup, which has been around since the toga. It is best made with your own rich bouillon, but cubes serve in a pinch. Some cooks also add a spoon or two of semolina flour, but I prefer the purist's version, thickened only by the eggs.

2 quarts Brodo di Carne or Brodo di Pollo (page 68 or 69)
4 or 5 eggs
Pinch of fresh grated nutmeg
2 tablespoons grated Parmigiano-Reggiano, plus more for serving
Salt and freshly ground pepper to taste
A few drops of fresh lemon juice

Bring the stock to a boil. Meanwhile, stir the rest of the ingredients together with a fork or whisk, but do not make them foamy. Quickly stir the egg mixture into the boiling stock, creating little *stracci,* or rags, of egg. Serve with more Parmigiano-Reggiano.

Variation:
For *zuppa pavese* (not to be confused with *zuppa inglese,* a sweet dessert based on English trifle), a variation of stracciatella that originated in Lombardy but that is sometimes found on Roman menus, bring hot beef stock to a boil, put a slice of toasted rustic bread in a soup plate, break a couple of very fresh eggs over the bread, and ladle hot broth over the eggs. Sprinkle with lots of Parmesan and fresh pepper and serve.

"If flour is silver, semolino is gold." Motto of Rome's Museo Nazionale delle Paste Alimentari. • Spend an afternoon in Rome's Museo Nazionale delle Paste Alimentari (Piazza Scanderbeg, 117) and you will be amazed by the vast history and complexity of one of the world's favorite foods. A museum publication sold in the gift shop, *Time for Pasta,* cites the existence of pasta from the time of the Etruscans and Romans, dispelling the myth that Marco Polo first brought noodles back from China. • For me, pasta and bread are the twin staffs of life. I always serve them together, as I

cannot see one without the other, contrary to some hostesses' view that bread is never to be served with the primo. The Romans I know happily eat bread with pasta, for with what else would one *fare la scarpetta?* This is certainly acceptable at home, but please think twice before wiping the Ginori china at a state dinner. Still, even the ambassador is probably longing to make his little shoe after the Spaghetti alla Boscaiola (page 122) has been consumed. Fortunately for me, my husband has the endearing habit of leaving precisely the right amount of pasta and sauce in his bowl to fit on my last crust of bread. For this alone, I would have married him.

Many people have the mistaken idea that pasta is only a backdrop, or worse, a bed for the sauce, but in fact the quantities of the two must be in perfect balance, with just enough sauce to barely coat each piece of pasta.

Fresh pasta, made well, served with just the right amount of butter or oil, is devastatingly good by itself. But—and this is law—any sauce you put on pasta should be perfectly compatible with the noodle underneath. This is why specific shapes of pasta often demand a particular sauce. For example, Bucatini all'Amatriciana (page 120) allows tomato sauce (see Pasta al Pomodoro o al Sugo, page 100) to seep gradually into the hollow opening of the pasta strand (making a bib imperative; a thrashing bucatino can hurl sauce in a 5-foot radius!). Clam sauce simply would not work with anything except spaghetti or, perhaps, in a pinch, linguine, an Italian-American combination. Clams slip all over the place when served over short pasta since there is no web of noodle threads in which to snare them. And imagine a rich, hearty rabbit or wild boar sauce lying heavily upon delicate, thin vermicelli. Unthinkable!

The Romans eat fresh and dry pasta interchangeably, depending on the sauce and season, and a trattoria will be surely be given thumbs up or down on the quality of its pasta. The more expensive durum wheat (called *semola di grano duro*) pasta is far superior to one made with common wheat or bread flour, which is why De Cecco, Barilla, and other strong *semolino paste* have stayed in first position, in both Italy and other countries. De Cecco has a good tooth when cooked, although Barilla is running a close second for producing imaginative shapes such as mini-rigatoni and *campane,* little bells, which children adore. Both are found almost everywhere, but even in regions without an abundance of Italian products you will find supermarkets that carry some form of acceptable pasta. Never cook pasta as long as the package suggests. Good pasta should be al dente in about 9 minutes, cooked at a full, roiling boil. Some rigatoni might take 10 minutes, but never more.

Most fresh pasta is made with semolina flour. Semolina is also the basis for Gnocchi alla Romana (page 108) and certain regional soups. I often hear people confusing *semolino* (called "semolina" in English) with polenta, the latter being made from corn, so keep this in mind when shopping for your flour. My trick is to mix fine semolina flour with unbleached white flour, half and half, for easily manageable pasta, as pure semolina creates a stiff dough, quite ragged on the edges, which has to go through the first large opening of the pasta machine several times to smooth it out.

Next to a food processor, the best and most enjoyable piece of equipment you can have in your kitchen is a hand-cranked pasta machine, preferably made by Imperia, expensive compared to most but worth every euro. If you have ever used and then tried to clean the modern electric pasta makers, resorting in exasperation to a toothbrush and a toothpick, you know why I am partial to the hand-cranked ones. Plus, they're just more fun to use, and kids can turn out their own pasta easily. The smooth movement of the rollers as they press the pasta ever thinner, the precision of the cutter as a pristine sheet of dough goes in one side and comes out the other in perfect fettuccine or pappardelle—here is magic in pasta making not to be missed.

TO COOK PASTA:

For most of my recipes, you may put the salted water on to boil and then start your sauce. Your sauce will often be ready before the water boils!

- Use I quart of water for each person.
- The pasta pot must be large enough to allow water to circulate around the pasta at a full boil. A 6-quart pot is a good size for starters.
- Use a scant $^1/_4$ cup salt to about 6 quarts water. Every Italian cook emphasizes that pasta must always be perfectly salted before it mingles with the sauce, so salt your pasta water well—most of the salt gets tossed out. The water should taste as salty as the sea. There is nothing more unappealing than bland, poorly seasoned pasta, which detracts enormously from the most perfect sauce.
- Al dente pasta cooks in I to 3 minutes less than the suggested time on the box.
- Fresh pasta cooks in I to 4 minutes, depending on its thickness and cut.
- Drain pasta in a large colander placed inside the serving bowl. Reserve a little pasta water if needed in a recipe, about 2 to 3 tablespoons. Lift out the colander and toss your sauce and pasta in the nice warm bowl. (Normally, I just put it back in the warm pasta pot, mix the sauce and pasta, then serve the plates from the kitchen.)
- Fresh pasta dough must never form a ball or mass in the food processor. When it does, you have used too much liquid.
- Fresh rolled pasta may be kept from sticking together with a dusting of cornstarch, semolina, or rice flour.
- If the first sheets of pasta are left too long before you cut them, they will not pass through the machine easily. Better to quickly cut the pasta while it is slightly moist and then dry the excess or store in the refrigerator.
- Fresh noodles and stuffed pasta may be made ahead of time, dusted with any of the aforementioned flours, and covered with a clean, dry cloth to use later that day. Stuffed pasta is best used within a couple of hours. Or dry the noodles on a clean towel and store in plastic bags.

Pasta all'Uovo

FRESH EGG PASTA

Serves 4

How I love the earthy, sexy smell of fresh pasta shops in Rome! On the way to my tiny bar in the via della Croce, I pass by a window filled with neat piles of fresh tagliatelle and pappardelle laid out on clean trays. The same little man who has been there for years tends his noodles with the same daily smudge of flour on his pink cheek. The lovely, eggy scent of pasta lingers just inside his door, luring innocent passersby even if they have just had their cornetto. At eight o'clock in the morning, I am imagining lunch.

There are four basic ways to make pasta. You can make a pasta all'uovo using the basic recipe. You can then enrich the dough by using more egg yolks for a special pasta—fettuccine with white truffles, for example. Or you may use fewer eggs and add a little oil for a lighter pasta. When chickens were scarce and oil was plentiful (during the war, for example), this combination was prevalent. I do not put oil in my pasta dough, but try one batch to see which you prefer. As a last resort, you may use no eggs at all, but pasta made from only flour and water will not expand as it cooks, and the resulting noodles simply do not have the taste and elasticity of egg pasta.

The secret to perfect pasta is mixing flour, egg, and scant water just long enough to form tiny granules resembling bee pollen, which can be gathered easily with the hands into a semisoft nonsticky mass of dough. The dough may even look a little dry to you, but it is deceptively moist and will come together as you press it into a flat cake. If your dough is sticky, you will have nothing but trouble.

Once you have mixed, rolled, and felt the granular texture of fresh pasta, you will have no trouble turning it out for the masses in minutes. In fact, with a little practice, you can always make fresh pasta before the water boils.

4 cups all-purpose unbleached flour, or 2 cups fine semolina flour plus 2 cups all-purpose
    unbleached flour
1 teaspoon salt
2 large or 3 medium eggs
$^{1}/_{2}$ cup warm water (you may need a few drops more or less, depending on your flour)

Put the flour, salt, and eggs into the bowl of a food processor. Add the water as you pulse, watching carefully to make sure the pasta does not leave the sides of the bowl. If the pasta seems too wet, add a tablespoon or two of flour; if too dry, add a few drops of water.

Gather some of the grainy dough together in your hand. The little granules should stick together as you press them and stay together in a soft lump that releases easily from your hand. The dough is now ready to roll.

Divide the dough into 8 pieces, forming each into a round, flattened cake about 3 inches in diameter and smoothing the edges of the cake as well as you can.

Set your pasta machine to the widest opening and place the edge of a cake at the opening. Begin to roll slowly as you feed the cake into the opening. The pasta will emerge with very ragged edges and may or may not tear a little, depending on how fast you have rolled it, but don't worry.

Fold the top third of the rolled pasta rectangle down one third of the way and the bottom third upward, making a little square with two ragged edges and two smooth sides.

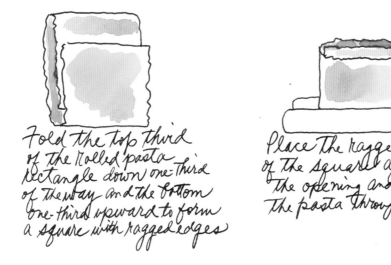

Fold the top third of the rolled pasta rectangle down one-third of the way and the bottom one-third upward to form a square with ragged edges

Place the ragged edge of the square against the opening and roll the pasta through again.

Place the ragged edge of the square against the opening and roll the pasta through the widest opening again. Repeat the folding once more, turning the ragged edge over the top third and the bottom third up to form a square with smooth edges. Repeat this rolling and turning process with the other seven cakes of pasta. Set aside the rectangles. They may not be perfect rectangles, but that's all right; they will still make beautifully cut noodles with no ragged edges.

Switch to the medium setting (about midway on the dial) and roll the squares through into longer sheets. Set aside the sheets, not overlapping, on a barely floured surface. If you have wooden countertops, you'll need no flour. Marble, granite, or any kind of manmade surface needs a little flour so that the pasta will not "sweat" and stick.

Switch to the next-to-narrowest opening and carefully roll the pasta squares through. You will have very long sheets of pasta almost like fabric, about 15 inches or so in length. Lay the sheets on a dry towel or on a wooden surface, making sure they do not overlap.

Now choose which shape you want: fettuccine, spaghetti, or simply flat pasta with which to make stuffed pasta or lasagna.

TO CUT THE NOODLES:

With one hand, feed the end of the long sheet into the fettuccine or spaghetti cutter of your pasta machine. As you turn the handle with your right hand, place the other hand under the noodles emerging from the blades, guiding the cut noodles out from under the cutter. To prevent sticking, lay them on a towel dusted with flour or put them in a large bowl with a little flour, semolina, or cornstarch and toss them with a light hand until all are coated.

Cut the pasta when it is fresh or, if you wish to keep the sheets fresh until cutting time, dust them with cornstarch and stack them on top of one another, then wrap them in a dry towel, place them in a plastic bag, and refrigerate. This works well for same-day cutting, but fresh pasta sheets left in the fridge over 2 days tend to discolor because of the egg.

To dry cut pasta, simply spread the noodles out on a floured cloth in loose individual serving bunches or flat for a day or two. Dried noodles keep very well in resealable plastic bags and tend not to stick together when cooked as fresh ones sometimes do. Both are delicious, but thoroughly dried pasta may be kept up to a month in an airtight resealable bag or container (although in our house, nothing stays around that long).

Fettuccine—Use the next-to-last opening to make fettuccine with a little more substance and the last opening to make a thinner noodle. Use the wide blade on the machine.

Pappardelle—There is a separate attachment that will enable you to cut a wider noodle. Barring that, simply roll out long, wide sheets of pasta on the narrowest setting. Lay the sheets out on a cutting board or counter and cut the pasta into 1-inch widths. Pappardelle are often used with sauces made from game.

Ravioli—Roll out on the narrowest setting and follow instructions for ravioli, folding the dough lengthwise over the filling (see Ravioli con Spinaci e Ricotta, page 106)

Spaghetti or Spaghettini—Roll dough through the narrowest setting on the machine.

Stuffed Pasta—Roll out on the narrowest setting and leave pasta in a sheet. Cut desired strips or squares for lasagna, or circles or squares for agnolotti, ravioli, tortellini, and other small stuffed pasta. Always boil the pasta for lasagna before assembling the dish. Pasta rolled very thin dries quickly and so must be filled or cut and used right away unless you wish to dry it for future use. If the sheets become too long to handle easily, simply cut each one in half and then proceed to cut the noodles. Slightly shorter noodles are easier to twirl on a fork!

Fettuccine al Limone

· ·

RIBBON PASTA WITH FRESH LEMON

Serves 4

When I serve this intense, lemony pasta, my guests practically faint with pleasure. It is one of those easy dishes that knocks your socks off. Lemon, cream with just a touch of garlic, and Parmesan will elevate any everyday fresh pasta to grandeur. You need not serve huge plates of this pasta if you are serving a second, because it is rich and filling. Use Eureka lemons, if possible, since their zest is thick and tasty.

2 tablespoons butter
1 very tiny dried hot red pepper, crushed
1 small garlic clove, quartered
3 cups heavy cream
3 large lemons
1 recipe Pasta all'Uovo (page 88), cut into fettuccine
2/3 cup grated Parmigiano-Reggiano
Freshly ground pepper or chopped fresh flat-leaf parsley for garnish (optional)

Bring a large pot of salted water to a boil and have 4 warm pasta bowls ready.

In a large skillet, heat the butter to bubbling, add the pepper and garlic, and cook over medium heat until the garlic is golden, about 2 minutes. Remove the garlic and add the cream. When the cream is simmering, add the pulp and grated zest (no white attached) of 2 of the lemons and let the sauce reduce by about one quarter, which should take about 4 to 5 minutes.

When the sauce has thickened, cook the fettuccine in the boiling water for a few minutes, until al dente, and while it is cooking add the juice of the remaining lemon and half the Parmigiano-Reggiano to the cream sauce. Drain the pasta well and toss with the lemon sauce. Sprinkle with pepper or parsley, if desired, and serve with the remaining Parmigiano-Reggiano.

Fettuccine all'Alfredo

. . . .

RIBBON PASTA WITH BUTTER AND PARMESAN

Serves 4

At Alfredo alla Scrofa, Mary Pickford and Douglas Fairbanks gaze dreamily at one another over their rich fettuccine, which the owner himself has just created in honor of their honeymoon. On a golden plate! Or tossed with golden spoons, depending on which storyteller is embellishing the legend. According to the *Grande Enciclopedia Illustrata della Gastronomia,* Fettuccine all'Alfredo contains cream, but I say, no, no, no! Perhaps the chef interviewed at the restaurant led the researchers astray, but there is *no* cream in this dish, cream being the prime ingredient used erroneously in so many Italian dishes. Although a case may be made for a shot of cream, I feel that it detracts from the real thing, which has no rival when executed properly.

Salt

1 recipe Pasta all'Uovo (page 88), made with 8 egg yolks instead of 2 or 3 whole eggs, cut into fettuccine

1 cup (2 sticks) butter, softened

1 cup very finely grated Parmigiano-Reggiano, plus more for serving

Have ready 4 warm plates and a large warm serving plate on which to toss the noodles. Bring a large pot of salted water to a boil. Cook the fettuccine for 3 to 4 minutes, until al dente (Alfredo says to remove them just as they rise to the top). Drain, leaving a couple of tablespoons of water with the noodles so that they do not stick together.

Put the butter, divided into small pats, on the warmed large plate and put the noodles on top of the butter. Sprinkle the Parmigiano-Reggiano on top of the noodles, and with 2 large forks, quickly begin to toss the fettuccine to mix in the butter and cheese, trapping as much air as possible (as you would when folding air into a soufflé) between the strands of pasta to make the mixture very light. Serve immediately with more Parmigiano-Reggiano. I like a pinch of pepper, too, but it's not in the original.

Fettuccine alle Noci

· ·

RIBBON PASTA WITH WALNUT SAUCE

Serves 4

La Ciotola, on the outskirts of Rome off the via Cassia, and now unfortunately closed, served these thick noodles with a creamy nut sauce, chops or little flattened chickens cooked on a large grill over wood from the vineyards, and a tiramisù or homemade torta to end a meal. Nut sauces, borrowed from Liguria, are often found on pasta.

Rustic home cooking (often labeled *cucina casereccia* on a restaurant's sign), several generations of family, an occasional dog and cat or two, lambs (and children) cavorting nearby, and of course, *la mamma* presiding over all are the ingredients for a perfect Sunday lunch—the essence of eating in Italy.

1 slice rustic bread, crusts removed, toasted
2/3 cup milk or heavy cream
8 tablespoons (1 stick) butter or 1/2 cup olive oil
2 garlic cloves, minced
1 pound walnuts or hazelnuts, toasted
A few drops lemon juice
1 recipe Pasta all'Uovo (page 88), cut into fettuccine
1/2 cup grated Parmigiano-Reggiano

Bring a large pot of salted water to a boil. Meanwhile, soak the bread in the milk or cream until soft. Melt the butter or heat the oil in a skillet, add the garlic and nuts, and toss together over medium heat for 3 to 4 minutes, just until the nuts and garlic are golden. Put the contents of the skillet in the bowl of a food processor with the lemon juice and blend to a smooth paste. Add a little warm milk, if necessary, to obtain the consistency you like for pasta, and reheat the sauce.

Cook the fresh fettuccine for 3 to 4 minutes, until just al dente. Drain and toss with the sauce. Serve with Parmigiano-Reggiano.

Variation:
This nut sauce may be served over cheese-filled ravioli or agnolotti, sometimes called *pansotti* in Liguria.

Fettuccine con Tartufi Bianchi

RIBBON PASTA WITH WHITE TRUFFLES

Serves 4

Now here is pure decadence. The Romans attribute many emotions to white truffles, including passion, and I must say that when I taught this recipe to a class one evening, the banter became more raucous and rowdy as we worked our way through several truffle courses.

In trattorie, the waiter will approach your fettuccine with a stainless-steel truffle cutter adjusted to a particular setting and proceed to slice what looks like a pale brown nut over your pasta until you stop him. Keep in mind that fresh truffles last year were going for about $600 a pound in the U.S., and although they always cost less in Italy, the longer you wait to cry *"Basta!"* the more euros you will pay.

Allow the waiter to slice until you have covered your fettuccine with a blanket of beige slivers and their earthy, sexy aroma has filled the air. Plunge in, banish thoughts of cost, and enjoy one of the greatest dishes (and perhaps a night of love) in Italy.

4 tablespoons butter
$^1/_2$ very small garlic clove, minced
2 cups heavy cream
$^1/_2$ cup grated Parmigiano-Reggiano, plus more for serving
1 pinch of fresh grated nutmeg
Freshly ground pepper (optional)
1 recipe Pasta all'Uovo (page 88), cut into fettuccine
4 to 6 ounces whole white truffles

Bring a large pot of salted water to a boil.

Melt the butter in a medium skillet, add the garlic, and cook over medium heat for a minute. Add the cream and simmer for 5 minutes, until thickened. Add the Parmigiano-Reggiano, nutmeg, and pepper and simmer for another few minutes, until thick. If you feel you need more sauce, you can always add a bit more cream.

Cook the pasta for 3 to 4 minutes, until al dente. Drain and toss with the sauce. Serve on warmed plates at once and shave truffles on each dish at the table so that guests can have the pleasure of their wonderful perfume. Serve with more Parmigiano-Reggiano.

Paglia e Fieno

. . . .

"STRAW AND HAY":
PLAIN AND SPINACH FETTUCCINE WITH
PROSCIUTTO AND PEAS

Serves 4

This lovely name refers to the two kinds of pasta with the colors of straw (plain fettuccine) and hay (spinach fettuccine) used in the dish. To make life easier, you may buy packages of the plain and green fettuccine, but they are best made fresh. You may put any sauce on the two pastas, but the classic one is made with Parma's famous salt-cured ham and fresh spring peas.

Salt
1 recipe Pasta all'Uovo, (page 88) $^1/_2$ recipe made with spinach (see Note), cut into fettuccine
2 tablespoons extra virgin olive oil
1 small onion, chopped fine
8 brown mushrooms, sliced very thin
4 thin slices prosciutto, chopped
1 cup heavy cream
1 cup shelled fresh spring peas
$^1/_2$ cup grated Parmigiano-Reggiano

Bring a large pot of salted water to a boil.

Meanwhile, heat the olive oil in a medium skillet and cook the onion over medium heat until translucent, 3 to 4 minutes. Add the mushrooms and cook until nicely browned. Add the prosciutto and continue cooking for 2 to 3 minutes, then add the cream and cook until heated through and the sauce has reduced and thickened, about 7 minutes. Stir in the fresh peas and a spoonful of the Parmigiano-Reggiano and cook for 3 minutes more. Cook the pasta for 4 to 5 minutes, until al dente. Drain and toss with the sauce. Serve with Parmigiano-Reggiano.

Note: For the pasta, make one-half recipe of Pasta all'Uovo using water. Make another half recipe substituting $^1/_4$ cup spinach purée for the water. You may need a few drops more water in the dough, depending on the wetness of the purée.

Pappardelle alla Lepre

. . . .

WIDE NOODLES WITH HARE OR RABBIT

We use chicken so much in our cooking that we forget there is domestic rabbit to be had in almost all upscale markets, dressed and ready for the pan. I urge you to try the succulent, mild meat if only to take an occasional break from our staple bird. Be the first on your block to serve these rich and delectable noodles. You may, of course, use a pound of commercial pasta in place of homemade.

One 2- to 3-pound rabbit, cut into 2- to 3-inch pieces
$^{1}/_{2}$ recipe marinade for Bresaola con la Rughetta (page 32), *without the salt*
1 small onion, peeled
1 carrot, sliced
$^{1}/_{4}$ teaspoon salt
$^{1}/_{2}$ cup flour mixed with $^{1}/_{8}$ teaspoon each salt, freshly ground pepper, and paprika in a paper bag
$^{1}/_{4}$ cup extra virgin olive oil
1 onion, chopped fine
3 shallots, sliced thin
1 carrot, chopped fine
2 tablespoons cognac
2 cups white wine
1 cup rabbit stock or Brodo di Pollo (page 69)
1 clove
1 recipe Pasta all'Uovo (page 88), cut into pappardelle
$^{1}/_{2}$ cup grated Parmigiano-Reggiano

Cover the rabbit pieces with the marinade in a glass or stainless-steel bowl, seal with plastic wrap, and marinate overnight or for 8 hours. Remove the pieces from the marinade and cut off as much meat as possible.

Place the rabbit bones in a pot with the peeled onion, sliced carrot, and $^{1}/_{4}$ teaspoon salt. Barely cover the bones with water, bring to a boil, and simmer until the liquid is reduced by half, about 15 to 20 minutes.

Meanwhile, toss the meat with the flour mixture, shaking off the excess. Heat the olive oil in a heavy casserole and brown the meat well on all sides. Transfer the meat to a plate. Cook the chopped onion, shallots, and carrot in the oil remaining in the pan, adding a little more oil if necessary, until the onion is translucent, 3 to 4 minutes. Add the browned rabbit meat and heat for a few minutes.

Stand back from the stove and add the Cognac, which will flame as you tilt the pan. When the flame dies out, add the wine, the stock, strained, and the clove and simmer over low heat, covered, for 40 to 50 minutes or until the meat is very tender. Cool, then pulse the sauce in the bowl of a food processor just until meat is minced—do not purée.

Bring a large pot of salted water to a boil. Cook the pappardelle for 3 to 4 minutes, until al dente, drain, toss with the sauce, and serve with Parmigiano-Reggiano.

Gnocchi di Patate

. . . .

POTATO DUMPLINGS

Serves 4

When gnocchi are made well, they are lovely light little ridged cylinders over which you may serve tomato sauce (see Pasta al Pomodoro o al Sugo, page 100) or only butter and cheese, but poorly made gnocchi can be heavy and leaden, in short, indigestible. The same light hand used for Fettuccine all'Alfredo (page 92) will keep gnocchi airy and digestible. Although served year-round, they are more attractive in winter than in warm months.

   You may add a little grated Parmesan and an egg yolk to gnocchi dough for a richer flavor. Cooked gnocchi may also be sautéed in butter until browned, then served with tomato sauce or Gorgonzola melted with cream (or milk) and butter.

1 1/2 pounds baking potatoes, peeled
Salt
1 egg (optional)
1 tablespoon softened butter (optional)
1 cup flour, sifted
Freshly ground pepper
4 tablespoons butter
1/2 cup grated Parmigiano-Reggiano

Boil the potatoes in salted water until soft. Drain and put them through a ricer or mash with a fork and mix with the egg and/or softened butter, if using. Season with salt and pepper to taste. On a very lightly floured board or surface, knead quickly to mix well, forming a smooth dough. Let the dough rest for a few minutes. Roll the dough into long ropes about 3/4 inch thick or as thick as your thumb. Cut 1-inch lengths with a sharp knife. Press each gnocco down onto the inside (or outside) curved tines of a fork dipped in flour to make the characteristic indentations on the gnocchi so that the sauce will adhere easily. Press lightly with a finger or thumb, then gently roll the gnocco up off the fork into a little cylinder.

   Bring a large pot of salted water to a boil, lower the heat until the water is simmering, and drop the gnocchi, one at a time, into the pot. When they turn over and float to the surface, they are ready, usually in 1 to 2 minutes. Remove with a slotted spoon and serve with butter and Parmigiano-Reggiano.

Orecchiette con Rapini

. . . .

LITTLE EARS WITH RAPINI

Serves 4

One of Rome's most popular dishes, probably because the broccoli rape (called *rapini* in Italian) that grows on farms south of the city is intense and sweet, with a subtle aftertaste of vanilla. Turnip greens (*cime di rapa,* called *rapini* in Tuscany) or young chard may be substituted for rapini.

$^{1}/_{2}$ cup extra virgin olive oil
4 garlic cloves, chopped fine
1 small dried hot red pepper, crushed
1 pound broccoli rape, chopped
4 anchovy fillets, chopped
1 cup Brodo di Verdure or Brodo di Pollo (page 71 or 69)
1 pound orecchiette
$^{1}/_{2}$ lemon
$^{1}/_{2}$ cup grated Parmigiano-Reggiano

Bring a large pot of salted water to a boil.

Heat the olive oil in a medium skillet and cook the garlic and hot pepper for a minute, until golden around the edges. Add the broccoli rape and cook it over medium heat until it is wilted and beginning to crisp, 7 to 10 minutes. Add the anchovies and stock, cover the pan, and cook for 5 to 7 minutes.

Cook the pasta in the boiling water until al dente. Drain and toss with the sauce and Parmigiano-Reggiano. Serve with a squeeze of lemon on each bowl.

Pasta al Pomodoro o al Sugo

PASTA WITH TOMATO SAUCE

Serves 4

On any Sunday morning as you join Romans in their true living room, the streets, you will smell onion and garlic sizzling in olive oil and the sweet, rich scent of simmering tomatoes coming from apartment windows. Almost every little street will have its own perfume, depending on whether the cook used meat or pancetta or kept it simple. Whatever the ingredients, a plain sugo, as it is called, is one of the basic sauces of Italy, kept on hand for a quick lunch or extra guests.

In fact, you will be using this sauce for so many things that I suggest you make a double recipe. In Rome, canned plum tomatoes are used in hundreds of sauces year-round, while uncooked sauces made with fresh tomatoes are made mostly in summer, when tomatoes are at their peak. I use the plain canned ones for this sauce (*never* those with added herbs or flavors), which I then ruthlessly pulverize with my bare hands as a Sicilian taught me to do for maximum flavor. Or, when short on squeezing time, I throw them into the food processor. Always use the pinch of sugar to balance the acid of the tomatoes. A plain sauce is more versatile than those made with garlic and other seasonings, and you can freeze the leftovers for other dishes. This recipe makes about four cups.

Salt
$^1/_2$ cup extra virgin olive oil
1 medium onion, minced
Two 18-ounce cans whole plum tomatoes, crushed or chopped
Generous pinch of sugar
1 pound dry pasta such as spaghetti or penne
$^1/_2$ cup grated Parmigiano-Reggiano

Bring a large pot of salted water to a boil.

Meanwhile, in a large skillet or casserole, heat the olive oil over medium heat, add the onion, and cook until translucent, 3 to 4 minutes. Add the tomatoes when the oil is still very hot, as this will affect their sugar and give the sauce a nice roasted tomato flavor. Add $^1/_2$ teaspoon salt and the sugar and lower the heat. Cook for 20 minutes, and your sauce is ready for any dish.

Cook any pasta in boiling water until al dente, drain well, toss with the sauce, and serve with Parmigiano-Reggiano.

Three Friends

Malfatti

·······························

"BADLY FORMED" RICOTTA AND SPINACH DUMPLINGS

Serves 4

I learned this delectable recipe from the mother of a restaurant owner outside the walls of
Assisi, but most trattorie in Rome serve some version of spinach gnocchi. Of course, the
Roman ricotta is practically still warm from the cow, and often Italian markets in the U.S. will
have a soft, rich ricotta made locally, but I like to use cottage cheese that has been left out for 8
hours to sour. As for any gnocchi, a light hand will serve you well. I use beet tops more often
than spinach because I feel they have more flavor, but your gnocchi may well turn out pink,
making this a perfect dish for the festival of San Valentino.

I pound spinach leaves or beet tops, steamed, drained until very dry, and chopped
I cup ricotta or cottage cheese left out for 8 hours with lid on loose, not sealed, to sour
2 eggs
I cup flour
I cup grated Parmigiano-Reggiano
Pinch of freshly grated nutmeg
Salt and freshly ground pepper
2 tablespoons butter, softened

Preheat the oven to 350°F. In a mixing bowl, combine the spinach, ricotta, eggs, $^1/_2$ cup of the flour (you may need a little more, but add enough to make a mixture that is not runny, like a very thick paste), $^1/_2$ cup of the Parmesan, the nutmeg, and salt and pepper to taste. Put the rest of the flour on a large plate or in a large shallow baking dish. With a teaspoon, drop balls of the ricotta mixture into the flour.

With your hands, toss the little balls of ricotta mixture in the flour, coating the outside, until you can handle them easily. Do not compact them. Make a few, leaving them on the floured plate, and bring a large pot of salted water to a boil. Lower the heat until the water is simmering and gently place the malfatti in the water. Let them simmer, but not boil, for 3 to 5 minutes or until they roll over and float to the top. Lift them out with a slotted spoon, draining well, and place them in a buttered baking dish. Continue making and poaching the balls until you've used up the mixture and the dish is full.

Dot the malfatti with the soft butter, sprinkle them with the rest of the Parmigiano-Reggiano, and bake for 10 minutes or until golden. You can also serve the malfatti with a *besciamella* (see Lasagna di Spinaci al Forno, page 104) flavored with truffles, mushrooms, or porcini, or with a tomato sauce (see Pasta al Pomodoro o al Sugo, page 100).

Lasagna di Spinaci al Forno

. . . .

BAKED PASTA WITH RICOTTA AND SPINACH

Serves 4 to 6

You may think it strange that my favorite recipe for lasagna comes from the Italian chef at the old La Rue restaurant in Los Angeles, but my ex-father-in-law ate at La Rue daily and could extract anything he wished from this marvelous cook, so I ended up with the coveted recipe. A layer of Parmesan-flavored béchamel sauce—*besciamella* in Italian—was the secret.

Béchamel is often found in *lasagne,* cannelloni, and other baked pasta dishes, a legacy perhaps from the *monzú* (corruption of *monsieur*) cooking developed when Sicilian aristocracy began importing French chefs. If you wish a richer sauce, you can use half-and-half in place of milk and add an egg yolk or two, a French habit I often adopt. Roman lasagna is often made without meat. I prefer the meatless one, but you may add a layer of the ragù from page 126 if you wish.

Salt to taste
3 cups milk, half-and-half, or heavy cream
2 tablespoons butter
2 tablespoons flour
2 egg yolks (optional)
Pinch of freshly grated nutmeg
1 recipe Pasta all'Uovo (page 88) cut into 1 $^1/_2$-inch-wide strips or 3- to 4-inch squares
Extra virgin olive oil
2 cups cooked, well drained, and chopped spinach
2 cups fresh ricotta
2 cups tomato sauce from Pasta al Pomodoro o al Sugo (page 100)
1 cup grated Parmigiano-Reggiano

Bring a large pot of salted water to a boil.

Meanwhile, make the *besciamella*. Heat the milk in a pan over medium heat just until little bubbles form around the edge, then remove it from the heat. Melt the butter until bubbling in a heavy saucepan. Sprinkle the flour over the butter and stir briskly with a whisk, cooking over low to medium heat until the butter and flour mixture, called a *roux*, is smooth and the flour is cooked through, about 2 minutes. Slowly add the warm milk, stirring well to remove any lumps, until the sauce is thickened slightly. Beat the egg yolks thoroughly and pour them slowly into the sauce, whisking the whole time. The sauce will become thick and smooth in a few minutes. Add the nutmeg, strain (optional), and cool. *Besciamella* may be kept for up to a week in the refrigerator, covered with plastic wrap directly on the surface to prevent a skin from forming.

Cook the pasta in the boiling water for 4 to 5 minutes, until al dente. Toss with a little olive oil to prevent sticking. Set aside.

Mix the spinach, ricotta, and cooled *besciamella* together.

Preheat the oven to 350°F.

Put a layer of pasta in a buttered baking dish large and deep enough to hold the layers, about 10 by 7 by 2 inches. Spread some of the spinach mixture over the pasta, spread some of the tomato sauce over the spinach mixture, and sprinkle Parmigiano-Reggiano over the tomato sauce. Repeat the layering, but end with a little spinach or tomato sauce rather than with Parmigiano-Reggiano, as the cheese will acquire a bitter taste if exposed to heat for a long time. Bake for 30 minutes or until brown and bubbling. Let cool for 10 minutes before cutting and serving.

Ravioli con Spinaci e Ricotta

RAVIOLI STUFFED WITH SPINACH AND RICOTTA

Serves 4

This classic dish is just about as good as ravioli get. Although we have fresh ricotta here in L.A., I find that cottage cheese, left out for 8 hours, will acquire a rich, slightly tangy taste that is far more interesting than most commercial *ricotte*. I sometimes use beet tops or young chard in place of spinach, which give the ravioli a more intense flavor. You can use this filling in cannelloni—cooked, flat 5-inch-square pieces of pasta rolled around the filling, covered with *besciamella* (page 104) or tomato sauce (see Pasta al Pomodoro o al Sugo, page 100), and baked like lasagna.

I recipe Pasta all'Uovo (page 88), cut for ravioli

1 $^{1}/_{2}$ pounds spinach, beet tops, or young chard, stalks and thick ribs removed

2 cups ricotta or cottage cheese left out to sour for 8 hours

3 tablespoons plus $^{1}/_{2}$ cup grated Parmigiano-Reggiano

2 egg yolks

Pinch of fresh grated nutmeg

Salt and freshly ground pepper

4 tablespoons butter

12 fresh sage leaves

Wash the greens well and, leaving the water on the leaves, steam in a pot with a little salt until just wilted. Drain very well, pressing out all the liquid (I save all vegetable liquids and have an instant vegetable stock on hand). Chop the greens very fine and mix with the 3 tablespoons Parmigiano-Reggiano, egg yolks, nutmeg, and salt and pepper to taste, or pulse in a food processor just until the ingredients are blended.

Follow the instructions for stuffed pasta as in Agnolotti di Carne (page 110), bring a large pot of salted water to a boil, and cook the ravioli for about 3 to 4 minutes until al dente.

Melt the butter in a small saucepan, add the sage leaves, and cook over medium heat just until the leaves are toasted, 3 to 5 minutes. Drain the ravioli and place in warmed bowls. Spoon the sauce over the ravioli and serve with the additional grated Parmigiano-Reggiano.

Variations:
Sauté 1 pound of any mushrooms, chopped fine, in $^{1}/_{4}$ cup extra virgin olive oil. Add a dash of Cognac or white wine and a squeeze of lemon. Use in place of ricotta stuffing.

Sauté 1 pound of any firm winter squash (turban, butternut, pumpkin, and so on), chopped, with $^{1}/_{2}$ cup chopped onion until tender, adding a little white wine if needed. Purée with a couple of crushed Amaretti biscotti, a spoonful of grated Parmigiano-Reggiano, and a few drops of lemon juice in the bowl of a food processor. Use in place of ricotta stuffing.

Gnocchi alla Romana

. . . .

SEMOLINA DUMPLINGS

Serves 4

I love cutting these gnocchi with my heart-shaped cookie cutter, especially for Valentine's Day, but you can use a drinking glass or any shape you like to form interesting gnocchi. The mixture must be very cool and firm before the process begins, and it helps to dip the cutter in ice water before each cut.

These gnocchi are very different from those made with potato, as are gnocchi made with polenta (my favorite).

1 quart milk
4 tablespoons butter, plus 2 tablespoons for buttering the dish and for the top of the gnocchi
1 ^{1}/$_2$ to 2 cups semolina
Pinch of fresh grated nutmeg
1 egg plus 2 yolks, beaten together
^{2}/$_3$ cup grated Parmigiano-Reggiano

Heat the milk slowly to a boil (be careful as milk scorches easily) in a heavy saucepan, add a spoonful of the butter, and with a whisk, begin stirring the semolina into the milk, taking care that lumps do not form. Cook for 15 to 20 minutes, until the mixture is very smooth and thick. Add the nutmeg and whisk in the eggs, the rest of the butter, and half the Parmigiano-Reggiano. Stir for a minute or two to blend. Turn the mixture out onto a smooth, oiled surface such as Formica, granite, or marble or use a large piece of oiled parchment paper, spreading the mixture evenly into a circle ^{1}/$_2$ inch thick. Let the mixture cool completely.

Preheat the oven to 350°F. Cut rounds (or whatever shapes you like) of gnocchi and lay them overlapping in a buttered baking dish. Dot with butter, sprinkle with the remaining Parmigiano-Reggiano, and bake for 30 minutes or until golden brown.

. . . .

Gnocchi alla Romana may be served as a more substantial dish with tomato sauce, meat sauce, or even a few spoons of pesto (page 113) on the top. They are also wonderful with a few slices of fresh mozzarella or fontina added to the dish, but not until halfway through the cooking, since soft cheeses often turn rubbery when cooked too long.

The semolina mixture, when cool, may be formed into long rolls like potato gnocchi, cut into 1-inch pieces with a knife dipped in cold water, and simmered in salted water until the gnocchi float to the top. Polenta (page 226), cooled and cut into shapes as for Gnocchi alla Romana, makes a delicious substitute.

Best not to call someone a gnocco. It means "really, really dumb."

Agnolotti di Carne

. . . .

LITTLE PASTA STUFFED WITH MEAT

Serves 4

The Roman filling for agnolotti is made from meat or ricotta, and both are kept as simple as possible so that the flavor of the meat or cheese does not overwhelm the delicacy of a light pasta.

2 tablespoons extra virgin olive oil

$^1/_2$ small onion, chopped fine

1 small carrot, grated

1 small celery rib, chopped fine

1 thin slice pancetta, chopped fine

$^1/_4$ pound ground raw chicken breast or ground cooked chicken

$^1/_2$ pound ground veal or beef

$^1/_4$ pound ground sausage or pork cheek (guanciale) if available

$^1/_2$ cup white wine

2 tablespoons tomato sauce from Pasta al Pomodoro o al Sugo (page 100)

2 egg yolks

2 tablespoons plus $^1/_2$ cup grated Parmigiano-Reggiano

Pinch of fresh grated nutmeg

Salt and freshly ground pepper

1 recipe Pasta all'Uovo (page 88), rolled according to directions for stuffed pasta

Heat the olive oil in a medium skillet. Add the onion, carrot, celery, and pancetta and cook over medium heat until the pancetta is crisp and the vegetables are translucent, about 5 minutes. Add the chicken, meat, and sausage or guanciale and brown well. Lower the heat, add the wine and tomato sauce, and simmer for 15 to 20 minutes or until the meat is cooked through and the liquid evaporated. Let cool. Put the meat mixture in the bowl of a food processor with the egg yolks, the 2 tablespoons Parmigiano-Reggiano, nutmeg, and salt and pepper to taste. Pulse just until mixed.

Fold the pasta over the filling and press out the air

METHOD I

With a cookie cutter or water glass with a thin edge, cut 2- or 3-inch circles from the pasta dough. Put a little of the filling slightly off-center on each circle, leaving enough dough to fold over and seal. Dip your finger in cold water and run it around the edge of the pasta. Fold the circle in half over the filling, pressing firmly around the edges. Cut around the edges with a ravioli cutter if desired.

METHOD II

On the long sheet of pasta, just off-center down the middle, place a spoonful of filling at 4-inch intervals (see illustration above). With a brush or your fingers, moisten the edges of the pasta sheet with a little cold water and carefully fold one edge to meet the other edge, pressing firmly down around the filling to eliminate air bubbles. With a ravioli cutter, cut semicircles from the fold around the filling to make little half-moons. Or use a large round ravioli cutter, placing only half of the cutter on the dough and pressing firmly to make a half-moon around the filling. Transfer each agnolotto to a floured dish towel, sprinkle very lightly with flour, and lay another towel over the pasta until ready for use. Bring a large pot of salted water to a boil. Lower the heat to medium and simmer the agnolotti for 4 to 5 minutes. Drain and serve with tomato sauce or ragù (page 126 or 100) and grated Parmigiano-Reggiano.

BASILICO

Spaghetti al Pesto

. . . .

SPAGHETTI WITH BASIL SAUCE

Serves 4

My stepdaughter adds a little milk to the pesto when she is tossing it with pasta, which aids in the digestion of garlic and the sometimes sharp oils in the basil when it is out of season. I add milk or whey from ricotta (see Ricotta con Cioccolato, page 252) to leftover pasta on the second day, when moisture without added flavor is needed. I have always used pistachio nuts, sautéed in a pan with the garlic for just a few seconds before being added to the basil leaves, in place of classic pine nuts. You can find the raw ones at health food stores. This technique takes the raw edge off the garlic, and the nuts give texture to the sauce. My secret is now out!

About 1 cup extra virgin olive oil
^{2}/$_3$ cup shelled raw pistachios
4 garlic cloves, chopped coarse
1 pound fresh basil, leaves only, or, if very fresh and young, the whole stem with leaves
^{1}/$_2$ teaspoon salt
1 pound spaghetti or short pasta such as penne or fusilli
^{1}/$_2$ cup grated Parmigiano-Reggiano

Bring a large pot of salted water to a boil.

Heat a tablespoon or two of the oil in a medium skillet, add the nuts, and cook over low heat, turning once or twice, until golden, 4 to 5 minutes. Add the garlic and cook for only 1 to 2 minutes more. Remove the nuts before cooking the garlic if they are browning too fast. Cool. Put the basil leaves in the bowl of a food processor or blender and add the cooled nut mixture. Add the remaining oil in a stream just until the sauce is nice and thick, not too liquid, then add ^{1}/$_2$ teaspoon salt.

Boil the spaghetti until al dente, toss with the pesto, sprinkle with Parmigiano-Reggiano and serve.

Pesto may be frozen or stored in the refrigerator for up to 1 month with a thin coating of olive oil over the surface.

Spaghetti Cacio e Pepe

. . . .

SPAGHETTI WITH PECORINO AND PEPPER

Serves 4

Talk about simplicity! This dish is one of Rome's greatest. It wraps around you and won't let you go. The best is in Porto Portese, a neighborhood named after the door through the walls of Rome leading to the port, at a lively trattoria called Dal Cordaro. The cordaro was the ropemaker whose shop was next to the fishing boats needing to be pulled into port. The waiters move like blurs with plates of this favorite and other Roman fare.

Buy the best pecorino Romano you can find in your neighborhood and get out your pepper grinder.

1 pound spaghetti
3/4 pound grated pecorino Romano
Freshly ground pepper

Bring a large pot of salted water to a boil. Cook the spaghetti until al dente and drain, reserving a couple of spoonfuls of pasta water. Return the pasta to the pot and toss with cheese and plenty of pepper.

Variation:
Some trattorie use fresh pasta such as taglierini (a square-cut spaghetti), but I prefer dried.

Spaghetti all'Aglio, Olio, e Peperoncino

SPAGHETTI WITH GARLIC, OLIVE OIL, AND HOT PEPPERS

Serves 4

This is the *spaghettata* (a little late-night spaghetti supper eaten after events or thrown together extemporaneously) prepared for us one late evening by the artist Alberto Burri after an opening of his works. Everyone should visit his spectacular, cracked art piece at Ghibellina, in Sicily, where an earthquake demolished a whole town in one fell swoop. You can walk through reconstructed streets and manmade walls in this ghostly city created at the leveled site of the disaster.

1 pound spaghetti
$^1/_2$ cup extra virgin olive oil
1 small dried hot red pepper, crushed
4 garlic cloves, chopped

Bring a large pot of salted water to a boil. Boil the pasta until al dente and drain, leaving a tablespoon or two of water in the pot. Return the pasta to the pot.

Heat the olive oil, add the red pepper and garlic, and cook over medium heat just until the edges of the garlic are golden brown and crispy, about 2 minutes. Watch that it does not burn, or the flavor will be bitter. Toss the oil and garlic mixture with the pasta and serve immediately in warm bowls. No cheese is used with this dish.

Rotelle alla Romana

· ·

LITTLE WHEELS WITH TOMATO AND BASIL

Serves 6

This is, above all others, my favorite summer pasta when tomatoes are fat and juicy and basil is pungent. People go crazy over this dish, and yet it is the simplest recipe in the world, which is, of course, why it is so good. A pound of rotelle goes a long way, feeding 6 people.

I was served a similar pasta at a Roman ladies' lunch and was delighted to find that just for me the hostess had spooned chopped avocado over the top, *alla californiana!* Add the avocado at the last minute, if you use one, because there is nothing worse than a cooked alligator pear.

1 pound rotelle
5 large ripe tomatoes
2 cups fresh basil leaves
$^{1}/_{2}$ teaspoon salt
2 garlic cloves, halved and slightly mashed to release the oils
$^{3}/_{4}$ cup extra virgin olive oil
$^{1}/_{2}$ pound Parmigiano-Reggiano, shaved
Salt and freshly ground pepper
Juice of 1 large lemon

Bring a large pot of salted water to a boil.

Meanwhile, in the bowl of a food processor, chop the tomatoes with the basil leaves, being sure not to purée them. Put the tomatoes in a strainer over a bowl, add the salt and garlic, and drain, reserving the juice. Remove the garlic from the tomatoes, drink the juice as a cocktail with or without vodka, and put the tomatoes and olive oil in a large bowl.

Cook the pasta in boiling water until al dente, which will take only about 7 to 8 minutes since rotelle cook faster than other pastas. Drain and put them back in the pot. Add the Parmigiano-Reggiano and toss the pasta with the tomato mixture. Add salt and pepper to taste and the lemon juice and serve.

Penne all'Arrabbiata

. . . .

"ANGRY" QUILLS

Serves 4

I once won a whole mortadella by gambling on a guinea pig who scrambled to safety in a numbered slot on a huge roulette wheel at a neighborhood food festival. "La Sagra della Gastronomia" featured bowls of peppery pasta served at communal tables to hundreds of lively locals, a pasta so simple you would think anyone could make it. Not so. I have tasted botched *penne all'arrabbiata* on numerous occasions and seen a multitude of incorrect recipes published in major newspapers and magazines. This dish contains no meat, no onions (except the small amount in the tomato sauce), no wine, no bell peppers, no cream, and for heaven's sake, do not serve it with Parmesan!

$^{I}/_{2}$ cup extra virgin olive oil
I or 2 small dried hot red peppers, depending on their heat, crushed
3 garlic cloves, minced
3 cups tomato sauce (from Pasta al Pomodoro o al Sugo, page 100) or canned plum tomatoes, drained and crushed
I pound penne (smooth, not rigate, with grooves, although some people prefer them)
Chopped fresh flat-leaf parsley

Bring a large pot of salted water to a boil.

Heat the olive oil in a medium skillet, add the pepper and garlic, and cook until barely golden, about 2 minutes. Add the tomato sauce or tomatoes (they should sizzle when they hit the oil) and stir well to mix. Simmer over low to medium heat until the sauce is shiny and thick, about 15 minutes.

Cook the penne in boiling water until al dente, drain well, and toss with the sauce. No cheese is served with this dish, but sometimes breaking my own purist rule, I sprinkle a little chopped parsley over each plate—not authentic, but pretty.

Spaghetti alla Puttanesca

. . . .

SPAGHETTI WITH TOMATO, OLIVES, AND CAPERS

Serves 4

When I was first in Rome many years ago, I marveled at the colorful prostitutes along the Appia Antica—yes, the very same Appian Way along which Caesar's chariot transported him to Rome and along which one can still drive (no chariots allowed) or walk. Prostitutes have their fascination, after all—the exotic makeup, the sequined and feathered miniskirts, everything straight out of Fellini, although sometimes it was hard to tell who were men and who were women, so beautiful were—and still are—the transvestites.

I loved to imagine the ladies (of both genders) of the night taking time out to make this delicious pasta for their humble dinner over little campfires along the road. It's lively, spicy, and seductive, just like its creators. A friend suggests that the wild mint growing along the via Appia would be the perfect garnish for this sauce.

$^1/_2$ cup extra virgin olive oil

3 garlic cloves, chopped coarse

4 anchovy fillets, chopped coarse

2 tablespoons capers

2 cups tomato sauce from Pasta al Pomodoro o al Sugo (page 100) or crushed canned tomatoes

$^2/_3$ cup pitted Kalamata olives, chopped coarse

1 tablespoon tomato paste mixed with a little water

1 pound spaghetti

2 tablespoons chopped fresh flat-leaf parsley or mint (optional)

Bring a large pot of salted water to a boil.

Heat the olive oil in a large skillet. Add the garlic and cook over medium heat until golden, about 2 minutes, then add the anchovies and capers and stir for a minute. Add the tomato sauce or canned tomatoes, the olives, and the tomato paste. Simmer the sauce for 10 to 15 minutes.

Cook the pasta in boiling water until al dente, drain, and return it to the warm pot. Add the sauce and toss well. Garnish with parsley or mint if desired.

Penne alla Vodka

. . . .

QUILLS WITH VODKA

Serves 4

I remember when this dish became fashionable in Rome some years ago. My stepdaughter served it at a gathering to celebrate the news that her father and I would be grandparents, a thrilling thought that also made us aware, as news of that sort sometimes does, that we might not be the spring chickens we thought we were. A nice shot of vodka in the pasta restored our illusions.

$^1/_2$ cup extra virgin olive oil
$^1/_4$ pound guanciale or pancetta, chopped fine
1 onion, chopped fine
2 garlic cloves, minced
3 cups tomato sauce from Pasta al Pomodoro o al Sugo (page 100) or drained and
    crushed plum tomatoes
2 tablespoons vodka
2 tablespoons butter
1 pound penne, smooth or rigate
$^1/_2$ cup grated Parmigiano-Reggiano

Bring a large pot of salted water to a boil.

Heat the olive oil in a medium skillet, add the guanciale or pancetta, and cook over medium heat until browned, about 5 minutes. Add the onion and garlic and cook until translucent, 3 to 4 minutes. Add the tomato sauce or canned tomatoes and vodka and simmer for 10 minutes, then swirl in the butter.

Cook the penne in boiling water until al dente, drain well, toss with the sauce, and serve with Parmigiano-Reggiano.

Bucatini all'Amatriciana o alla Gricia

. . . .

HOLLOW PASTA WITH PORK CHEEK AND ONION

Serves 4

Guanciale is the succulent cheek of the pig, used specifically for this recipe and for *bucatini alla gricia* (see variation), Spaghetti alla Carbonara (page 123), or any recipe calling for pancetta. Despite the well-stocked Italian markets in Los Angeles, guanciale is not easy to come by, so I pick one up in Rome at an alimentari on the via della Croce, where many delicacies are wrapped to travel. The vacuum-packed guanciale fits nicely in a purse or carry-on bag and will weather a 15-hour flight without damage. You may also order guanciale from Niman Ranch, an organic supplier in the U.S. (see Sources and Seeds).

While you are there, pick up a fresh *caciotta*, the cheese made near Rome, some marinated anchovies, a couple of Rome's famous rolls (*rosette* or *michette*, depending on which part of Rome you are in) from the baker next door, and make everyone on the plane wish he were in your seat.

$^{1}/_{4}$ cup extra virgin olive oil

1 medium onion, chopped fine

$^{1}/_{4}$ pound guanciale or 4 slices pancetta, cut into $^{1}/_{2}$-inch pieces

1 small dried hot red pepper, crushed

$^{1}/_{2}$ cup dry white wine

3 cups tomato sauce from Pasta al Pomodoro o al Sugo (page 100) or crushed canned plum tomatoes

1 pound bucatini

$^{1}/_{2}$ cup grated pecorino Romano

Bring a large pot of salted water to a boil.

Heat the olive oil in a medium skillet, add the onion and guanciale, and cook over medium heat until the meat is crispy around the edges, 5 to 6 minutes. Add the pepper to the hot oil and cook for a few seconds to toast it, then add the wine and tomato sauce or tomatoes. Simmer the sauce for 10 to 15 minutes, until thick.

Cook the bucatini in boiling water until al dente, drain, toss the sauce with the pasta, and serve with pecorino.

Variation:

Bucatini alla gricia, according to every cook I know in Rome, is simply the "white" version *(in bianco,* which always means no tomatoes) of *bucatini all'amatriciana.* Bucatini were originally made in Naples, but all of Italy has adopted them. *Bucatini alla gricia* are best in winter, but good Roman pecorino and guanciale are hard to pass up, so I eat this dish year-round. To make *bucatini alla gricia,* omit the tomatoes, using a little more olive oil, white wine, or a few spoons of pasta water if needed for the sauce. Serve with pecorino.

Spaghetti alla Boscaiola

. . . .

SPAGHETTI WITH WILD MUSHROOMS

Serves 4

Many trattorie serve fresh pasta with mushrooms, but my favorite versions are the homemade pasta at Dal Cordaro and another small neighborhood trattoria outside the walls of the Piazza del Popolo in via Flaminia called Orsetto. Their mushroom dishes are exceptional, so if you are a mushroom fanatic like me, you may want to start at Orsetto with the lemony mushroom antipasto to pave the way for even more mushrooms on your noodles. I find here that, lacking porcini, any good cremini, shiitake, or portobello mushroom will do nicely.

$^{1}/_{2}$ cup extra virgin olive oil

$1^{1}/_{2}$ pounds wild or exotic mushrooms, sliced very thin or chopped fine

3 garlic cloves, minced

1 small dried hot red pepper, crushed

2 tablespoons Cognac

3 cups Brodo di Verdure or Brodo di Pollo (page 71 or 69)

1 cup yogurt or heavy cream

Juice of 1 lemon

1 pound spaghetti

$^{1}/_{2}$ cup grated Parmigiano-Reggiano

Bring a large pot of salted water to a boil.

Meanwhile, heat the olive oil in a skillet, add the mushrooms, and sauté over high heat until just browned, about 6 minutes. Add the garlic and hot pepper and stir briskly. Stand back, add the Cognac, tilt the pan to ignite, and let the flame burn off. Add the stock and cook for about 5 minutes, until reduced just a little. Stir in the yogurt or cream and lemon juice.

Cook the spaghetti in boiling water until al dente, drain, toss with the sauce, and serve with Parmigiano-Reggiano.

Variation:

This sauce may be puréed in a food processor and then tossed with the pasta. The mushroom flavor is a little more intense in this creamy version. You may also use any fresh pasta in place of dried.

Spaghetti alla Carbonara

. . . .

SPAGHETTI WITH PANCETTA AND EGGS

Serves 4

First, let me emphasize that there is *no* cream or butter in this dish, contrary to what chefs in this country might think.

My husband, uninterested in doing anything else in the kitchen (except cleaning up), makes the best *spaghetti alla carbonara* I have tasted. Mine never comes out as creamy or rich as his, perhaps because I guiltily pour off some of the pancetta fat before mixing it into the eggs, and he uses every drop. Make *spaghetti alla carbonara* with abandon, and to hell with fat and cholesterol! This is a winter dish, and there is plenty of time to do penance in the spring.

3 tablespoons extra virgin olive oil
Six $^{1}/_{2}$-inch-thick slices pancetta or lean bacon, cut into small dice
6 large eggs
1 cup grated Parmigiano-Reggiano
Salt and freshly ground pepper
1 pound spaghetti

Bring a large pot of salted water to a boil.

Meanwhile, heat the olive oil, add the diced pancetta or bacon, and cook over medium heat until crisp, about 5 minutes. In a separate bowl, whisk the eggs and half the Parmesan together well, adding a little salt and a generous pinch of pepper.

Cook the pasta in the boiling water until al dente, drain, and reserve a few spoonfuls of the water. Return the pasta and water to the pot. Heat the pancetta quickly and immediately whisk the pancetta mixture (including all the fat!) into the eggs, then quickly add the egg mixture to the pasta, tossing well to "cook" the eggs with the warmth of the pasta. Serve in warmed bowls with more Parmigiano-Reggiano. The pasta should be creamy and shiny.

Variation:
Al Moro, one of the oldest and best ristoranti in Rome, adds zing to its famous *spaghetti alla Moro* with a small dried red pepper sautéed in the bacon fat.

Rigatoni alla Toto

. . . .

RIGATONI WITH CREAM, SAUSAGE, AND BASIL

Serves 4

Toto, a trattoria in the *centro storico,* center of Rome, on via delle Carrozze, used to be our affordable neighborhood hangout, the sweet owner making sure that each plate was perfect and that when I ate there alone at lunch occasionally, I had a table where I would be comfortable and not too conspicuous. A woman dining alone could be perceived to be up to no good.

Toto now caters to tourists with its "creative" menu, but the antipasto table is one of the best in Rome and lures us despite the tourists.

I pound rigatoni
3 tablespoons extra virgin olive oil
I small onion, chopped fine
I pound pork sausage, flavored with fennel or plain, removed from the casing
I cup white wine
A few fresh basil leaves, chopped
Pinch of ground fennel seed, if using plain pork sausage
I $^{1}/_{2}$ cups heavy cream
$^{1}/_{2}$ cup grated Parmigiano-Reggiano

Bring a large pot of salted water to a boil.

Heat the olive oil in a large skillet, add the onion, and cook over medium heat until translucent, 3 to 4 minutes. Add the sausage meat, brown it on all sides, then add the wine and cook for a minute. Add the basil leaves, ground fennel (if using), and cream and simmer over low heat for 20 minutes, until the sausage is cooked through.

Cook the rigatoni in boiling water until al dente, drain well, toss with the sauce, and serve with Parmigiano-Reggiano.

Spaghetti alle Vongole Veraci

....

SPAGHETTI WITH REAL CLAMS

Serves 4

This is a dish (like Carciofi alla Romana, page 44) by which I ruthlessly judge a trattoria. The dish is a Roman favorite found everywhere, but it can be drastically wrong if the clams are not the ones with two little dark horns coming out of their bodies. They really should be no larger than a fingernail, which is why I use cockles here at home when tiny clams cannot be found.

Without even recovering from jet lag, I rush to one of my favorite trattorie, La Campana, where I tasted my first vongola on pasta. If I can't quite make it that far, I stumble to 31, via delle Carrozze, a tiny trattoria near our apartment at which we have eaten so often that the waiter now kisses me on both cheeks and the busboy looks mortally offended if I forget to shake his hand.

4 pounds cockles or tiny clams
1 pound spaghetti
$^2/_3$ cup extra virgin olive oil
1 small dried hot red pepper, crushed
6 garlic cloves, chopped coarse
A handful of fresh flat-leaf parsley, chopped
Lemon wedges (optional)

Rinse the cockles or clams well in a colander. Bring a large pot of salted water to a boil. Add the pasta and cook until al dente.

Meanwhile, heat the olive oil in a very large skillet over medium-high heat, add the pepper and garlic, then quickly add all the clams and immediately cover the pan. Cook for 3 to 4 minutes over medium heat, then lower the heat to medium-low. The clams should open in less than 5 to 6 minutes, just when the pasta is done. Do not overcook the clams or they will get rubbery.

When all the shells are opened and the garlic is golden, drain the pasta, put it back in the warm pasta pot, and toss with the clam mixture and chopped parsley. Serve with lemon wedges if desired.

Pasta al Ragù o alla Bolognese

. . . .

PASTA WITH MEAT SAUCE

Serves 4

We are so used to Italian-American meat sauces often made with inferior hamburger meat, tomato paste, and dried herbs that we don't realize how good an authentic one can be. An example is the *ragà alla bolognese,* which may be attributed to Bologna but has been adapted by practically every city in Italy, including Rome. The Roman housewife is fortunate in having meat available that still tastes like the animal and does not have all the fat bred out of it. I use top sirloin, tritip, or eye of round for the beef.

Dal Bolognese, one of Rome's favorite and most enduring restaurants for *buongustaia* (gourmets), serves this quintessential meat sauce and other favorites from Bologna, including mixed boiled meats with green sauce (Bollito Misto con Salsa Verde (page 178).

3 tablespoons extra virgin olive oil

Two $^1/_4$-inch-thick slices pancetta, minced

$1^1/_2$ pounds lean ground beef or veal or a mixture (my preference)

$^3/_4$ pound ground pork

2 tablespoons butter

1 large onion, chopped fine

2 carrots, chopped fine

1 celery rib, chopped fine

1 cup red wine

1 quart Brodo di Carne (page 68)

$1^1/_2$ cups tomato sauce from Pasta al Pomodoro o al Sugo (page 100)

Very small pinch of fresh grated nutmeg

Salt and freshly ground pepper

1 pound spaghetti

$^1/_2$ cup grated Parmigiano-Reggiano

Heat 2 tablespoons of the olive oil in a large, fairly deep casserole or skillet, add the pancetta, and cook over medium heat until brown around the edges, about 3 minutes. Add the ground meats and cook over medium-high heat until nicely browned on all sides. Transfer to a plate. Add the rest of the olive oil and the butter to the pan and cook the onion, carrots, and celery quickly over medium-high heat to brown. Return the meat to the pan, add the wine, and cook over low heat until the liquid is absorbed, about 5 minutes. Add the stock, tomato sauce, nutmeg, and salt and pepper to taste and cook over very low heat for 1 hour. You may need to add a little stock.

Meanwhile, bring a large pot of salted water to a boil. Cook the spaghetti until al dente, drain well, toss with the sauce, and serve with Parmigiano-Reggiano.

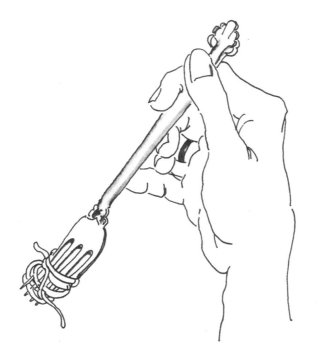

Farfalle al Radicchio

. . . .

BUTTERFLY PASTA WITH RADICCHIO

Serves 4

Radicchio is used all over Rome in risotto, pasta, and salads and is grilled, braised, or roasted. The long heads from Treviso are my favorite for grilling, while the little compact red and white balls with their bittersweet flavor are best for salads and cooking.

The regulars at Settimio all'Arancio, a warm and lively neighborhood trattoria in the center of Rome, exchange both-cheek kisses with the owner as he cuts prosciutto by hand while the chef peers out every now and then to make sure everyone is happy with his farfalle. For risotto, simply chop radicchio fine and stir it into the basic risotto recipe along with the stock, adding a spoon of yogurt or mascarpone and a squeeze of lemon to the rice just before serving.

$^1/_4$ cup extra virgin olive oil

1 small onion, chopped fine

1 garlic clove, minced

1 large head radicchio, shredded and chopped fine

2 cups Brodo di Verdure or Brodo di Pollo (page 71 or 69)

Juice of 1 lemon

2 tablespoons butter

1 pound farfalle

$^1/_2$ cup grated Parmigiano-Reggiano

Bring a large pot of salted water to a boil.

Meanwhile, heat the olive oil in a large skillet and add the onion. Cook over medium heat until translucent, 3 or 4 minutes, then add the garlic and cook for another minute. Add the shredded radicchio and sauté until wilted and browning on the edges, about 5 minutes. Add the stock, cover, and simmer for 10 minutes. Remove the lid and add the lemon juice and butter. Cook the pasta in the boiling water until al dente, drain, toss with the sauce, and serve with Parmigiano-Reggiano.

Spaghetti al Tonno

. . . .

SPAGHETTI WITH CANNED TUNA

Serves 4

Fresh tomatoes are all right, but canned are better in this recipe. I fixed this for my stepson's Italian friends, who were visiting for a month in the summer and were, I think, anticipating days of "American" food: hamburgers, perhaps, or tuna fish sandwiches. It was such fun to serve bowls of this wonderfully pungent pasta and hear audible sighs of relief. After all, a month is far too long be away from Roman cooking.

$^1/_4$ cup extra virgin olive oil

1 small onion, chopped fine

2 garlic cloves, chopped

1 small dried hot red pepper, crushed

2 anchovy fillets, chopped

3 cups tomato sauce (from Pasta al Pomodoro o al Sugo, page 100) or crushed plum tomatoes

3 tablespoons capers, mashed a little with a spoon

Two 8-ounce cans tuna packed in olive oil or water (see page 24)

1 pound spaghetti

Juice of 1 large lemon

A little chopped fresh flat-leaf parsley

Bring a large pot of salted water to a boil.

Heat the olive oil in a large skillet, add the onion, and cook over medium heat until translucent, 3 to 4 minutes. Add the garlic and cook just until golden, another minute, then add the pepper and anchovies and cook for few seconds. Add the tomato sauce or canned tomatoes and capers and cook over low heat for 10 minutes. Add the tuna, drained, and cook just until heated through and bubbling, 2 to 3 minutes (cooking canned tuna too long makes it tough and tasteless).

Cook the spaghetti in boiling water until al dente, drain, toss with the sauce, lemon juice, and parsley, and serve.

Variation:
For a cold tuna sauce, pulse two 8-ounce cans or jars imported tuna or two 8-ounce cans or one 16-ounce can domestic tuna in water, drained, $^2/_3$ cup extra virgin olive oil, 1 small onion, 3 tablespoons capers, leaves from 3 fresh mint sprigs, the juice of a lemon, and $^1/_4$ teaspoon freshly ground pepper in a food processor. Toss with hot pasta and garnish with a few leaves of mint, chopped.

Il riso leva la fame e mette appetito.— Rice takes away your hunger and gives you an appetite. • Many of my cooking students have questions about the care and feeding of risotto, but I assure them that Italian rice is sturdy and forgiving. When I do not wish to commit to a full 20-minute constant stirring session with risotto, I simply cook my rice halfway (in defiance of those who insist it will not work), turn off the fire, partially cover the pot, and then finish it off just before serving. The rice is always al dente, and this process shaves about 6 or 7 minutes off the stirring time. So much for the stirring myth. Many Italian

risotto

cooks (my stepdaughter, for one) use pressure cookers! • If your risotto does have to wait longer than you anticipated and appears too dry, stir in about $^1/_2$ cup of stock to revive the creamy texture. • Carnaroli, arborio, and Roma rice are all excellent types for risotto, and Beretta and Gallo are brands that can be found almost everywhere, but any round-grain rice will do. There are many subtle differences in risotto rice, so you must experiment and find the one you like best. Beretta rice has a creamy texture and a good tooth when fully cooked.

Always sauté vegetables, such as mushrooms, radicchio, artichokes, zucchini, and others before stirring them into risotto. I sauté everything separately before assembling any dish, including soups, stews, pasta sauces, and so on. That way the individuality of the ingredient remains intact, even though mixed with several others.

For perfect risotto:

- Heat the vegetable, chicken, beef, or fish stock before using it.
- Heat the oil or butter and cook the onion first until translucent.
- Next, coat the rice well with butter or oil, whichever you are using, and sauté to seal the starch coating on the rice.
- Next, add the wine and cook until absorbed.
- Next, add the stock gradually, just a cup or two at a time, and stir until absorbed before adding the next liquid.
- Add the vegetables near the beginning of the cooking, but add seafood toward the end so as not to overcook it.
- Finish any risotto with a spoonful of butter or a swirl of cream (or yogurt, which works very well and imparts a subtle tartness; even so, everyone thinks it's cream).

Risotto ai Funghi Porcini

. . . .

RICE WITH PORCINI MUSHROOMS

Serves 4

I once buried porcini in my yard near an elm tree, hoping for spore miracles, but alas, raccoons (clearly gourmets) interfered with my experiment.

Mushrooms are sponges. They soak up every bit of butter or oil in which you cook them, which is why most chefs "sweat" them over low heat to evaporate their moisture. I instead seal in their juices with a quick sauté in a little olive oil before adding them to any dish. Fresh porcini are preferable, but dried work well, too, and sometimes have richer flavor.

$^{1}/_{4}$ cup extra virgin olive oil

1 pound porcini, cremini, or portobello mushrooms, chopped fine (a food processor does a great job), or $^{1}/_{2}$ pound dried porcini, soaked in warm water or broth for 15 minutes until soft (reserve the broth for risotto liquid)

2 cups arborio or Carnaroli rice

3 garlic cloves, minced

2 tablespoons Cognac or white wine

5 to 6 cups Brodo di Pollo (page 69)

$^{1}/_{2}$ cup heavy cream

2 tablespoons butter

A few drops of lemon juice

$^{1}/_{2}$ cup grated Parmigiano-Reggiano

Using half the olive oil, cook the mushrooms in a heavy casserole over fairly high heat until they start to brown on the edges, about 5 minutes. Add the rest of the oil, then the rice, and cook, stirring to coat and seal the grains, for 2 to 3 minutes. Add the garlic and cook until golden, a minute or two. Stand back and add the Cognac, tilting the pan to ignite. On an electric stove, use a match to ignite. When the flame dies out, add the stock, a cup or two at a time, stirring until all the liquid is absorbed. Repeat until all liquid is used and the rice is creamy, about 15 to 18 minutes total. Stir in the cream, butter, lemon juice, and a spoonful of Parmigiano-Reggiano. Serve with additional Parmigiano-Reggiano.

Variation:

Add 2 slices of pancetta, diced fine, to the olive oil before the garlic. Eliminate the cream if you prefer and use a spoonful of butter or yogurt.

Risotto alle Mele

. . . .

RICE WITH APPLES

Serves 4

My Italian stepdaughter, Nicole, first served this to us in Santiago, Chile, as a farewell lunch, and now she makes it each time we are departing from a visit to wherever she and her traveling family happen to be. Her mother made this dish for Nicole and her then boyfriend, Ciallo, who evidently was so impressed by the mamma's risotto that he married the daughter. I have added crisp fried apples and onion as garnish (and a little cream or yogurt for body).

6 tablespoons butter
2 tablespoons extra virgin olive oil
2 small onions, 1 chopped fine and 1 sliced thin
2 cups arborio rice
Pinch of curry powder
4 apples, preferably Fuji or Braeburn, peeled and cored, 3 chopped fine and 1 sliced thin
$^1/_2$ teaspoon salt
1 $^1/_2$ cups white wine
1 quart Brodo di Pollo (page 69)
1 cup grated Parmigiano-Reggiano
Juice of 1 lemon
$^1/_2$ cup heavy cream or yogurt
Freshly ground pepper

Melt 4 tablespoons of the butter in a heavy casserole, add the oil, and sauté the chopped onion over medium heat until translucent, 3 to 4 minutes. Add the rice and stir for a minute or two, until well coated. Add the curry powder, chopped apples, and salt and cook, stirring, until soft, 3 to 4 minutes. Add the wine and stir until absorbed. Add a third of the stock and stir until absorbed. Continue to add stock as needed until the rice is creamy and just al dente, about 15 to 20 minutes total. In a small skillet, melt the rest of the butter and sauté the apple and onion slices until very crisp and browned, about 8 minutes. Add half the Parmigiano-Reggiano, lemon juice, and cream or yogurt to the risotto and serve with pepper and the apple and onion slices as garnish. Serve with more Parmigiano-Reggiano.

Risotto al Nero di Seppie

. . . .

RICE WITH CUTTLEFISH AND THEIR INK

If you can find tiny seppie about the size of a finger, called *moscardini* in Italy, by all means use them, but they do not seem to be prevalent on the West Coast except at Japanese or Chinese markets. Fresh or frozen small squid will do as well.

You will need extra squid ink for this risotto since the little sacs inside of seppie or our larger squid are not quite large enough to blacken a dish for 4. I buy my ink at the fish market and keep the sealed packets in the freezer, where they last for months.

2 pounds cuttlefish or squid, cleaned (page 37)

$^1/_2$ cup extra virgin olive oil

1 small onion, chopped fine

2 cups arborio or Carnaroli rice

2 garlic cloves, chopped

1 cup dry white wine

2 tablespoons squid ink (2 packets)

5 to 6 cups shellfish stock or Brodo di Pesce (page 70)

Juice of 1 large lemon

1 tablespoon butter

2 tablespoons minced fresh flat-leaf parsley

Clean and chop the cuttlefish into small pieces, reserving the ink sacs if possible if using squid. Heat the olive oil in a casserole, add the onion, and cook over medium heat until translucent, 3 to 4 minutes. Add the cuttlefish, the ink sacs, and the rice, and cook for a few minutes to coat and seal the rice. Add the garlic and cook until golden, another minute. Add the wine and stir until the liquid is absorbed. Add the squid ink, then the stock, a cup or two at a time, stirring after each addition until all the stock is absorbed and the rice is black and creamy, 15 to 18 minutes total. Stir in the lemon juice, butter, and parsley and serve in warm bowls.

Risotto alla Zucca

RICE WITH SQUASH

Serves 4

I first tasted this risotto, enhanced by a nice dollop of mascarpone, at one of the many meals we have enjoyed at the home of my husband's ex-wife. Cream will do as well, but mascarpone is a hard act to follow. I often use yogurt in place of heavy cream for its tangy flavor, which no one has ever identified. A final spoonful of butter enriches the taste of squash.

Various dense, orange-fleshed squash are best for this risotto, the same kinds used for pasta fillings. I like to use a medium-sized Turk's Cap, Marina de Chioggia, Piena di Napoli, Cushaw, or a cut piece of dense yellow banana squash.

$1\,^1/_2$ pounds raw or 3 cups cooked winter squash
$^1/_2$ cup extra virgin olive oil
1 onion, chopped fine
2 cups arborio or Carnaroli rice
2 garlic cloves, chopped
1 small dried hot red pepper, crushed
1 cup dry white wine
5 to 6 cups Brodo di Pollo (page 69)
A few fresh rosemary or basil leaves, chopped fine
2 tablespoons mascarpone, heavy cream, or whole-milk yogurt
1 tablespoon butter
Juice of 1 lemon
$^1/_2$ cup grated Parmigiano-Reggiano

If using raw squash, bake it in the oven at 350°F until soft, then scoop out the pulp and reserve. Or cut peeled squash into chunks and steam them in a little stock until soft, then purée.

Heat the olive oil in a heavy casserole, add the onion, and cook over medium heat until crisp around the edges, 5 to 6 minutes. Add the rice and cook, stirring to coat and seal the grains, for 2 to 3 minutes. Add the garlic and pepper and cook until golden, then stir in the squash pulp. Add the wine and stir until it is absorbed. Add the stock, a cup or two at a time, stirring until all the liquid is absorbed. Repeat until all the liquid is used and the rice is creamy, 15 to 18 minutes. Stir in the herbs, mascarpone, butter, and lemon juice, plus a spoonful of Parmigiano-Reggiano. Serve with more Parmigiano-Reggiano.

Risotto alla Crema di Scampi

....

RICE WITH SHRIMP AND CREAM

Serves 4

I am always amazed at the intense sweetness of Italian scampi (the ones with the little pincers known as *langoustines* in France, also called *Dublin Bay prawns* elsewhere), but I must admit that sweet Santa Barbara, Japanese, and some Mexican shrimp, called *gamberi* in Italy, run a pretty close second. Truly, any shrimp will do nicely.

2 pounds scampi, langoustines, shrimp, crayfish, bay shrimp, or prawns of any kind in their shells
7 cups cold water
2 onions, chopped fine
1 carrot, chopped
2 celery ribs, chopped
4 garlic cloves, chopped
Salt and a few peppercorns
Juice of 1 lemon
2 cups dry white wine
$^1/_4$ cup extra virgin olive oil
2 cups arborio or Carnaroli rice
$^1/_2$ cup cream
3 tablespoons butter
3 tablespoons minced fresh flat-leaf parsley

TO PREPARE THE STOCK:
Shell the shrimp, keeping any heads or claws for the stock. Reserve the raw shrimp and put the shells, along with the water, half of the chopped onion, the carrot, celery, half of the garlic, the salt, peppercorns, lemon juice, and half of the white wine in a medium pot with a lid. Bring to a simmer and cook for 25 minutes, covered, or until reduced by a cup or so. Strain and reserve. This may be done ahead of time and the raw shrimp kept for up to 2 days in the refrigerator. You will need 6 cups stock. Add Brodo di Verdure (page 71), Brodo di Pesce (page 70), or bottled clam juice if needed to make 6 cups.

TO PREPARE THE RISOTTO:

Heat the olive oil in a heavy casserole, add the rest of the onion, and cook over medium heat until translucent, 3 to 4 minutes. Add the rice and cook, stirring to coat and seal the grains, for 2 to 3 minutes. Add the remaining garlic, cook until golden, about a minute, then add the rest of the wine and stir until it is absorbed. Add the shrimp, then begin adding the stock, a cup or two at a time, stirring until all the liquid is absorbed. Repeat until all the liquid is used and the rice is creamy, 15 to 20 minutes total. When the rice is al dente, add the cream, butter, and parsley and cook for 2 to 3 minutes more to incorporate the cream and butter. Serve in warm bowls.

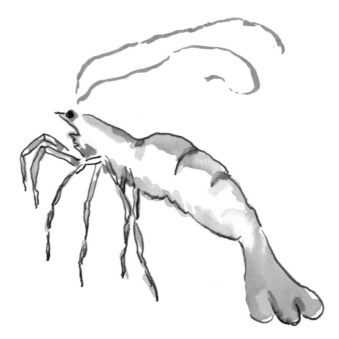

Risotto alla Pescatora

. . . .

RICE WITH SEAFOOD

Serves 4 to 6

A spectacular dish, especially for dinner parties, worth all of the time it entails, although the preparation is shortened by practice. This is a version using California seafood, so adjust yours to whatever is available in your area. Chinese or Japanese fish markets often offer many exotic items similar to the ones found in Rome, but almost every city has clams, mussels, shrimp, lobster, and scallops.

I cook my mollusks, crustaceans, and squid separately from the risotto so that they will be very tender in the final dish and because the reserved juices they exude as they cook are essential to the stock used in the risotto.

$^1/_2$ cup plus 1 tablespoon extra virgin olive oil

1 pound squid, cleaned (page 37), and their ink or 1 tablespoon commercial squid ink (found at fishmongers)

4 garlic cloves, chopped fine

2 cups dry white wine

1 $^1/_2$ pounds tiny clams or cockles

1 $^1/_2$ pounds mussels

1 small onion, minced

2 cups arborio or Carnaroli rice

Pinch of cayenne pepper

6 cups Brodo di Pesce (page 70), including the liquid from the squid and shellfish

1 pound medium shrimp, peeled and chopped coarse

$^1/_2$ pound bay scallops

$^1/_4$ pound rock shrimp

Juice of 1 large lemon

1 tablespoon butter

2 tablespoons minced fresh flat-leaf parsley

TO PREPARE THE SQUID:

Heat 1 tablespoon of the olive oil in a pan, add the squid and their ink sacs, and cook for 5 minutes. Add 1 teaspoon of the chopped garlic, 1 cup of the white wine, and a little salt. Simmer, covered, over very low heat for 20 minutes. Reserve the squid and the liquid.

TO PREPARE THE CLAMS AND MUSSELS:

Heat 1 tablespoon of the remaining olive oil in a large shallow skillet with a lid. Add 1 teaspoon of the remaining chopped garlic, then add the clams or cockles and mussels and cover, lowering the heat to medium. The moisture in the mollusks will steam them open in 5 to 6 minutes. Remove the meat from the shells and discard the shells. Reserve the liquid.

TO PREPARE THE RISOTTO:

Heat the rest of the olive oil in a heavy casserole, add the onion, and cook over medium heat until translucent, 3 to 4 minutes. Add the rice and cook, stirring to coat and seal the grains, for 2 to 3 minutes. Add the rest of the garlic and the cayenne and cook until golden, another minute, then add the remaining wine and stir until it is absorbed. Add the stock, including the liquids from the squid and shellfish, a cup or two at a time, stirring after each addition. Add the clams, mussels, medium shrimp, scallops, and rock shrimp about halfway though. Continue cooking until the shrimp are pink and most of the liquid is absorbed, 12 to 15 minutes. The rice should be creamy and still al dente. Stir in the lemon juice and butter and serve in warm bowls with parsley sprinkled over each serving.

. . . .

To ease the pain of cleaning so many sea creatures, buy everything cleaned at your local fish market. The taste will not be quite as intense, but the time saved may be worth it.

Supplì al Telefono

....

RICE BALLS WITH MOZZARELLA

Serves 4

At many of Rome's "hot tables," the cafeteria-style eateries called *tavole calde,* you will find a tray of crunchy, cone-shaped or round croquettes of rice, deep-fried and golden. *Supplì al telefono* contain a piece of mozzarella in the center, which melts and forms a long string like a telephone wire as you attempt to get a piece from your fork to your mouth. Others contain meat sauce, even chicken livers, but the ones I like best are made with cheese and leftover risotto or rice into which an egg or a couple of yolks are stirred to bind the mixture. The original Sicilian rice balls, called *arancini* because they were formed into shapes resembling little oranges when deep-fried, are the meat-filled ancestors to supplì. I always make enough risotto to generate supplì the next day.

4 cups leftover risotto (see Risotto alla Zucca, page 139, or Risotto ai Funghi Porcini, page 135)
3 eggs, beaten
Salt
Eight 1-inch cubes mozzarella
2 cups fine bread crumbs
Extra virgin olive oil

Mix the risotto well with half of the egg mixture and salt to taste. Rinse your hands with cold water, then cup your hand and press a soupspoon of rice into the cavity. Press a piece of mozzarella into the rice, then cover with another spoonful of rice, making a ball about 2 inches across (you may make supplì any size you wish, but these are manageable). Dip in the remaining beaten egg, then roll in bread crumbs and set aside on a plate. Repeat the process until all the rice is used.

Heat about $1/2$ inch of olive oil until it begins to smoke in a large skillet and add the supplì, keeping them separated and flattening each one slightly so that they will be easier to turn over. Fry each one on both sides until golden, about 4 minutes in all, and transfer to paper towels to drain before serving. Sometimes I roll the supplì in flour, then egg, then crumbs. Both techniques work well.

Variation:
For meat-filled supplì, use a teaspoon of ragù (see Pasta al Ragù o alla Bolognese, page 126) or chicken liver mixture (see Crostini di Fegato, page 50) in place of the mozzarella.

Risotto al Pomodoro e Basilico

RICE WITH FRESH TOMATO AND BASIL

Serves 4

I created this recipe one summer when my tomatoes were practically throwing themselves off their vines, the broad-leafed basil was organizing a major demonstration of foliage, and jars of pesto had almost pushed me out of my kitchen. We all needed a change. You will see that this is the sauce for Rotelle alla Romana (page 116) simply stirred into risotto. This dish starts the juices flowing for grilled meats or Galletto Ruspante alla Diavola (page 166) as a second course. The leftovers make delicious Supplì al Telefono (page 144) for yet another first course, or if made smaller in little rounds, they are tasty and substantial appetizers with drinks.

3 large tomatoes
I cup fresh basil leaves
$^1/_2$ garlic clove
$^1/_2$ teaspoon salt
Juice of I large lemon
$^1/_4$ cup extra virgin olive oil
I small onion, chopped fine
2 cups arborio or carnaroli rice
$^1/_2$ cup white wine
4 to 5 cups Brodo di Pollo (page 69)
$^1/_2$ cup grated Parmigiano-Reggiano

In the bowl of a food processor, pulse the tomatoes, basil, garlic, salt, and lemon juice until almost puréed.

Heat the olive oil in a large skillet, add the onion, and cook over medium heat until translucent, 3 to 4 minutes. Add the rice and cook, stirring to coat and seal the grains, for 2 to 3 minutes. Add the wine and stir until it is absorbed. Add the tomato mixture alternately with the stock, a cup or two at a time, stirring until all the liquid is absorbed. Repeat until all liquid is used and the rice is creamy, 15 to 20 minutes total. The rice should be al dente but cooked through. Serve with Parmigiano-Reggiano.

Secondi

2ND courses

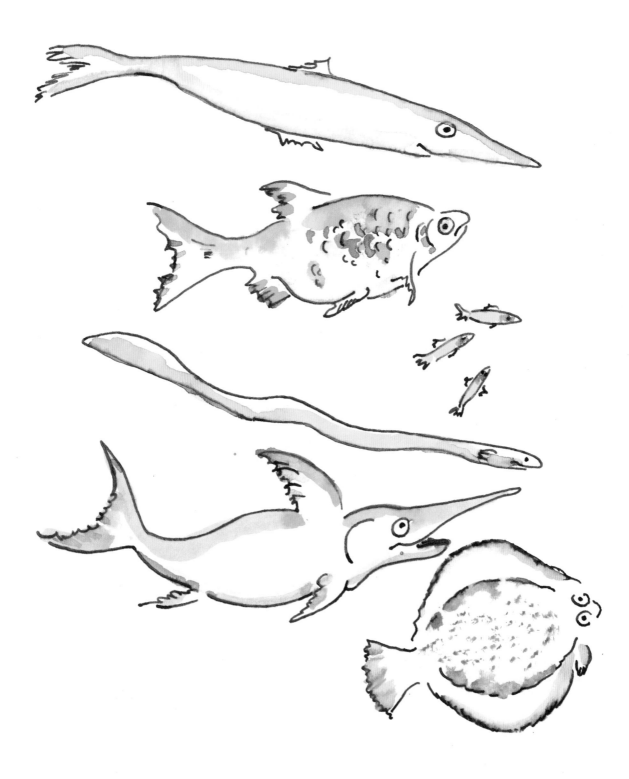

Gli ospiti sono come pesce. Doppo tre giorni, puzzano. — *Guests are like fish. After three days, they stink.* • Buy fresh, bright-eyed fish on the day they were caught. I always make good friends with a fishmonger I trust and ask what special catches he might be receiving that week, such as anchovies, sardines, or cockles. Many Mediterranean fish have a different flavor from ours, but we have such a bounty of fish, crustaceans, and tentacled creatures from our coastal waters and even from streams and lakes in the middle of the country that it's easy to find salmon, sea bass, catfish, and sole almost everywhere. • Choose a whole fish, with clear

eyes, pink gills, and the tail still flopping. Many Japanese, Mexican, or Chinese markets offer tanks of live fish and you can also order whole fish at most fish markets. Fish steaks with the bone in are tastier than fillets and usually less expensive. • For pasta sauces, cockles are preferable to larger clams. Where there are simply no clams to be had, a passable *spaghetti alle vongole* can be made with cans of tiny clams from Asia found at supermarkets. Avoid bottled clam sauces, because they are often tasteless and contain starchy thickeners. Your own quick sauce made with canned clams will be far superior to any commercial sauce.

Branzino, Orata, Dentice, Salmone, o Triglie alla Griglia

. . . .

GRILLED SEA BASS, SEA BREAM, RED SNAPPER, SALMON, OR MULLET

Serves 4

The fish dishes of *la cucina romana* are never complicated. Pick out the freshest fish you can find. Brush it with the best olive oil you can buy. Add salt and pepper and cook it. *Basta!* Enough!

One 3 ^{1}/$_2$- to 4-pound branzino or two 2-pound branzini
   (or any other whole fish you like), cleaned and gutted
Extra virgin olive oil
1 garlic clove, sliced
1 fresh rosemary sprig
Salt and freshly ground pepper
Lemons

Light a grill or preheat the oven to 425°F. If your fish is large, make shallow diagonal slashes on each side. Brush the fish liberally with olive oil. Put garlic slices with a few leaves of rosemary in the slashes. Grill on both sides for about 8 to 10 minutes, depending on thickness, or until the flesh is firm but still moist. Serve with lemon. Or place the fish on a baking sheet and bake for 18 to 20 minutes. Test for doneness by inserting a sharp knife at the thickest point and pulling away the flesh gently to see if the fish is cooked to your desired doneness.

. . . .

I roast all fish at 425°F, but your oven may require slightly more or less heat. For every inch of thickness, a fish needs 8 to 10 minutes of cooking time. So if you have a 2-inch-thick fish, it should cook for 16 to 20 minutes, more or less, whole or filleted. A salmon fillet 1 inch thick does indeed take about 10 minutes. Dense fish may require a few more minutes, but I like my fish slightly undercooked by a few seconds rather than dried out. A piece of foil laid loosely over the fish for the first 5 minutes will help keep the flesh moist. Remove and cook for 5 minutes more without the foil to brown the fish, or brown quickly under a broiler.

Baccalà alla Romana
con Pinoli e Uvetta

. . . .

SALT COD IN THE ROMAN MANNER WITH PINE NUTS AND RAISINS

Serves 4

Fried baccalà pieces cooked in a tomato sauce with raisins and pine nuts must be derivative of a Sicilian preparation, but the Romans think it is theirs. No matter where it's from, it is delicious. I like the addition of lemon juice or balsamic vinegar, because I feel the saltiness of the fish is balanced well by a little acid. I suggest serving this with slices of grilled polenta.

$2/3$ cup extra virgin olive oil

$1 1/4$ pounds prepared salt cod (page 160), cut into 8 pieces

Pastella I or II from Alici o Latterini Fritti (page 30)

1 large onion, chopped

2 tablespoons chopped celery or a few leaves, chopped

2 garlic cloves, chopped

$1/2$ cup sultanas or golden raisins

3 cups drained canned plum tomatoes, crushed

A few fresh basil leaves, chopped

A few drops lemon juice or balsamic vinegar

$1/2$ cup toasted pine nuts (see page 23)

2 tablespoons chopped fresh flat-leaf parsley

4 slices grilled Polenta (page 226)

Heat half the olive oil in a wide skillet until smoking, dip the pieces of cod in the pastella, and fry until golden brown, about 3 minutes on each side. Remove the pieces and drain on a grocery bag or paper towels. Add a little more olive oil to the pan if necessary, add the onion and celery, and cook over medium heat until translucent, 3 to 4 minutes. Add the garlic and cook until golden, another minute. Add the raisins, tomatoes, basil, and lemon juice or vinegar and simmer for 10 minutes. Add the pieces of cod and the pine nuts and simmer until heated through, 5 to 6 minutes, taking care not to break up the fish. Sprinkle with parsley and serve over grilled polenta slices.

Variation:
A creamy alternative to this savory dish is made by simmering the fish pieces, without batter, with 2 diced potatoes, in milk to cover, until the potatoes are soft, about 15 minutes. Season and serve.

Sogliola al Burro

. . . .

SOLE WITH BUTTER

Serves 4

Whole sole is available at almost all fish restaurants in Rome. Sometimes it is dusted with flour, sometimes not, and then grilled or panfried in butter. The little California sand dabs I buy at my weekly open market are nothing more than sole without its swimming fins, and I prefer to cook my sole whole, as its tail and side fins get very crisp and tasty when sautéed or grilled. The females often contain delicious roe, so when choosing, look for a salmon-colored strip down the underbelly.

Six $3/4$-pound sole
1 cup flour, seasoned with 1 teaspoon salt and $1/2$ teaspoon freshly ground pepper
8 tablespoons (1 stick) butter
Lemon wedges

Shake the sole in a bag containing the seasoned flour, coating all sides. In a skillet large enough to hold 2 fish if possible, melt the butter until bubbling, then add the fish and cook on each side for 4 to 5 minutes, until golden and crisp. Serve with butter spooned over each and lemon wedges.

Variation:
Add a spoonful of onion chopped fine to the melted butter and cook for a minute before adding the fish. When the fish is cooked, remove it to a platter. Add $1/4$ cup white wine or dry vermouth, $1/4$ cup fresh orange juice, and a squeeze of lemon to the pan. Reduce slightly, stir in 1 teaspoon of butter, and serve.

Purée di Baccalà

. . . .

SALT COD PURÉE

Serves 4 to 6

This purée is the equivalent of the French brandade and is eaten on toasted bread accompanied by a strong red wine. The air-dried cod, *stoccafisso,* is traditionally used for stewed dishes at Christmas, but I like this spread as part of my holiday antipasti.

1^1/4 pounds prepared salt cod (page 160)
A few slices onion, carrot, and celery
Extra virgin olive oil
3 garlic cloves, chopped
1 baking potato, peeled and cooked
A few drops lemon juice
Freshly ground pepper
8 slices rustic bread, toasted

Make sure there are no bones in the baccalà or stoccafisso. Put the fish, onion, carrot, and celery in a pot and cover with cold water. Bring to a simmer and cook for 20 minutes. Drain, saving the broth for fish soups.

Heat a spoonful of olive oil in a small pan and cook the garlic for a few minutes, until golden. Put the fish, potato, and garlic in the bowl of a food processor and pulse a few times to mix. With the motor running, add olive oil in a thin stream until the mixture is like soft mashed potatoes or of spreading consistency. Add the lemon juice, taste for seasoning, and serve on toast.

Calamari o Moscardini al Tegamino

. . . .

SQUID OR BABY OCTOPUS IN TOMATO SAUCE

Serves 4 to 6

Any fish or shellfish may be prepared with this wine and tomato sauce. Octopus and calamari benefit from slow cooking over very low heat, because their flesh is dense and can become rubbery if cooked too quickly. A sushi chef taught me to tenderize calamari by soaking it in milk for half an hour before using. Discard the milk.

$^{1}/_{2}$ cup extra virgin olive oil
3 garlic cloves, chopped
Pinch of cayenne pepper
2 pounds squid, cleaned and cut into rings (page 37), or cleaned whole baby octopus
1 cup white wine
2 cups tomato sauce from Pasta al Pomodoro o al Sugo (page 100)
A few fresh flat-leaf parsley sprigs, chopped
Juice of 1 large lemon

Heat the olive oil in a large skillet, add the garlic, and cook until golden, about 1 minute. Add the cayenne, squid or octopus, wine, tomato sauce, parsley, and lemon juice and simmer over low heat for 20 to 30 minutes. This dish, if there are any leftovers, is also very good served over pasta.

Cozze al Vapore

. . . .

STEAMED MUSSELS

Serves 4

The mussels in Italy are sweet, almost buttery, and best when steamed quickly in a little oil, wine, and garlic. Some trattorie add tomato to the broth, which can be delicious, but the object is not to overpower a flavor that is already very good.

I would be circumspect about eating mussels known to be from a bay or anyplace where sewage might be in the water. In this country, you are best off buying farm-raised mussels, already cleaned, which are plump, sweet, and flavorful. The New Zealand green-lipped mussels are extraordinarily good, too. Don't forget to serve plenty of good bread for the sauce.

$^1/_2$ **cup extra virgin olive oil**
4 to 6 pounds mussels, scrubbed well, beards removed if necessary
4 garlic cloves, chopped coarse
2 cups dry white wine
A few fresh flat-leaf parsley sprigs, chopped

Heat the olive oil in a very large skillet with a lid. When it is hot, put in the mussels and garlic, cover, and steam for 2 minutes. Add the wine and let the mussels steam quickly over medium heat until just opened, 6 to 7 minutes. Divide the mussels and broth among bowls and serve, sprinkled with parsley.

Variation:
Add 2 cups tomato sauce from Pasta al Pomodoro o al Sugo (page 100), thinned with a spoonful or two of wine, just after the garlic; bring to a boil and add the mussels. Lower the heat, cover, and steam as directed. Use a mixture of mussels and clams to dress up this dish.

Fritto Misto di Mare

. . . .

MIXED FRY OF SMALL FISH, SHRIMP, AND CALAMARI

Serves 4

A fritto misto, also called *frittura di paranza*, contains anything small that is fresh that day at the fishmonger, but calamari and little *latterini*, a tiny sliver of a fish similar to our whitebait, are almost always included. You may order whitebait and sometimes fresh anchovies from your fishmonger, but in a pinch, frozen whitebait work very well.

Extra virgin olive oil for frying
1 pound whitebait
1 pound squid, cleaned and cut into rings (page 37), tentacles left whole
1 pound small shrimp
Pastella II from Alici o Latterini Fritti (page 30)
Lemon wedges

Heat 1 inch of olive oil until just beginning to smoke in a large deep skillet. Dip the fish in the batter and fry for 3 to 4 minutes, until very crisp and golden. Place a napkin on each plate, divide the fish among the plates, and serve with lemon wedges.

. . . .

To tenderize larger, possibly tougher, calamari for frying, simmer the pieces in 2 tablespoons extra virgin olive oil, 1/2 cup white wine, and a little salt, covered, over low heat for about 15 minutes. Drain and reserve the broth for another dish such as Risotto alla Pescatora (page 142) or Zuppa di Pesce (page 80). Dip the calamari in the batter and fry.

Baccalà Fritto

. . . .

FRIED SALT COD

Serves 4 to 6

Near the Campo dei Fiori, just off the via dei Giubbonari (a paradise for young shoppers because of all the shoe stores, tops and pants shops, sporting goods havens, and numerous little inexpensive pizza places and bars), there is a tiny piazza where baccalà is king. At Dar Filettaro in largo dei Librari, where we lived for one summer, fried, boiled, steamed, and whipped codfish is dished out in huge quantities every day to waiting lines of cognoscenti. Diners eat cheek by jowl, sharing their enjoyment of dried cod, rough wine, and this particularly lively neighborhood.

Italian markets carry dried codfish and an air-dried version without salt called *stoccafisso* or stockfish, tougher than baccalà, more delicate in flavor, and traditionally eaten at Christmastime as a paste on bread.

TO PREPARE BACCALÀ:
Dried cod used to be put under slowly running water for a week to remove the salt, but those were the days when water bills and droughts were nonexistent. Several changes of cold water over 48 hours will be fine, then test for saltiness. No refrigeration is needed during the soaking except during very hot weather. After 48 hours, dry the cod with a paper towel and remove all skin and bones, leaving the fish in whole pieces if possible. The fish is now ready to use.

TO PREPARE STOCCAFISSO:
Beat the dried fish with a mallet to break down its fibrous texture. Soak the fish in cold water for 5 to 6 days, changing the water regularly. The fish will be almost double its size after the soaking. Take out all the bones, leaving the flesh as intact as possible. The fish is now ready for recipes.

This is the dish for which hundreds stand in line each week: simple, crispy cod served with potatoes or salad and half a liter of flagrantly unrefined but fresh local wine, red or white, to cut the olive oil. You will welcome a Fernet Branca after this feast.

1 cup extra virgin olive oil
Eight 3- to 4-ounce pieces prepared salt cod
Pastella I or II from Alici o Latterini Fritti (page 30)
Lemon wedges

In a large skillet, heat the olive oil to smoking. Coat the baccalà slices with Pastella I or II and slide them carefully into the hot oil. Cook on one side until golden brown, 3 to 4 minutes, then turn over the slices and repeat. Drain on a brown paper grocery bag or paper towels. Serve with lemon wedges.

. . . .

Fernet Branca (Fernet pronounced as in tennis net, not fernay) is the secret weapon against practically all travel ailments above, below, or behind the belly button, including car sickness. Formulated from a good healthy dose of soothing wormwood and other potent herbs, this bitter bombshell tranquilizes the churning acids of indigestion while the body attached to the stomach slips into a delightful, soporific anticipation of the next meal. One of the great pleasures of sharing a Fernet is to watch the face of someone sipping it for the first time. It has a formidable kick, and you might wonder why you have subjected yourself or anyone else to this experience, but the perverted part of me really likes the flavor, and Fernet and I have struck a balance after all these years. I have actually become a bit masochistically attached to its unsubtle whack on the tongue and more than willingly attached to its effect. To be used sparingly, but if an occasional quick fix is needed to carry on with gastronomical research, this is the ticket.

Rombo, Branzino, o Salmone al Forno con Patate

....

ROASTED TURBOT, SEA BASS, OR SALMON WITH POTATOES

Serves 4

The turbot of the Mediterranean are huge and fleshy, unlike the small, flat flounder we have here. Every Roman cook agrees that a fresh fish, roasted only with a few potatoes, garlic, and rosemary, is one of the best dishes on any menu. It is also often the most expensive due to the diminishing supply of fish in the Mediterranean.

One 3-pound turbot or sea bass, cleaned and scaled, or $1^1/2$ pounds salmon fillet
$^1/2$ cup extra virgin olive oil, plus a little more to brush on the fish
Salt and freshly ground pepper
2 tablespoons butter
2 pounds Yukon Gold or waxy potatoes, cut into 1-inch dice or $^1/2$-inch slices
4 garlic cloves, halved
4 or 5 fresh rosemary sprigs

Preheat the oven to 400°F. Place the fish in a pan large enough to hold the fish and potatoes. Make shallow slashes in the fish if it is very thick, brush liberally with olive oil, and season well with salt and pepper.

Heat the rest of the oil and the butter in a skillet. Add the potatoes and cook over medium heat on all sides until golden and half cooked, about 10 minutes. Add the contents of the skillet, plus the garlic and rosemary sprigs, to the baking pan and roast the fish for 10 minutes for every inch of thickness, about 30 minutes in all. The potatoes and outer skin of the fish should be crisp and golden brown. If you like, you can add a splash of white wine to the pan halfway through the cooking time.

Variation:
Mash 8 anchovy fillets with 1 stick softened butter until very smooth. Brush a little on each cooked portion of roast fish.

Scampi alla Moro

. . . .

GRILLED LANGOUSTINES

Serves 4

At one of our favorite restaurants, Il Moro, the scampi are split like little lobster tails and grilled quickly over coals to preserve their fresh sweetness. You can use large shrimp in place of scampi, or even lobster tails if you are so fortunate as to have several lying around.

2 tablespoons melted butter
$^{1}/_{4}$ cup extra virgin olive oil
1 very small garlic clove, mashed
3 pounds scampi, split down the middle and opened flat
Juice of 1 large lemon
2 tablespoons minced fresh flat-leaf parsley

Preheat the broiler. Mix the butter, olive oil, and garlic in a dish and let sit for 10 minutes.

Place the scampi on a baking sheet and brush them liberally with the butter and oil mixture. Squeeze a few drops of lemon juice over the scampi, and broil them close to the heat source for 3 to 4 minutes, until the edges of the shells brown a little and the scampi are golden. Spoon the juices in the pan over the scampi, dust with parsley, and serve.

Pollo, coniglio, e agnello, meglio senza coltello.— Chicken, rabbit, and lamb, best when no knife is needed. • In Rome, chicken tastes the way chicken used to taste at my grandmother's farm on Sundays (dispatched with a firm grip and a swing around her head—painless and quick). There is actual flavor in the meat, unlike some of the plastic chickens we find at supermarkets. Of course, some brands here are better than others, especially the free-range birds that acquire some flavor simply through living normal lives out in the world. • I keep boned chicken breasts on hand for a quick dinner on the grill or for Pollo alla

pollame

Parmigiana (page 171), a crowd pleaser. I also suggest that you buy Cornish game hens every now and then instead of chickens, because they have a different flavor and because they are quick and easy to split, flatten, and grill or panfry. Poussins, the small chickens found easily in Europe, are also becoming popular here. They are very expensive but certainly worth serving for a special dinner since they are sometimes even more flavorful than game hens. • I keep quail and duck in my freezer for a change of pace and because quail are the perfect size for individual servings at dinner parties and a duck is perfect for a romantic dinner for two (see Sources and Seeds).

Galletto Ruspante alla Diavola

. . . .

GRILLED SMALL FREE-RANGE CHICKEN WITH HOT PEPPERS

Serves 4

The now-defunct La Ciotola prepared very small chickens with a zing of hot pepper. They were weighted down with heavy metal blocks to keep them flattened and the skin crisp. I sometimes cook these in a wide, shallow pan on the stove (when it's cold outside and difficult to barbecue), which works as well as a grill but without the smoky taste. You may prepare any small bird in this manner, using a heatproof plate placed over the flattened chicken and a 3- to 5-pound barbell on top. A brick or heavy stone works well, too.

4 very small chickens or 2 Cornish game hens, split
$^{1}/_{4}$ cup extra virgin olive oil
4 garlic cloves, minced
$^{1}/_{4}$ teaspoon hot red pepper flakes
Salt
Lemon wedges

Light a grill or heat a griddle or heavy skillet. Cover the split chickens with wax or parchment paper and pound them ruthlessly (especially the legs) with a mallet to flatten them to about $^{3}/_{4}$-inch thickness. Brush liberally with olive oil and sprinkle both sides with garlic, hot pepper flakes, and salt. If you are using a barbecue, cook the chicken halves over medium heat for 6 to 7 minutes on each side with the lid on, controlling the fire with a squirt bottle so that the outside skin does not become overly blackened. If you are using a griddle or skillet, place a heatproof dish or a smaller heavy skillet over the flattened chicken and place a weight on top. Cook over medium heat on one side, then turn and repeat. Serve with lemon wedges.

Pollo alla Cacciatora

CHICKEN IN THE HUNTER'S STYLE

Serves 4

Chicken, lamb, and rabbit are often served *alla cacciatora* in Rome—literally, in the style of the hunter. Regional differences call for mushrooms in one, rosemary and vinegar in another, but this lovely fall or winter dish, succulent and hearty, has suffered greatly because of all the liberties taken with the recipe by cooks who might not have been to Italy to taste the real thing. Artusi's famous cookbook, *La Scienza in Cucina e L'Arte di Mangiar Bene,* a sort of Italian *Joy of Cooking,* passed down from generation to generation, mentions that this dish is "not for those with weak stomachs." Perhaps the lard used in the original contributed to his opinion.

2 small chickens or 1 large roasting chicken, about 3 pounds
$1/4$ cup white lard, chicken or goose fat, or extra virgin olive oil
4 slices pancetta, diced
1 large onion, chopped
2 garlic cloves
1 $1/2$ cups red wine
3 cups tomato sauce from Pasta al Pomodoro o al Sugo (page 100)

Cut the small chickens into 8 pieces or the large bird into 8 to 10 pieces. Heat the lard, fat, or olive oil in a wide, heavy casserole, add the pancetta, and cook over medium heat until it begins to crisp, about 4 minutes. Add the onion and cook until translucent, about 4 minutes, then add the garlic and cook just until golden, another minute or so. Remove everything from the pan except the oil and brown the chicken on all sides. Return the pancetta mixture to the casserole, add the wine, and bring to a simmer. When the wine has reduced by half, add the tomato sauce, cover, and cook for 25 to 30 minutes, until the chicken is cooked through.

Variations:
Sauté $1/2$ pound brown or white mushrooms, sliced thin, along with the onions or the chicken.

After browning the chicken, add 1 $1/2$ cups raw rice and stir to coat with the oil. Add 3 cups chicken stock, return the pancetta mixture to the casserole, and proceed with the recipe.

Pollo Arrosto con Patate

. . . .

ROAST CHICKEN WITH POTATOES

Serves 4

This is the best and easiest chicken dish in Italy or anywhere. If you really wish to impress your guests at a dinner party, serve this dish. Even if you can't boil water, you will be able to make this classic, since everything is simply tossed with olive oil, placed in a pan, and roasted. The potatoes are suffused with oil and fresh rosemary, the chicken is crisp and juicy, and the sauce in the pan is perfect for a last crust of bread.

Buy the best chicken and the freshest potatoes, steal fresh rosemary from your neighbor's yard if you have to, and use extra virgin olive oil. I promise you success and sighs of appreciation at the table.

One 3-pound roasting chicken or 2 Cornish game hens
$^1/_2$ cup extra virgin olive oil
Salt and freshly ground pepper
$^1/_2$ teaspoon paprika
2 lemons, quartered
2 pounds waxy potatoes, cut into $^3/_4$-inch slices or diced
5 or 6 fresh rosemary sprigs, leaves only
1 cup white wine

Preheat the oven to 400°F. Brush the chicken or game hens liberally with some of the olive oil and season with salt and pepper inside and out. Sprinkle with paprika. Place the lemon quarters in the cavity, giving each a little squeeze to release the oil from the skins. Season the potatoes with salt and pepper and toss them with the rest of the olive oil and the rosemary leaves. Spread them around the chicken in a large baking pan. Fold a piece of aluminum foil double into a rectangle about the size of the chicken. Crease it down the middle, making a little tent, and lay the foil loosely over the breast. Roast the chicken for 45 minutes, basting 2 to 3 times with the fat in the pan. Add the wine (it will quickly evaporate in the hot oven, leaving a lovely flavor in the potatoes), remove the foil, and cook for 15 to 20 more minutes. If the breast is not browned enough, turn on the broiler for a few seconds to crisp the skin, but watch carefully so as not to burn your masterpiece. Carve the large chicken or split the game hens and serve with the potatoes and the pan juices poured over the chicken.

Pollo alla Romana

· ·

CHICKEN WITH SWEET PEPPERS

Serves 4 to 6

I do not use green bell peppers in anything. This is the only vegetable about which I am dogmatic, stubborn, fiercely opinionated, and also obstinate. Well, there are a few more, but green peppers are definitely on my hit list. I prefer sweet red, yellow, orange, and even chocolate-brown peppers.

Lacking fresh peppers, you may successfully substitute an 8-ounce jar of commercially roasted and peeled red bell peppers or pimientos.

3 bell peppers, any color but green
^{1}/$_2$ cup extra virgin olive oil
One 2- to 3-pound chicken, cut into 8 to 10 pieces
Salt and freshly ground pepper
I small onion, chopped fine
2 garlic cloves, chopped
^{1}/$_2$ cup white wine
4 ripe tomatoes, chopped coarse

Cut the peppers in half and remove all seeds and white membranes. Flatten them and char under a broiler, over a gas burner, or on a barbecue grill. When they are charred on all sides, transfer them to a plate and throw a damp dish towel over them to allow them to sweat, then slip off the blackened skin and cut the peppers into strips.

Heat the oil in a heavy skillet or casserole and add the chicken, seasoned well with salt and pepper. Brown on all sides, transfer to a plate, then add the onion and cook until translucent, 3 to 4 minutes. Add the peppers and garlic and cook for a minute or two. Return the chicken to the casserole and add the wine. Cook for a minute to reduce the wine a little, then add the tomatoes and simmer over low heat, uncovered, for 30 to 40 minutes.

Pollo alla Parmigiana

CHICKEN WITH PARMESAN SAUCE

Serves 4

Chicken bathed in Parmesan sauce draws nothing but admirers. The success of this dish depends on the quality of the Parmesan, so buy the very best and freshest you can find and grate it by hand, as any good Roman would.

I cup grated Parmigiano-Reggiano
2 eggs, beaten and seasoned with salt and freshly ground pepper
6 medium chicken breasts, flattened (page 166)
I cup cracker crumbs
$^1/_2$ cup extra virgin olive oil
I tablespoon butter
$^1/_2$ garlic clove, minced
I $^1/_2$ cups heavy cream
2 egg yolks
Juice of I large lemon

Add a spoonful of the Parmigiano-Reggiano to the eggs, then dip each chicken breast in the egg mixture and coat with cracker crumbs.

Heat the oil in a large skillet and brown the chicken breasts on one side. Cover, lower the heat, and cook for about 5 minutes. Remove the cover, turn the breasts, and cook on the other side for 4 to 5 minutes, until done but still moist.

In a saucepan, heat the butter, add the garlic, and cook until golden, about a minute. Add the cream and egg yolks and whisk over low heat until thickened. Stir in the rest of the Parmigiano-Reggiano and the lemon juice and serve the sauce over each breast.

Note: To make really tasty cracker crumbs for this dish (or any other), use Stoned Wheat Thins, a few sprigs of parsley, and a garlic clove and chop them in a food processor or blender until pulverized.

Chi non apprezza il vitello ha perso il cervello.—He who does not appreciate veal has lost his marbles. • In most of Europe, veal is a staple, and eating meat of any kind is not an issue. • I love good meat. When I am in the company of those who adhere to strict vegetarian diets, or are members of animal rights groups, I simply keep my preferences to myself. I enjoy all foods, with rare exceptions, and relish tasting whatever is offered to me, wherever I may be, although I'm still not quite comfortable with cannibalism. • Italians do not spend much time on examination of their consciences. Vegan and

carne

antifur groups are sometimes in the news, but freezing Italian winters have not yet dissuaded people from donning their pelts. • I search for meat with taste, try to make friends with duck hunters, and keep myself under control when a deer appears in my backyard to munch on my roses. • Meat in Italy tastes of the animal rather than a commercially standardized product with the flavor bred out and no character whatsoever. Even Italian pancetta brands are different from one another, while, with few exceptions, most of our commercial bacons taste alike. For most purposes our bacon is acceptable, but you may want to explore gourmet or health food stores for pancetta or bacon that contains no nitrates and offers varying degrees of smokiness or saltiness and more pronounced flavor.

Some lesser cuts of meat are best for braising or stewing, while recipes requiring a good steak or quickly cooked meat strips, *straccetti,* must be made with lean prime cuts if possible. Even when I am preparing a stew, I admit to sometimes using steak tips or top sirloin, just because I know the results will always be tender. And I have searched for good lamb for years, only to end up buying Australian or New Zealand lamb racks at my local Costco, where many chefs shop. I am on a search for good, fat pork as it used to be, but in general I find pork at ethnic markets is far superior to pork at supermarkets. Niman Ranch also offers good pork, although with less fat than, for example, Gloucester Old Spot, a delicious English heritage breed that is being bred again after a hiatus. Here in Los Angeles we have Hispanic and Asian markets, both of which offer a large selection of beef, pork, lamb, and even goat, which I love to grill or roast. Look around your city for new sources or visit a nearby farm where you might find a willing purveyor.

Abbacchio al Forno con Patate

ROAST LAMB WITH POTATOES

Serves 4 to 6

If ever there was a dish that exemplifies Roman cooking in all its glory, this is it. *"Stupendo,"* as Italians say about anything that boggles the mind, or *"È una poesia"*—this dish is a poem. The lamb is often milk-fed, although not always, but in either case the meat is tender, the skin crisp, and the potatoes perfect enough for the pope himself and all his cardinals.

You may use a boned leg of lamb to speed the cooking time, but the bone will always impart more flavor to the meat. I just throw everything in a roasting pan and let it rip.

1 leg of lamb, about 3 ^{1}/$_2$ to 4 pounds (anything larger is approaching mutton)
Salt and freshly ground pepper
4 or 5 garlic cloves, sliced
4 to 5 fresh rosemary sprigs, leaves only
2 pounds waxy potatoes, cut into 1-inch slices or medium dice
^{1}/$_4$ cup extra virgin olive oil
1 ^{1}/$_2$ cups white wine

Preheat the oven to 400°F. Season the lamb all over with salt and pepper. With a sharp knife, make incisions in the meat and push a slice of garlic and a little piece of rosemary into each. Toss the potatoes with some of the olive oil, salt, and pepper. Spread the potatoes in a roasting pan and put the lamb on top. Pour the rest of the oil over the meat. Roast for 10 minutes, then lower the heat to 350°F, add the wine, and continue roasting for 17 to 20 minutes to the pound, about 1 hour more depending on size, until the meat is very tender. Turn the potatoes once or twice if necessary to ensure even browning.

Variation:
You may put slivers of 5 or 6 anchovies into the incisions along with the garlic and add ^{1}/$_4$ cup capers to the pan during roasting to add flavor to the juices.

Or use a veal roast in place of the lamb for *vitello al forno.*

Abbacchio alla Cacciatora

LAMB IN THE HUNTER'S STYLE

Serves 4 to 6

Any good, inexpensive chunks of lamb (or beef, for that matter) may be used for this dish. Be sure to serve enough rustic bread to mop up the juices.

$^{1}/_{4}$ cup extra virgin olive oil

2 pounds boneless lamb, cut into $1^{1}/_{2}$-inch cubes

1 onion, chopped

2 garlic cloves, chopped

3 red or yellow bell peppers, roasted (page 54) and sliced

2 tablespoons red wine vinegar

1 fresh rosemary sprig

4 anchovies

1 cup white wine

1 cup Brodo di Carne or Brodo di Verdure (page 68 or 71)

2 tablespoons chopped fresh flat-leaf parsley

Heat the oil in a large casserole and brown the meat on all sides. Add the onion, garlic, and peppers and cook for a few minutes, until the onions are soft. Add the rest of the ingredients except the parsley, cover, and simmer over low heat for 1 hour or until the meat is very tender. Serve sprinkled with parsley.

Abbacchio alla Scottadito

· ·

FINGER-BURNING LAMB CHOPS

Serves 4

And they do. Best to let them cool a bit before handling, but it's hard to keep your hands off these delicious morsels. These very simple chops need only a few grilled onions, a few slices of grilled rustic bread, and a green salad as accompaniments. In Rome the chops can be so small that there is only one bite of meat at the end of a slender rib, or they can be *di una certa età* (of a certain age), as the Romans say of women who have just passed the apex of youth. In fact I find I prefer the older chops, which offer far more character and flavor than the others. Just like some women.

Allow 2 to 3 chops per person, depending on size (of chops, not of person, but that, too, should be taken into consideration).

8 to 12 rib lamb chops
2 tablespoons extra virgin olive oil
Salt and freshly ground pepper
3 large onions, cut into $^1/_2$-inch slices
6 slices rustic bread, brushed with olive oil
1 large garlic clove, peeled and halved

Light a grill or heat a large skillet. Brush the chops with some of the oil and season them well. Brush the onions with olive oil and place on the grill (or in a separate heated and oiled skillet on the stove) about 4 minutes before the chops. Cook on one side, turn, and add the chops. Grill very quickly over a hot fire or in the hot skillet, turning once after 2 to 3 minutes for rare meat, depending on thickness, or 4 minutes for medium-rare. Put the bread on the grill (or in the onion skillet after they come out—sauté on each side for a minute or so to toast) after the chops are ready, as it will toast in about 1 minute on each side. Rub the toast with the cut garlic before serving.

Bollito Misto con Salsa Verde

· ·

BOILED MEATS WITH GREEN SAUCE

Serves 8 to 10 with leftovers

Dal Bolognese is the place for this dish, the very trattoria where, after having eaten many courses at both lunch and dinner in Rome for ten days straight (something I rarely do), I easily managed an enormous plate of bollito misto and salsa verde while my husband watched in amazement, sipping his meager cup of broth. (Salsa verde is also very good spread on chicken, meat, or fish before broiling or used as a sauce for cooked fish or shrimp.)

As always, every ingredient must be top quality. There is more meat here than 8 people can eat, but believe you me, as my mother used to say, many other dishes can be made from the leftovers, or you can freeze them for yet another round with fresh salsa verde.

I have substituted plain sausage for *cotechino* (a fairly heavy Italian sausage eaten on New Year's Eve but not easily found here), but any sausage you like will do, even chicken or turkey. Remember that the large cuts of beef and veal cook first and the chicken follows about an hour later. The tongue and sausages cook separately and then go into the communal pot to finish cooking. I have left out the calf's head, but something tells me you won't miss it.

1 $^{1}/_{2}$ to 2 pounds tritip roast or brisket
1 $^{1}/_{2}$ to 2 pounds boneless veal roast
I beef tongue
4 large onions, chopped
4 carrots, chopped
4 celery ribs, chopped
2 tablespoons coarse salt
I tablespoon peppercorns
Pinch of ground cloves for each pot or I clove stuck in one of the meats
One 1 $^{1}/_{2}$-pound Italian sausage (fennel flavored, hot, or mild) or several smaller sausages adding
   up to the same weight
One 2-pound frying chicken (skinned if you would like to omit some fat)

FOR THE SALSA VERDE

1 thick slice rustic bread, crusts removed

3 tablespoons red wine vinegar

2 cups fresh flat-leaf parsley leaves or 1 small bunch

2 garlic cloves, peeled

2 tablespoons capers

3 anchovy fillets

$^1/_4$ teaspoon salt

$^2/_3$ cup extra virgin olive oil

Put the beef and veal in a large pot that will also accommodate the chicken. Put the tongue in another large pot that will also accommodate the sausage. Divide the vegetables and seasonings between the pots and add cold water to cover the meats to both. Heat to simmering, skimming and discarding the gray foam that rises to the top often during the cooking, and keeping the meats at a very low simmer.

After 30 minutes add the sausage to the tongue and continue cooking. After another 30 minutes, add the chicken to the meat pot. Check the tongue; it should be tender after an hour of cooking, and the sausage should be cooked after its 30 minutes of simmering. If so, turn off the heat under this pot while the chicken and meat continue to cook for 45 to 50 minutes. If they will fit, add the tongue and sausage to the meat pot for the last 10 minutes of cooking.

Meanwhile, make the salsa verde. Put all the salsa verde ingredients except the oil in the bowl of a food processor. Add the oil in a thin stream, but stop pulsing when you have a thick but still fairly liquid consistency. You may need a little more or less oil, depending on the bread used.

Serve the strained, combined broth in bowls and the meats arranged on a platter, sliced and sprinkled with parsley. Pass the salsa verde separately.

Braciole di Maiale o Vitello

GRILLED PORK OR VEAL CHOPS

Serves 4

My Roman stepson, upon moving to a bachelor apartment, had to learn to cook. Every time I called to ask what he was fixing, he would say, "*Una braciola*" [a chop]. For several years now the same answer has prevailed, not because he hasn't branched out but because a perfectly grilled chop is hard to beat when prep time is short, meat is a staple, and the best pork in Italy is available. Anyone on his or her own will never starve knowing this easy recipe.

A thick porterhouse grilled in the same way, minus the sage and garlic, becomes *bistecca alla fiorentina,* a favorite of Romans.

Four 5- to 6-ounce pork chops, bones in
Salt and freshly ground pepper
3 tablespoons extra virgin olive oil
8 to 10 fresh sage leaves
2 garlic cloves
Fresh lemon juice
2 tablespoons chopped fresh flat-leaf parsley

Season the chops with salt and pepper. Heat the oil in a large skillet, add the sage, and cook until toasted. Transfer the sage to a plate, add the garlic, and cook until golden. Transfer the garlic to the sage plate, add the chops, and sauté over medium-high heat for about 3 to 4 minutes on each side, until well browned. Add the garlic and sage back to the pan, sprinkle a little lemon and parsley over the chops, and serve.

Variation:
Sauté a few sage leaves and 2 to 3 garlic cloves in 1 tablespoon extra virgin olive oil or butter and spoon over grilled or broiled pork, lamb, or veal chops.

Fegato ai Ferri

· ·

GRILLED CALF'S LIVER

Serves 4

Along with brains, kidneys, and sweetbreads, liver is standard fare at most trattorie. Cesarina, one of Rome's top restaurateurs for many years, presided over our first visit to her establishment, insisting that of all the wonders she offered we were to have the grilled fegato, cooked for only seconds on a hot grill. The thin liver slices, perfectly crisped, pink in the middle but still juicy, are something we still talk about twenty years later.

We were unable to revisit her trattoria for almost four years. As we entered, Cesarina (in the same simple, faded green house dress that set off the four-carat emeralds she always wore) greeted us again, seating us at the same table. *"Volete prendere il solito fegato?* Are you having your usual fegato?" she asked. Which is why, of course, she was one of Rome's greats.

1 ^{1}/$_2$ pounds calf's liver, cut into ^{1}/$_2$-inch-thick slices
2 tablespoons extra virgin olive oil or melted butter
Salt and freshly ground pepper
2 tablespoons chopped fresh flat-leaf parsley

Light a grill or heat a skillet until very hot. Brush the liver on both sides with oil or butter and season well. Cook for 1 to 2 minutes only on each side and serve sprinkled with parsley.

Variation:
Cut the liver into 1-inch cubes, toss with 1 cup flour mixed with ^{1}/2 teaspoon pepper and 1 teaspoon paprika, and sauté in extra virgin olive oil over high heat for 1 minute on each side. Add 1 cup red wine to the pan, reduce quickly, for a minute or two, and serve dusted with parsley.

Coda di Bue alla Vaccinara

BRAISED OXTAIL

Serves 4

When I first tasted this luscious dish in Rome, I remembered that my father loved oxtails, and that my mother had braised them first and then made oxtail soup for him each winter. The familiar smell in Roman restaurants where oxtails were cooking was one from my childhood.

It is said that this dish originated at Checchino dal 1887, one of Rome's oldest trattorie (as you can see upon entering). The restaurant is from an elegant bygone era, with walls constructed from ancient amphora shards, most likely the same ones that make up the famous mountain in the neighborhood.

Make this dish ahead of time, put it in the refrigerator overnight, covered, and remove the fat. Then reheat, add the celery, finish the cooking, and serve. Oxtails also make a hearty winter pasta sauce. Serve with grated pecorino Romano.

^{1}/$_2$ cup extra virgin olive oil

2 onions, chopped

2 carrots, sliced

2 tablespoons chopped fresh flat-leaf parsley

2 garlic cloves, peeled and crushed

1 small bunch celery, sliced

2 pounds oxtails, cut into 1^1/$_2$-inch pieces (about 3 tails)

Salt and freshly ground pepper

1 beef cheek (optional, but your butcher may have one—ask)

1 thick slice pancetta, diced

2 cups dry white wine

2 cups tomato sauce from Pasta al Pomodoro o al Sugo (page 100)

1 cup Brodo di Carne (page 68)

Heat the oil in a heavy casserole large enough to hold the meat and vegetables. Add the onions, carrots, parsley, garlic, and half the celery and cook over medium heat until starting to brown, 6 to 7 minutes. Remove the garlic, add the oxtails, salt and pepper to taste, beef cheek if using, and pancetta, and cook until browned on all sides. Add the wine and simmer over low heat, covered, until the wine is almost gone, about 10 minutes. Add the tomato sauce and broth and cook, covered, for about 2 hours, until the oxtails are almost tender. Cool and refrigerate overnight, removing the congealed fat in the morning. Cook for another 30 minutes over low heat, adding the rest of the celery (for texture) to cook with the meat.

Note: For a thicker sauce, sprinkle 1 tablespoon flour over meat before browning.

Coda di bue

Involtini alla Romana

. . . .

ROLLED STUFFED BEEF OR VEAL IN TOMATO AND WINE SAUCE

Serves 4

So many cooks have versions of this dish—with bay leaf or cloves or without, with or without garlic, with canned tomatoes or fresh tomatoes, and so on—that you may pick and choose your own favorite ingredients, including whatever cut of meat seems appropriate. Essentially, involtini are made from lesser cuts such as skirt steak or top round pounded very flat (my choice). Ask your butcher what he has on hand for rolling and stuffing.

$^{1}/_2$ cup extra virgin olive oil

2 onions, chopped fine

2 carrots, chopped fine

2 celery ribs, chopped fine

1 garlic clove, minced

1 teaspoon fresh thyme leaves

2 pounds top round boneless beef cutlets, pounded very thin, or any very thin lean beef or veal cutlets

8 thin slices prosciutto

1 cup flour seasoned with 1 teaspoon salt, $^{1}/_2$ teaspoon freshly ground pepper, and 1 teaspoon paprika

1 cup dry white wine

2 cups canned plum tomatoes, crushed, or tomato sauce from Pasta al Pomodoro o al Sugo (page 100)

Pinch each of freshly grated nutmeg and clove (optional)

Chopped fresh flat-leaf parsley

Heat half the oil in a skillet, add the onions, carrots, and celery, and cook over medium heat until soft, about 5 minutes. Add the garlic and thyme and cook until the garlic is golden, another minute. Transfer the mixture to a plate to cool slightly. Using half the mixture, put a spoonful on each cutlet, then a slice of prosciutto, and roll up the meat, enclosing the filling. Secure with a toothpick.

Heat the rest of the oil in a skillet, dust the involtini with seasoned flour, and brown them well in the oil, adding a bit more if needed. Add the rest of the vegetables and the wine to the pan and simmer over low heat until a little of the wine evaporates, about 5 minutes. Add the tomatoes, nutmeg, and clove, if using, cover, and simmer over very low heat for 50 to 60 minutes, until the meat is tender, adding a little meat stock or wine if needed. Serve sprinkled with parsley.

Variation:
For Involtini di Maiale al Forno (Rolled Stuffed Pork), follow the recipe for Involtini alla Romana, substituting very thin pork slices—from a boneless pork roast or tenderloin, for example. Use Calvados instead of wine and finish off the sauce with the juice of a lemon and 1 teaspoon butter.

Maialino al Forno

. . . .

ROAST SUCKLING PIG

Serves 8 to 10

My grandfather butchered a pig once a year, as do many Italians. The by-products are infinite, and best of all, pork simply tastes good in Italy. The fat has not been bred out of the animal, and the meat is slightly less expensive than bistecca or vitello. You may find a pig through your butcher or Niman Ranch, a purveyor of delicious, humanely raised pork products (see Sources and Seeds). Cooking it is simple: season a young pig well and roast in a hot, then moderate oven. The outer skin of the pig will be very crispy as most of the fat cooks off, and the meat will be flavorful, succulent, and memorable.

1 small pig, 10 to 15 pounds, cleaned
10 garlic cloves, peeled and slightly mashed
4 to 6 branches rosemary and sage leaves
Salt and freshly ground pepper

Preheat the oven to 350°F and make sure your pig fits the pan. Wipe the pig with a vinegar-soaked rag. Make incisions all over the body and insert garlic slices. In the cavity of the pig, place several branches of rosemary and the sage and season exorbitantly with salt and pepper, inside and out. Roast the piglet for 17 to 18 minutes to the pound, about 3 to 4 hours, turning up the oven to 400°F for the last 20 minutes to crisp the skin well. Drain off the fat several times during the roasting.

Porchetta alla Romana

. . . .

SLOW-ROASTED PORK BELLY MEAT, STUFFED WITH HERBS AND GARLIC

Serves 6 to 8

When in Rome, you must stroll along the Appia Antica and marvel at the chariot grooves worn into ancient stones, gaze upon ruins of splendid villas, and dream of those worthy (and unworthy) Romans who traveled the same road: senators, housewives, gladiators going about their daily lives but, unfortunately for them, without a thick, fragrant midday sandwich from the little white cart selling *porchetta* that has been a fixture on the via Appia for years.

You can make your own facsimile right at home with help from a sympathetic butcher. This recipe (with Roman adjustments) came from Alessandro Possanzini, whose luscious porchetta I tasted in Torino at the huge Slow Food fair, which fills an entire former Fiat factory. An abbreviated version follows for those who do not have a good-sized pig on hand.

5 to 6 pounds pork belly meat, skin attached, or pork shoulder, butterflied and pounded flat by the
   butcher
2 tablespoons coarse salt, plus a little more for the outside of the meat
1 tablespoon freshly ground pepper
6 or 7 fresh rosemary sprigs, leaves only
3 garlic cloves
Tops of a fennel bulb or a spoonful of fennel pollen (available at gourmet or health food stores) or
   crushed fennel seed (optional)
²/₃ cup extra virgin olive oil
2 to 3 cups white wine

Preheat the oven to 500°F. Rub the meat with the salt and pepper. Chop the rosemary leaves with the garlic and fennel, if using, and mix with the extra virgin olive oil, using a mortar and pestle, to make a paste. Spread the paste over one side of the meat and roll up tightly, tying off at the ends and middle with kitchen string. Rub with a little more salt and roast for 20 minutes to seal the exterior. Lower the heat to 350°F and roast for about 2 hours, basting with a cup or two of dry white wine 2 or 3 times. When done, the skin should be crisp and a lovely caramel color, and the juice will run clear.

Ossobuco in Bianco

. . . .

VEAL SHANKS IN WHITE WINE

Serves 4 to 6

Yes, yes, I know this is a Milanese dish, but ossobuco is never omitted from Roman menus. I make ossobuco the day before because it tastes even better on the second day than when just out of the oven, as so many braised dishes do. You can serve this with any simple risotto or thumb your nose at the Milanesi and serve polenta or mashed potatoes instead.

Some chefs add tomatoes, carrots, peas, and all sorts of extraneous innovations, but I feel that tomatoes and vegetables draw attention away from the lovely marriage of meat, wine, garlic, and lemon, and they are generally not used in Rome.

The juice from ossobuco is a grand substitute for demi-glace, but having any leftovers is unlikely. Toasted rustic bread slices for the marrow are a must, and gremolata always accompanies ossobuco. I sometimes serve it with other braised dishes as well such as Stracotto di Vitello o di Manzo (page 194).

12 to 15 pieces meaty veal shank (ossobuco)

1 cup flour seasoned with 1 teaspoon salt, $^{1}/_{2}$ teaspoon freshly ground pepper, and 1 teaspoon paprika

$^{1}/_{2}$ cup extra virgin olive oil

4 tablespoons butter or $^{1}/_{4}$ cup extra virgin olive oil

6 large garlic cloves, chopped coarse

$^{3}/_{4}$ bottle dry white wine

4 to 5 cups rich Brodo di Pollo or Brodo di Carne (page 69 or 68)

Grated zest of 2 lemons

1 small bunch fresh flat-leaf parsley, chopped fine (about $^{2}/_{3}$ cup)

1 small garlic clove, chopped fine

6 slices rustic bread, toasted

Preheat the oven to 350°F. Put the seasoned flour in a brown paper bag and toss the meat in the flour mixture, shaking off the excess. Heat the oil and butter in a very large heavy casserole (or use a large skillet and transfer the browned meat to the casserole—you may need 2 if your largest casserole won't hold everything—before baking). Sauté on both sides over moderate heat until well browned. Add the coarsely chopped garlic and sauté until golden, another minute, then add the white wine to deglaze the pan. Add the stock and half the lemon zest, cover, transfer to the oven, and bake for $1^1/2$ hours. To generate a bit more juice, you may add a little wine or stock during the cooking.

To prepare the gremolata, mix the chopped parsley, finely chopped garlic, and remaining lemon zest and serve sprinkled over the ossobuco. Serve the toasted bread on which to spread the marrow from the bones.

Polpettone alla Romana con Purée

MEAT LOAF WITH MASHED POTATOES

Serves 4 to 6

My stepdaughter's recipe for polpettone came from her Sardinian-Roman mother, who got it from an Australian friend, who, it turns out, tinkered with a recipe from Marcella Hazan. So after considering all this, I have thrown in some elements from my mother's and mother-in-law's recipes to come up with a polpettone of which all six of us may be proud!

The optional hard-boiled egg is for looks (and taste). I am sure that at least a few Roman cooks might have borrowed this trick from the Piemontese on occasion.

1 thick slice white bread

$^2/_3$ cup milk or Brodo di Carne (page 68)

2 tablespoons extra virgin olive oil

2 slices pancetta or bacon, chopped fine

1 large onion, minced

1 celery rib, minced

1 garlic clove, minced

$^1/_2$ pound each ground pork, veal, and beef

2 ounces mortadella, chopped fine

2 eggs

1 egg yolk

$^1/_2$ cup grated Parmigiano-Reggiano

2 tablespoons chopped fresh flat-leaf parsley

Salt and freshly ground pepper

2 hard-boiled eggs (optional)

A few fresh rosemary, thyme, or basil leaves, chopped (optional)

$^1/_4$ cup flour mixed with a little salt and pepper

6 tablespoons butter

2 cups white wine

4 large baking potatoes, peeled and cut into 1-inch dice

$^1/_2$ cup heavy cream, milk, or yogurt

Preheat the oven to 375°F. Soak the bread in the milk or stock. Heat the oil, add the pancetta or bacon, cook until crisp, and transfer to a large bowl. Add the onion and celery to the pan and cook over medium heat until translucent, 3 to 4 minutes. Add the garlic, cook until golden, another minute, and add to the bowl. Add meats, eggs, cheese, parsley, salt and pepper to taste, and herbs if using and mix well with your hands. Form the mixture into a nice oblong loaf around the two hard-boiled eggs, if using. Roll in the seasoned flour, and brown on all sides in 2 tablespoons of the butter. Place the meat loaf in a baking pan and bake for 45 to 50 minutes, adding the wine after 30 minutes, or until the juices run clear when a sharp knife is inserted.

Meanwhile, cook the potatoes in salted simmering water until cooked through, 15 to 20 minutes. Drain, reserving the water for other dishes, and mash with the remaining butter and the cream, milk, or yogurt. Keep warm until the polpettone is ready.

Scaloppine di Vitello al Limone

. . . .

THIN VEAL SLICES WITH LEMON

Serves 4

Not to be confused with *scalpellino,* a stone mason.

During my first days of being a stepmother in Italy, I marveled at Italian prices. I could serve veal scaloppine to the children, who were used to them, and not make a terrible dent in the budget. For adults I add a little Marsala or a few capers to finish the sauce.

$^1/_4$ **cup extra virgin olive oil or 4 tablespoons butter**
8 veal scaloppine, pounded very thin
I cup flour seasoned with I teaspoon salt, $^1/_2$ teaspoon freshly ground pepper, and I teaspoon paprika
Juice of I large lemon
2 tablespoons butter
Chopped fresh flat-leaf parsley (optional)

Heat the oil or 4 tablespoons butter in a large skillet. Dredge the veal in the seasoned flour and sauté over medium-high heat until crisp and brown, about 2 to 3 minutes on each side. Add the lemon juice and 2 tablespoons butter and serve immediately, sprinkled with a little parsley if desired.

Variation:
When the veal is done, transfer it to warm serving plates and add $^1/_2$ cup Marsala to the pan. Reduce for a few seconds until shiny, swirl in the butter and a few capers, and pour over the veal.

Straccetti con la Rughetta

. . . .

"TATTERED" STRIPS OF BEEF WITH ARUGULA

Serves 4

This meat dish (*stracci,* rags, are also uneven pieces of pasta) appeared in Rome a few years ago quite suddenly, a fashionable menu item, which was welcomed by those eating lighter fare. The dish took off and is now seen everywhere except in cookbooks, as far as I know. Del Sostegno at via delle Colonnelle, 5, makes straccetti with artichokes (see variation below), a great match.

You may have to cook the meat in two batches since the strips are very thin and there will be many to contend with. Steak tails are very good in this dish.

1 $^{1}/_{2}$ pounds lean sirloin, cut into $^{1}/_{4}$-inch by $^{1}/_{4}$-inch by 2-inch-long strips
Salt and freshly ground pepper
$^{1}/_{4}$ cup extra virgin olive oil or 4 tablespoons butter
1 large bunch arugula leaves, chopped if large, left whole if small

Sprinkle the meat with salt and pepper. Heat the oil or butter in a large skillet, add the meat, and brown quickly on all sides over high heat, about 5 minutes. Add the arugula to the skillet, turn off the heat, toss with the straccetti, and serve immediately.

Variations:
Substitute cooked slivers of artichoke from Carciofi alla Romana (page 44) or thin strips of *zucchine,* sautéed until crisp, for the arugula.

Stracotto di Vitello o di Manzo

. . . .

VEAL OR BEEF POT ROAST IN WINE

Serves 4 to 6

Most stews are made with less expensive cuts of meat, as they were the food of the frugal peasant class. Use whatever stew meat you like for stracotto, but your stew will not be the poorer for having been assembled, if you choose, with choice meat such as the sirloin used for Straccetti con Rughetta.

Stews are so often the basis for great pasta sauces that it is wise to generate enough liquid in your stew by adding, if needed, an extra cup or two of meat stock or a little more wine, red or white.

2 pounds stew meat (veal or beef shoulder, chuck steak, top round, or sirloin), cut into $1^{1}/_{2}$-inch cubes

I cup flour seasoned with I teaspoon salt, $^{1}/_{2}$ teaspoon freshly ground pepper, and I teaspoon paprika

$^{1}/_{2}$ cup extra virgin olive oil

I large onion, chopped

2 carrots, chopped fine

I celery rib, chopped fine

2 garlic cloves, chopped

A few fresh sage or thyme leaves or a $^{1}/_{2}$-inch piece bay leaf

I bottle dry red wine, such as Merlot, Syrah, or Cabernet Sauvignon

2 cups Brodo di Carne (page 68), if necessary

$^{1}/_{4}$ cup tomato sauce from Pasta al Pomodoro o al Sugo (page 100)

Juice of $^{1}/_{2}$ lemon

Gremolata from Ossobuco in Bianco (page 188, optional)

Toss the meat in a paper bag with the seasoned flour, shaking off the excess. Heat the oil in a large casserole and brown the meat well on all sides. Remove from the pot and add the onion, carrot, and celery. Cook over medium heat until the onion is translucent, 3 to 4 minutes, then add the garlic and cook until golden, another minute. Return the meat to the pot, add the herbs and wine, lower the heat, cover, and simmer for about 1 hour, checking to see if stock or more wine is needed. Add the tomato sauce and lemon juice and serve with the gremolata if desired.

Variation:

Stufatino alla romana, a similar Roman stew made with beef, may be generated from much the same ingredients as in stracotto, although $^1/_2$ cup chopped pancetta is cooked with the onions, 1 tablespoon chopped fresh marjoram is used in place of the thyme, and 2 cups tomato sauce from Pasta al Pomodoro o al Sugo (page 100) is added along with the meat.

Trippa alla Romana

. . . .

TRIPE IN TOMATO SAUCE

A la trippa la menta, ar pisello er prosciutto; e su tutte dua mettece un gotto.—
For tripe use mint, for peas, use ham; and with them both down a swig of wine.

Serves 4 to 6

Wine will definitely help. Tripe, which is part of a cow's stomach, is an acquired but delicious taste. Romans eat trippa as if it were a bowl of pasta, which it resembles but isn't. You must try it once if only out of curiosity. Eating tripe is a kind of initiation into *la cucina romana*. One of the best renditions is served at Gigetto al Portico d'Ottavia, where offal things happen daily.

The tripe you buy will probably come ready to use, but if not, the preparation is easy. Many ethnic markets also carry tripe, ready for recipes.

FOR THE TRIPE
2 pounds honeycomb tripe from veal or beef
1 small onion stuck with 2 cloves
2 carrots, sliced
2 celery ribs, sliced
A little fresh flat-leaf parsley
A $1/2$-inch piece of bay leaf (stop right there, no more!)
A few peppercorns
Salt

FOR THE DISH
3 tablespoons butter or extra virgin olive oil
1 onion, chopped fine
1 carrot, chopped fine
1 celery rib, chopped fine
2 garlic cloves, minced
$1/3$ cup white wine
2 cups canned plum tomatoes, crushed, or 2 cups tomato sauce from Pasta al Pomodoro o al Sugo
   (page 100)
Pinch of fresh grated nutmeg

A few fresh mint sprigs, chopped fine
1 cup grated pecorino Romano

TO PREPARE THE TRIPE:

Cover the tripe with cold water in a pan and add the onion, sliced carrots, sliced celery, parsley, bay leaf, peppercorns, and salt to taste. Bring to a simmer, skimming off any foam that rises to the top during the cooking. Simmer for 3 hours, adding a little more water if needed, or until very tender. Drain, straining and reserving the stock. Cut the tripe into small bite-sized pieces and reserve.

TO PREPARE THE DISH:

Heat the butter or oil in a skillet or casserole, add the chopped onion, carrot, and celery, and cook over medium heat until the onion is translucent, 3 to 4 minutes. Add the garlic and cook until golden, another minute. Add the tripe and wine and cook until the wine is absorbed, 6 to 7 minutes. Add the tomatoes and nutmeg and simmer over very low heat, covered, 20 to 30 minutes. Serve in bowls with chopped mint and lots of pecorino. In earlier times, this was served over toasted bread.

Vitello Tonnato

. . . .

VEAL WITH TUNA SAUCE

Serves 4 to 6

When I make this very easy summer dish, I think of sexy underwear. My first taste of *vitello tonnato* was at the Casina Valadier, just above the Spanish Steps, a beautiful villa perfect for lunch on a summer Sunday. Many weddings used to be held on the spectacular terrace overlooking Rome. I remember the day, too, because my husband and I were on our first trip to Italy together, as yet unmarried but in love with everything Italian and each other. We shared our pergola with another smitten couple, he of a certain age and she, around 23, dressed as so many Roman women are (at any age) in a see-through blouse with great lingerie underneath. I went straight out and added a few little items to my own wardrobe . . .

Every restaurant serves this dish in summer, with varying degrees of quality. Use the best tuna in olive oil that you can find and do not thin the sauce too much. To enhance domestic tuna packed in water, see page 24.

This is yet another way to generate veal stock for soups and stews or to reduce for demi-glace. All can be frozen.

You may also eliminate the mayonnaise and simply blend $^1/_2$ cup extra virgin olive oil with the rest of the tonnato sauce ingredients, thinning the sauce slightly with the veal stock.

3 pounds lean boneless veal roast
6 anchovy fillets, 4 chopped
I garlic clove, peeled and sliced
I onion, chopped coarse
2 carrots, chopped coarse
I celery rib, chopped coarse
Pinch of ground cloves
A $^1/_2$-inch piece bay leaf
I teaspoon salt
A few peppercorns
2 cups white wine
I $^1/_2$ cups homemade or commercial mayonnaise
One 6-ounce can imported tuna in olive oil or domestic tuna in water, drained
2 tablespoons capers, plus a few for garnish

Make incisions in the veal with a sharp knife and push pieces of the chopped anchovy and slices of garlic into the slits. Place the veal in a deep pot and add the vegetables, seasonings, wine, and cold water to cover. Bring to a boil, skimming off any foam with a perforated spoon. Simmer, covered, over very low heat for 1 to 1^{1}/2 hours, until very tender. When the veal is cooked, remove the pot from the heat and cool the veal in its stock. Reserve the veal and strain the stock. (Refrigerate overnight if you wish to remove the fat from the stock.)

TO PREPARE THE SAUCE:

Put the mayonnaise, tuna, capers, and remaining two anchovies in the bowl of a food processor. Pulse until smooth, adding about ^{1}/2 cup of the cooled veal stock to thin the sauce to the consistency of a thick pancake batter.

Slice the cooled veal very thin and arrange the slices on plates. Spread the tuna sauce over the meat, garnish with a few capers, and serve.

Variation:

Serve the tuna sauce over thick slices of tomato, on a bruschetta, or with little crackers as an hors d'oeuvre.

Prendere due piccioni con una fava.—You can kill two birds with one stone. • In Italy, hunting is not done just for sport, although that is surely a part of it. During wartime, deer, rabbit, and game birds often kept families from starving, just as they did in our country during the Depression, and game was often the only meat on the table unless one was fortunate enough to have a pig or lamb. Hunters are part of the landscape, and Romans do not balk at feathers, hooves, claws, or beaks, relishing their game dishes in winter as they do gelato in summer. Many trattorie feature delicious game creations, such as sauces of wild

cacciagione

boar or rabbit over wide noodles and roast pheasant, partridge, duck, or the classic quail with polenta. • In my opinion, game requires few frills. You salt and pepper it, roast it, and eat it. If you really want to go crazy, a couple of onions and carrots, a few juniper berries, and some wine will take care of just about any woodland creature. The following are some of my favorite Roman game recipes, which I encourage you to try, as they are, if not the heart of *la cucina romana,* the ventricles.

Anatra Selvatica alle Mele

. . . .

WILD DUCK WITH APPLES

Serves 4

A hunter friend here in L.A. used to bring me fresh teal ducks in exchange for hazelnut sage bread from my bakery. He always had a freezer full of game, and his wife simply grew tired of cooking it. Teal is some of the best meat you'll ever eat, succulent and as tender as a chicken breast but with the flavor of autumn and the hunting season in its flesh. If you do not have access to wild game, you may, of course, use domestic ducks. They will throw off copious fat, which you should strain and keep on hand in the refrigerator for cooking. Duck fat, like goose fat, is far better for your health than butter and gives vegetables, especially potatoes, a lovely, nutty flavor.

4 teal or two 3- to 4-pound domestic ducks (some will be left over for other dishes)
Salt and freshly ground pepper
$^1/_4$ cup extra virgin olive oil
4 slices bacon (omit for domestic duck)
2 onions, sliced thin
2 tablespoons butter or extra virgin olive oil
1 $^1/_2$ pounds tart apples, peeled and sliced thin
Juice of 1 lemon
1 cup dry white wine
1 $^1/_2$ cups Brodo di Pollo (page 69)

FOR WILD DUCK—ROASTING TIME 20 TO 30 MINUTES, DEPENDING ON SIZE:

Preheat the oven to 400°F. Season the ducks with salt and pepper. Put the ducks in a roasting pan, brush with the $^1/_4$ cup olive oil, and lay the bacon over the duck breasts. Add the onions to the pan and brown the duck in the oven for 15 minutes. Meanwhile, heat the butter or oil in a skillet, add the apple slices, and cook over medium-high heat until browned and crisp around the edges, about 10 minutes. Sprinkle with lemon juice and add to the roasting pan along with the wine. Roast the ducks for about 15 minutes more or until the breast meat is semifirm but not soft. Transfer the ducks to a platter, scrape down the pan, and add the broth to deglaze. Cook over medium heat until reduced by half. Serve some onion and apple with each portion of duck and spoon the reduction over the slices.

FOR DOMESTIC DUCK—ROASTING TIME ABOUT 1 TO 1$^1/_2$ HOURS:

Omit the bacon and do not precook the apples. Roast without the vegetables for 15 minutes, then pour off the fat. Add the white wine and broth. Continue roasting, pouring off the fat as needed. Add the onions and apples, sprinkled with lemon juice, during the last 25 minutes of roasting; they will cook in the duck fat and be absolutely delicious.

Fagiano Arrosto

. . . .

ROAST PHEASANT OR PARTRIDGE

Serves 4

In the fall you will often see hunters walking along back roads near Rome, their colorful game birds slung over their backs. I am always tempted to stop and ask to buy one, but I know that they would be compelled, by their generous Italian nature, to give me the whole lot, and so I drive on.

1 large or 2 medium pheasant (females are best), cleaned
$^1/_4$ cup olive oil
3 or 4 slices bacon
1 onion, sliced
2 carrots, sliced
1 $^1/_2$ cups red wine
1 cup Brodo di Pollo (page 69)
1 tablespoon butter

Preheat the oven to 400°F. Season the bird inside and out with salt and pepper. Place it in a roasting pan, brush with olive oil, and lay the strips of bacon over the breasts. Place the vegetables around the bird and roast for 30 to 45 minutes, depending on size, adding the wine and stock to the pan after 15 minutes. Transfer the bird to a platter to rest. Put the roasting pan on the stove and heat the juices, scraping down any bits that have clung to the pan. Swirl in the butter and serve with the pheasant.

Variations:
- Before roasting, the pheasant may be marinated overnight in 1 cup red wine with the vegetables, a fresh rosemary sprig, and a fresh thyme or lemon thyme sprig.
- If you have access to black or white truffles, morels, or any strongly flavored mushroom, slice 2 or 3 very thin and push them under the breast skin. Let the bird sit overnight in the refrigerator before cooking.
- Cut slices of rustic bread and butter both sides. Toast both sides in a skillet and serve under slices of the pheasant and its juices.

- Sauté diced potatoes, parsnips, or turnips in butter or olive oil until golden, sprinkle them with fresh rosemary, and add them to the vegetables in the pan to finish cooking.
- Sauté 1 pound of mushrooms (cremini, morels, chanterelles, or porcini) in butter or olive oil and add to the pan along with or instead of the vegetables. Substitute white wine for red.

Quaglie alla Griglia con Polenta

. . . .

GRILLED QUAIL WITH POLENTA

Serves 4

I grew up with quail on the grill, baked quail, roasted quail, quail in casseroles—you name it. Quail are as plentiful in Italy as they are in Texas and an essential part of the hunters' bounty along with venison and boar. I try to keep farm-raised quail in my freezer since they are the perfect single-serving size for dinner parties and quick to prepare.

Many commercial quail come boned with convenient little skewers stuck through them, ready for the grill. I remove the skewers when cooking in the pan since they get in the way, but you may skewer your own quail with bamboo sticks or short metal skewers to make them easier to handle.

Grilled sausages may be used in place of quail in this recipe.

Polenta (page 226)
2 tablespoons extra virgin olive oil or butter
8 quail
$^1/_4$ cup extra virgin olive oil mixed with 1 garlic clove, minced
Salt and freshly ground pepper
Fresh rosemary leaves (optional)

While it's still hot, spread the polenta $^1/_2$ inch thick on a smooth surface, let cool, and cut into 8 squares or whatever shape you like.

Light a grill, preheat the broiler, or heat 2 tablespoons of oil or butter in a large skillet. If using a grill or the broiler, brush the polenta with the oil or the butter, melted. Cook on an oiled fine grill over the regular barbecue grill, under the broiler, or in a hot skillet until browned on both sides.

Brush the quail with the garlic oil, season with salt and pepper, sprinkle a few rosemary leaves over them, and grill quickly along with the polenta, turning after 3 to 4 minutes. The birds are done when the breast meat is pink and only slightly firm to the touch, not fully cooked and hard.

Variation:

To cook the quail on the stove, toss them in 1 cup flour seasoned with 1 teaspoon salt, $^1/_2$ teaspoon freshly ground pepper, and 1 teaspoon paprika and sauté them over medium-high heat in 2 tablespoons extra virgin olive oil for 3 to 4 minutes on each side, until nicely browned but still pink inside. Add $^2/_3$ cup red or white wine to the pan to deglaze, a few drops of lemon juice, and 1 tablespoon butter. Serve with lemon wedges.

Cinghiale alla Cacciatora

· ·

WILD BOAR IN THE HUNTER'S STYLE

Serves 4 to 6

When I first lived in Italy I was charmed by the Christmastime displays in spotless tiled butcher shops of wild boar whose coarse fur was festooned with bright red ribbons or ornaments. Their long, formidable tusks formed a porky kind of smile, tempting me to experiment with the lean, intensely flavorful meat in stews, roasted in the oven, and in pasta sauces.

A rich cinghiale sauce is not to be missed at Mario, in via della Vite (the same Mario who is also the expert on zolfino beans; see Pasta e Fagioli o Ceci, page 78). My first visit years ago to this crowded neighborhood trattoria was inspired by having stopped in my tracks to watch through the restaurant window as two portly priests attacked plates of wide noodles and what looked like chocolate sauce—of course, in we went. This dense, meaty sauce was our reward. Serve it over pappardelle (page 90), with rice, or with grilled polenta slices (page 226).

1 $^1/_2$ pounds wild boar or lean beef or pork roast

$^1/_2$ bottle dry red wine

2 tablespoons red wine vinegar or balsamic vinegar

3 onions, sliced

3 carrots, sliced

3 garlic cloves, minced

A few celery leaves

Pinch of ground cloves

1 small piece bay leaf

Salt and freshly ground pepper

$^1/_2$ cup extra virgin olive oil or $^1/_4$ cup oil and $^1/_4$ cup lard

2 slices pancetta, diced

1 cup Brodo di Carne (page 68)

1 or 2 fresh thyme sprigs

1 cup pitted prunes, chopped

1 tablespoon softened butter blended with 1 tablespoon flour

Place the meat in a deep dish and add the wine, vinegar, one of the onions, one of the carrots, 2 of the garlic cloves, the celery leaves, cloves, bay leaf, and salt and pepper to taste. Cover and let sit overnight in the refrigerator. Pat dry before using.

Preheat the oven to 350°F. Heat the oil and lard, if using, in a heavy casserole and brown the meat on all sides. Transfer to a plate. Add the pancetta and remaining onions, carrots, and garlic to the casserole and cook until the bacon begins to crisp and the onions are translucent, 3 to 4 minutes. Add the meat to the casserole along with the marinade, broth, thyme, and prunes. Cover and bake in the oven for $1\frac{1}{2}$ hours, or until the meat is very tender.

Transfer the meat to a platter. In a small skillet, melt the butter and flour and cook just until golden brown and thick, about 2 minutes. Add a little of the meat juices and blend, then add the contents of the skillet to the juices in the casserole. Cook until thickened and serve.

Variations:
- Use 1 tablespoon crushed juniper berries in the marinade, omit the prunes, and add 1 teaspoon grated orange zest and $\frac{1}{2}$ cup fresh orange juice to the pan during roasting.
- Substitute dried apricots for prunes and add 1 tablespoon unsweetened cocoa powder or grated dark unsweetened chocolate to the pan during roasting. A splash of strong espresso works well, too.

Lepre al Marsala

. . . .

HARE OR RABBIT WITH MARSALA

Serves 4

Italians often cook with Marsala, a perfect complement to the taste of rabbit. This recipe takes very little time once the rabbit pieces are cut up (by you or the butcher). You may choose not to bone your rabbit, in which case simply cut it into manageable serving pieces, but be sure to warn guests of the small bones therein. You may substitute chicken for rabbit, but I encourage you to branch out and try a good domestic rabbit at least once for a savory change.

Marinating rabbit (or any meat) in milk will leave the flesh tender and eliminate the soapy taste a rabbit can sometimes have, as lactic acid breaks down the fibers.

One 2- to 3-pound rabbit, boned and cut into 1-inch pieces or not boned and cut into
 2- by 2-inch pieces
1 cup milk mixed with 1 garlic clove, mashed, and $^1/_4$ teaspoon each salt and freshly ground pepper
$^1/_2$ cup pine nuts
$^1/_2$ cup extra virgin olive oil
1 cup flour, seasoned with 1 teaspoon salt, $^1/_2$ teaspoon freshly ground pepper, and 1 teaspoon
 paprika
2 tablespoons butter
2 tablespoons onion, chopped fine
1 garlic clove, minced
$^1/_2$ cup Marsala
A few basil leaves, shredded

Soak the rabbit in the milk mixture for about an hour (or overnight if you wish). Meanwhile, sauté the pine nuts in 1 teaspoon of the oil in a skillet over medium heat for 2 minutes, just until they are golden. Set aside.

In a paper bag, toss the drained rabbit pieces with the seasoned flour. Heat the remaining oil and the butter in a wide skillet and brown the pieces on all sides over medium heat. Add the onion and cook for a few minutes, until golden. Add the garlic and cook until golden, another minute. Add the Marsala and cook over low heat, covered, for 20 to 30 minutes or a little longer if the pieces have not been boned. Remove the lid, add the pine nuts and basil, and serve.

. . . .

To cut up a rabbit, use a cleaver to split the rabbit in two down each side of the backbone, removing the backbone for stock. To grill, flatten the rabbit as you would Galletto Ruspante alla Diavola (page 166) or cut the rabbit into serving pieces as for fried chicken. You can bone out the saddle, as the tenderloin is called, and cut it into small medallions for special recipes, but normally I cut the saddle into 4 nice, meaty pieces, bone in, and then cut the rest of the rabbit into serving pieces.

Zucchine e melone sono buoni di stagione.—*Zucchini and melon are best in season.* •

Oh, the wealth of vegetables in and around Rome, although some are elusive, such as the tart, beet-flavored *agretti,* also known as *barba di frate,* "beard of the priest," because of their tangled appearance. Ask for agretti at restaurants or markets in some parts of Rome, and faces will go completely blank. Even in some of Rome's nurseries, where I searched for seeds to bring back to the growers at the Santa Monica Farmers Market, *Lepidium sativum* was unknown. • According to a farmer I know, agretti are of the tumbleweed family. Growers in the U.S. are

contorni

beginning to discover the profits from these jewels, but they germinate easily in a home garden and will come up again if left to form new seeds. Keep an eye out for this amazing vegetable (or pick up seeds on your next trip to Italy). • The intense flavor of vegetables in Rome is attributable to the volcanic soil of the region of Lazio. Vegetables play such an enormous role in the Italian menu that I can only encourage you to try as many as possible, steamed or grilled and dressed with only a little lemon and olive oil. I love to roast vegetables; cauliflower, beets, potatoes, onions, carrots, parsnips, and celery are good candidates. I also grill many vegetables, peeling bell

Barba di Frate

peppers after the first grilling, then putting them back on for a second time to caramelize. I urge you to try cooking vegetables a little longer than usual, in the Roman manner. String beans and asparagus should not squeak or resist when you chew them, and all greens should be cooked thoroughly until limp or even crispy or caramelized, if you are roasting them. The Italian diet is weighted toward vegetables and fruits, rarely punctuated with salty, high-fat snacks or sweets, making it one of the world's most healthful.

Bieta, Spinaci, o Cicoria in Padella

. . . .

CHARD, SPINACH, OR CHICORY WITH GARLIC AND HOT PEPPERS

Serves 4

Sautéed greens are quick and easy. You can take this dish in another direction by cooking the greens for another 15 to 20 minutes until they become brown and crisp around the edges, well worth the wait. You will need twice the amount of greens for this method since they shrink to nothing.

1 to 2 pounds spinach, chard, or radicchio
4 tablespoons extra virgin olive oil
2 cloves garlic, chopped
1 small dried hot red pepper, crushed
Lemon wedges

Wash the greens and drain well. Put 2 tablespoons of the olive oil in a skillet, add the greens, chopped, toss with the oil, and cook, covered, until wilted. Remove the cover, make a little space in the middle of the greens, and add another 2 tablespoons of olive oil to the space, then the garlic and hot pepper. Cook, uncovered, until the chard is very soft. Serve with lemon wedges. Or continue cooking, uncovered, until most of the moisture has evaporated and the greens are crispy and slightly browned all over. You may need an additional tablespoon or two of olive oil.

Variation:
Use butter in place of olive oil for a truly decadent dish. Spinach is particularly good in butter, with just a pinch of nutmeg stirred in at the end.

Fave con Salvia e Aglio

· ·

FAVA BEANS WITH TOASTED SAGE AND GARLIC

Serves 4

Just as a small percentage of Italians (mostly those with Sardinian blood and some others of Mediterranean heritage) suffer from a rare but serious reaction to fava beans, I, too, suffer from inverse *favismo,* as the unfortunate affliction is called. If I do not get my *fave* almost daily during their season, I become flushed, hot, grow short-tempered, and become obsessed with farmers' markets.

When *fave* are young, they are eaten raw accompanied only by a good pecorino and fresh pepper, although I can eat them young or old, raw or cooked, mashed or deep-fried and be almost as happy as I am with a white truffle.

Now comes the debate: to peel or not to peel a shelled fava. I have *never* peeled my *fave,* not once, and this recipe gets raves. Of course, there is something to be said for using spring's baby fava beans, and denuded, they melt like gelato in the mouth, but I happen to love the texture of the skins and feel it's part of the real taste and character of the bean.

Deep-fry the older ones in olive oil until very crisp. Add salt and serve with aperitivi.

$^1/_2$ teaspoon salt

1 pound shelled fava beans, about 3 pounds in the shell

$^1/_4$ cup extra virgin olive oil

8 to 10 fresh sage leaves

2 garlic cloves, chopped coarse

Juice of 1 lemon

Put $1^{1}/_{2}$ inches of water in a saucepan with the salt. Bring to a boil and add the fave. Cover and simmer until tender, 6 to 7 minutes if the beans are young, a few minutes longer if not.

In a small skillet, heat the olive oil over medium heat and cook the sage leaves until just crisp, 5 to 6 minutes. Add the garlic and cook quickly until golden, about 1 minute.

Drain the *fave* (saving the water for soups), toss with the sage and olive oil mixture and the lemon juice, and serve.

Variation:
Purée the beans in a food processor with $^{1}/_{2}$ cup of the cooking water, the juice of a large lemon, and a little more olive oil as needed until they are a smooth paste. Serve on bruschette or as a purée with meat or chicken.

Puntarelle con Salsa di Alici

. . . .

CHICORY SPEAR SALAD WITH ANCHOVY SAUCE

Serves 4

Puntarelle are the thin, tender, pale green stalks of young chicory plants, which arrive in Rome's markets in spring. They are split and cut into spears, then refreshed in ice water, where they curl into crisp tendrils. Fortunately for cooks in Rome, puntarelle come already cleaned, crisped, and ready for salads. I have recently grown my first crop from seed in Los Angeles (see Sources and Seeds) and I'm sure they will appear soon in our farmers' markets along with agretti.

You may bring faux puntarelle to your table by cutting very young celery stalks into very fine strips. Place them in ice water until they curl, then dress and serve. Some restaurants use too much anchovy in their sauce, some not enough, but at Tullio near Piazza Barberini and La Campana near Piazza della Fontanella Borghese, the puntarelle are perfect. I like a few drops of lemon to punctuate the sauce.

2 garlic cloves, minced
6 anchovy fillets
Juice of $^1/_2$ lemon
$^2/_3$ cup extra virgin olive oil
1 $^1/_2$ pounds puntarelle, ready for salads, or young celery stalks, deribbed, sliced lengthwise into very thin strips, and placed in ice water to curl

Mash the garlic and anchovies into a paste. Add the lemon juice, then slowly add the oil, whisking all the ingredients into a smooth sauce. Toss with the puntarelle and serve.

Vignarola

. . . .

FAVA BEANS, ARTICHOKES, AND PEAS

Serves 4

In spring, when young *fave,* artichokes, lettuce, and little green peas are fresh and tender, a *vignarola* can be a work of art. It must not be cooked too long but only just enough to soften the vegetables and encourage them to release their delicate flavors. Roman recipes for *vignarola* cook everything together at the same time (sometimes too long), so I add the peas at the end to preserve their sweet taste and firm texture.

$^{1}/_{2}$ cup extra virgin olive oil
Two $^{1}/_{4}$-inch-thick slices pancetta or guanciale, diced fine
2 spring onions or 1 small sweet onion, chopped fine
2 cups shelled fava beans
8 to 10 baby artichokes, cleaned and quartered (page 42)
$^{1}/_{2}$ cup white wine
Leaves of 1 small head romaine lettuce
2 cups fresh green peas
2 tablespoons chopped fresh flat-leaf parsley

Heat the olive oil in a heavy casserole with a lid, add the pancetta, and cook over medium heat until it is beginning to crisp, about 5 minutes. Add the onion and cook until translucent, 3 to 4 minutes. Add the fave and artichokes and stir to coat with oil. Add the wine, cover, and cook over the lowest heat, braising the vegetables for 10 to 15 minutes, until they are very soft. Add the lettuce leaves and peas, stirring them into the vegetables, and cook for about 5 minutes, until the peas are just tender. Add the parsley at the end.

Cipolline in Agrodolce

· ·

YOUNG ONIONS IN A SWEET AND SOUR SAUCE

Serves 4

These little tart and sweet onions are good on the antipasto table or as an accompaniment to game, roast meat, or chicken. Other vegetables can be cooked this way, including carrots, celery, turnips, and parsnips. I use butter instead of olive oil in this dish because olive oil does not caramelize as well when mixed with sugar.

8 tablespoons (1 stick) butter
1 $^1/_2$ pounds small white onions, trimmed and peeled (flat cipolline are perfect for this dish)
$^1/_4$ cup sugar
$^1/_4$ cup wine vinegar or balsamic vinegar
A few drops of fresh lemon juice

Heat the butter in a heavy saucepan large enough to hold the onions. Cook the onions in the butter, sprinkle with the sugar, add the vinegar and enough water to barely cover the onions, and bring to a boil. Simmer over low to medium heat until the liquid is completely gone, about 15 minutes, watching carefully to prevent scorching. The onions will become glazed and caramelized. Sprinkle with lemon juice and serve.

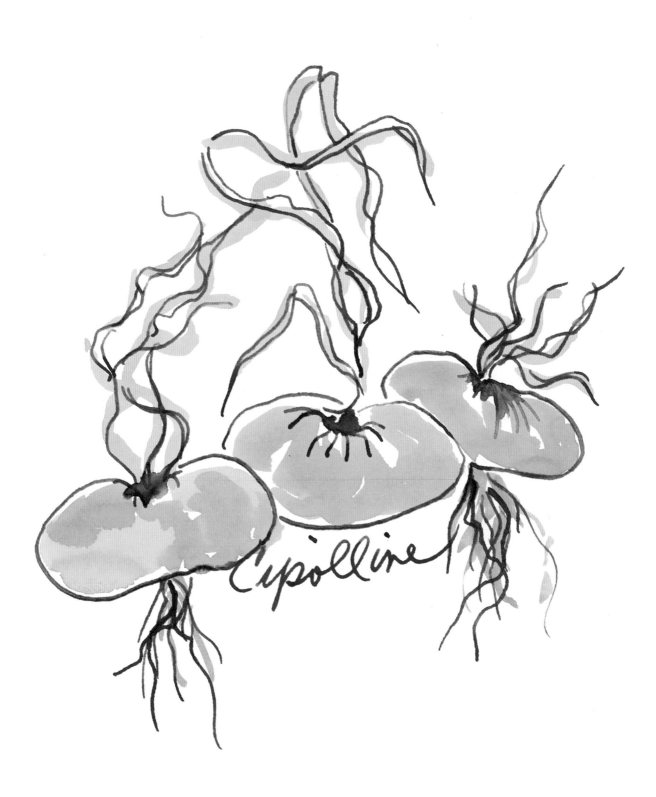
Cipolline

Funghi Porcini Arrosti

. . . .

SAUTÉED PORCINI MUSHROOMS

Serves 4

Not really a contorno, roasted porcini are ordered as a serious main course when the first ones arrive in trattorie after a fall, spring, or summer rain. Near Rome, in Città di Castello, the heady scent of the November porcini and truffle festival can make you swoon. After watching a mushroom and truffle auction at the restaurant Il Bersaglio, where tables were piled high with baseball-sized funghi, we managed to work our way through a 12-course porcini and tartufi menu, which left us unfit for anything except a nap.

David's Mushrooms in Los Angeles carries a domestic version of porcini, along with many other funghi, so I can easily relive my moments in Rome savoring their meaty flavor. Fresh porcini may appear occasionally in your own neighborhood markets, but please do *not* go hunting for them in the wild without a mycologist along. Every fall in Italy after the first rains, you will read at least one story of a whole family being wiped out because of a tiny mistake. Certainly one *amanita* can ruin your whole day!

8 fresh porcini with stems or any other large, meaty mushroom such as portobello
$^1/_4$ cup extra virgin olive oil
Salt
2 tablespoons chopped fresh flat-leaf parsley
Lemon wedges

Heat a grill or large skillet. Remove any loose dirt on the mushroom caps or stems with a toothbrush or a mushroom brush (found at kitchen shops). Remove the stems from the mushrooms and reserve them for other dishes, or slice, sauté along with the caps until golden, and serve together. Brush the porcini with olive oil and season with salt. Place the caps stem side down and cook over medium heat on one side until golden brown, about 3 minutes. Turn over, place a plate on top of the porcini and a 5-pound weight on the plate, and cook for a few minutes more, until well browned and slightly crisp on the outside. Remove the weight and plate and continue cooking until nicely browned, 2 to 3 minutes. Serve sprinkled with parsley and surrounded by lemon wedges.

Variation:
For porcini *trifolati,* slice or chop 8 fresh porcini and sauté over medium heat in 1 tablespoon butter or extra virgin olive oil until well browned and almost crispy. Add 2 tablespoons each of white wine and cream, continue cooking for 1 minute, and serve with chopped parsley.

Note: If you are in Rome in spring or fall when *ovoli* (egg mushrooms) are available, be sure to order them. They are sliced thin and served raw with celery, olive oil, lemon, and slivers of Parmigiano-Reggiano.

Patate Arroste con Rosmarino

. . . .

ROASTED POTATOES WITH ROSEMARY

Serves 4

Potatoes are, for me, the king of the vegetable bin. I can eat them prepared any way except raw, and when they are cooked in olive oil with rosemary or sage, they could almost be a light supper, with a salad and some cheese.

When using tiny new potatoes, leave them whole or cut the larger ones in half and roast only for 30 to 40 minutes.

Vegetables such as beets, parsnips, sweet potatoes, yams, cauliflower, and even young broccoli can be cut into $^{1}/_{2}$-inch slices and roasted in this manner, but I leave out the rosemary with beets and cauliflower. Serve sprinkled with lemon juice.

2 pounds waxy potatoes, peeled or unpeeled, cut into $1^1/_2$-inch dice
$^1/_4$ cup extra virgin olive oil
Salt and freshly ground pepper
4 to 5 fresh rosemary sprigs, leaves only
A few fresh sage leaves (optional)

Preheat the oven to 400°F. Toss the potatoes with the oil, salt and pepper, and herbs, if using, in a large bowl. Transfer to a shallow pan and roast for 45 minutes to 1 hour, until very crisp and brown.

Variation:
Use the same amount of melted butter instead of olive oil and experience nirvana.

Note: Diced beets and cauliflower take only 30 minutes to roast.

Polenta

· ·

CORNMEAL GRITS

Serves 4

Is it having grown up with creamy, buttered grits and hush puppies that makes me crazy for polenta? I love all forms of soft cereals, but polenta is queen. In Rome, polenta is a winter dish, cooked and cooled, then cut into shapes and grilled. It is often served with game and sausages or simply spread on a plate with Parmesan or a soft cheese like fontina melted over the top. I will dissuade you from using instant polenta, as it does not have the taste or character of the real grain. Everyone seems to think that polenta requires at least an hour of stirring, but it doesn't—trust me.

Polenta comes in fine grain, medium grain, and coarse grain, as do our commercial cornmeals. I recommend Albers golden cornmeal if you cannot find an imported, medium-grain polenta.

I quart water or 2 cups water and 2 cups stock
$^1/_2$ teaspoon salt
2 cups polenta
2 tablespoons butter
I tablespoon grated Parmigiano-Reggiano

Bring the water and salt to a boil in a large pot. Stir in the polenta with a whisk and continue stirring over low heat (the polenta will "spit" at you as it bubbles, so stand back) for about 5 to 10 minutes, adding stock or water as necessary, then stir in the butter and Parmigiano-Reggiano and serve.

Variation:
Spread on a smooth surface (like granite or marble) to cool, cut into circles or other shapes with a cookie cutter, and grill, broil, or sauté in butter or olive oil until crisp and golden brown.

Note: Look for *polenta integrale* in Italian markets as it has more texture than others.

Radicchio alla Griglia

. . . .

GRILLED RADICCHIO

Serves 4

There are several kinds of bitter Italian radicchio. One is the ball-shaped variety used for salads or, shredded and cooked, in risotto or pasta sauces; another is the elongated head from Treviso, still nicely compact in the center, making it easy to split and grill. All types may be sliced and sautéed in olive oil until wilted, then cooked until crisp and brown around the edges.

2 large heads radicchio from Treviso or any variety available
$^1/_4$ cup extra virgin olive oil
Salt and freshly ground pepper
Lemon wedges

Light a grill or heat a skillet. Cut the radicchio down the center, then again in quarters, or, if using the ball-shaped one, cut slices about $^1/_2$ inch thick with a little of the stem attached to keep the leaves from separating. Brush the slices with olive oil, season with salt and pepper, and grill quickly on a fine grill on both sides, taking care not to lose any leaves through the grill. Serve with lemon wedges.

To cook in a skillet, heat the olive oil over medium heat and sauté the radicchio on each side until very wilted and browned.

Variation:
Cut radicchio into $^1/_2$-inch slices and sauté with 2 slices diced pancetta or bacon until very crispy. Add a few drops of red wine vinegar and serve with chicken or meat. My mother called this "wilted lettuce."

Chi semina buon grano raccoglie buon pane.—One who uses good grain makes good bread • I may have begun baking at the age of five, but nothing in my childhood prepared me for the delight of Rome's focaccia, pizza bianca, and what is known as *pane casereccio* or "housewives' bread," those enormous loaves baked in wood ovens and meant to last a few days, even in large families. Hardly anyone makes these dense, gargantuan loaves anymore, but in the little town of Genzano outside Rome, the bakers at Antichi Sapori still create huge wheels of bread for restaurants. Their pizza is like lengths of savory fabric, which food shops,

pane, focaccia, e pizza

alimentari, then sell by the piece to customers. • In hot weather a baker in Rome might sport his boxer shorts and what used to be called "undershirt" before it became a fashionable "tank top," a cigarette dangling from the corner of his mouth and a long ash about to fall into the dough but caught just in time to be flicked aside on the rough stone floor. • After having eaten much of Antichi Sapori's bread in Rome, I spent the night with the bakers, observing that few technical rules are followed (bakers after my heart!) and that much intuition goes into preparing and baking these dark, fragrant loaves. The wood oven is four hundred years old, fueled by cuttings from a nearby vineyard, and the temperature is kept at around 600°F. • The dough seemed alive, pulsing and jiggling in its

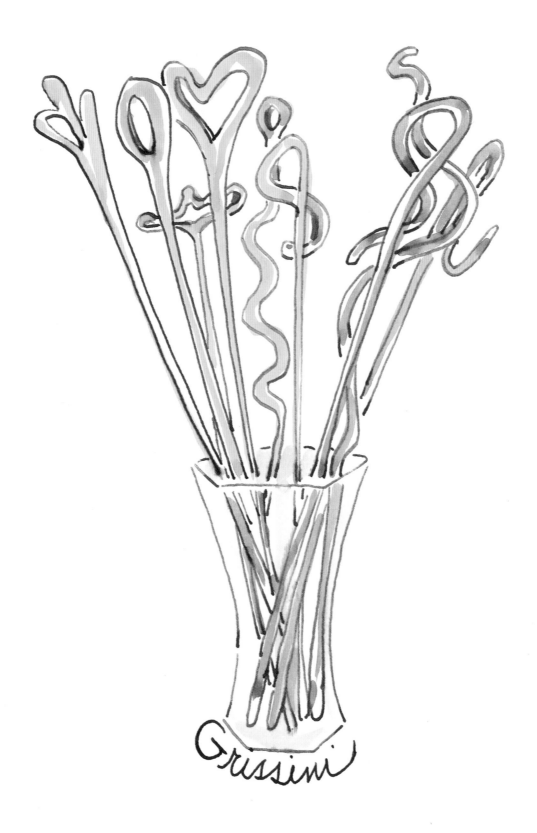

Grissini

linen-lined mangers, exuding the heavy perfume of yeast gone mad. All is done by hand. There is very little kneading of the very moist, almost wet dough, and bran is thrown onto the wooden baking peels so that the loaves will not stick as they are thrust into the oven.

At eleven o'clock in Rome, the rich smell of pizza bianca wafts through the streets and all partake. A particularly good example can be found at Pizza House at via del Corso, 51. This tavola calda serves simple but impeccably prepared rare roast beef, veal roll stuffed with olives, little flattened, grilled chickens, and a memorable pizza bianca with prosciutto. The rich, buttery taste comes from sunflower oil, *olio di girasole,* a beautiful word that means "turns toward the sun." Other *pizze* are sprinkled with fresh rosemary, a thin coating of tomato sauce, or various cheeses. This tasty square of paradise is a midmorning stepping-stone between a morning cornetto with espresso, and lunch. Antico Forno, off via de' Giubbonari, also sells excellent pizza bianca.

When you have chosen your slice, eat it warm, standing up at the counter with the Romans. Or better yet, bake your own pizza bianca at home and enjoy it sitting down with family and friends.

Pizza Bianca

. . . .

PIZZA WITH OLIVE OIL AND SEA SALT

Makes 2 thin 13- by 17-inch pizze (or 1 thick one)

My basic pizza bianca dough was the result of poking my head through the open window of a tiny pizza bakery on via della Frezza and asking the secret, one baker to another, of his perfect crust. It could have been my short skirt or the enthusiasm of a fellow bakery owner, but I was given an instant lesson, which corresponded exactly to what I had been doing at home, except for the use of Italian flour, all-purpose and unbleached, with a little high-gluten flour added for strength. The baker let me feel the dough, watch the rolling and poking process, and chatted with me about the pleasures of baking as we waited for results. He then sent me off with a golden slice, glistening and glittering with olive oil and sea salt, a warm piece of Rome right in my hand—and now in yours.

Quick-rising yeast will cut the rising time by half. If the dough is ready and you must wait to bake it, cover it with a light towel for up to 30 minutes, then turn it out and form it, quickly making indentations all over the dough just before baking. This will deflate the dough temporarily and keep the texture chewy instead of fluffy. The texture and flavor of pizza bianca, as with many doughs, benefit from an overnight stay in the refrigerator, but this is not necessary.

1 $^1/_2$ teaspoons active dry yeast
4 cups unbleached all-purpose flour
$^1/_2$ cup unbleached high-gluten bread flour such as Arrowhead or King Arthur (found at health food stores)
$^1/_4$ teaspoon malt, found in health food stores, or 1 teaspoon sugar if malt is not available
1 teaspoon salt
1 $^1/_2$ cups lukewarm water (85°F to 95°F)
$^1/_4$ cup extra virgin olive or sunflower oil
2 teaspoons coarse sea salt

Put the yeast, flours, malt, and salt into the bowl of food processor. Pulse for a few seconds, add the water, and blend just until the dough pulls away from the sides of the bowl. Do not overmix, or the dough may heat up too much, which will kill the yeast. The dough will be barely tacky but not sticky to the touch.

Dip your fingers in a little olive oil, lift the dough from the bowl, and shape it into a ball. Put the dough in an oiled bowl and cover with plastic wrap. Or place in a large resealable plastic

Pizza Bianca

bag and refrigerate until needed. The dough will rise in a bowl in about an hour or in the refrigerator in about 3 hours or overnight and be ready for use.

Preheat the oven to 525°F. Oil two 13- by 17-inch baking sheets for thin pizza, one for thick, with olive oil. Divide the dough in half and let it rest for 10 minutes on the baking sheet. Then stretch each piece into a rectangle the length of the pan by using your palms and starting from the center of the dough, gently pressing and stretching the dough outward until it is about $^1/_4$ inch thick. Make indentations all over the dough with your fingertips, as if you were a fork making holes in pie crust. Brush generously with olive oil and let rise for 25 to 30 minutes. Sprinkle with sea salt or any of the suggested toppings. Put the pizza in the oven, lower heat to 500°F, and bake on the rack closest to the bottom element of your oven for 10 to 12 minutes, until golden brown. If your oven bakes hot, you may need to lower the temperature to 450°F.

FOR THE TOP OF PIZZA BIANCA

Thin slices of prosciutto and fresh mozzarella or fontina
Thin slices of potato browned in olive oil with a little rosemary
Thin slices of onion cooked in olive oil
Artichoke hearts, sliced thin and cooked in olive oil with a little garlic and salt
Canned tuna in olive oil mixed with capers
Very thin slices of ham and hard-boiled eggs

TO PREPARE PIZZA BIANCA ON THE GRILL:

Heat a grill to the maximum heat. When the coals are red-hot, place a baking stone that will take high temperatures directly on the barbecue grill to heat. Meanwhile, stretch the pizza dough to a circle slightly smaller than your pizza stone, keeping the pizza at about $^1/_2$-inch thickness. Place the shaped pizza on a peel (or a piece of thick cardboard) dusted with flour or cornmeal to rise for 15 to 20 minutes.

Slide the pizza off onto the hot stone and quickly close the lid of the barbecue. Lower the heat, if possible, and cook the pizza for about 10 minutes, checking once after 8 minutes or so to see the progress. Cooking this way imparts a lovely wood-oven flavor to the pizza bianca or any pizza. I use a squirt bottle of water to control heat.

. . . .

Your oven heat may not crisp the underside of a pizza. If not, simply place the pizza on its baking sheet on a stove burner over medium heat, moving the pan continually back and forth over the heat and watching carefully until the pizza begins to send off steam. At this point, lift the pizza with a spatula to see that the bottom is well browned. A wood-burning oven would really do the trick, but alas, not many of us have that luxury. By cooking the bottom of the pizza on the stovetop, you duplicate as well as you can the stone floor of a wood-burning oven. This technique works beautifully for other dishes, such as a pie or pie shell that has not browned enough on the bottom.

Pizza

. . . .

BASIC PIZZA DOUGH

Makes 2 thin 13- by 17-inch pizze (or 1 thick one)

This is the simplest, tastiest, most user-friendly pizza dough you will ever encounter. It may be frozen up to 6 months. With the addition of oil, pizza dough is crispier than pizza bianca when cooked. I like my dough stretched very thin and topped with very little, like Roman pizza.

1 to 1$^{1}/_{2}$ teaspoons active dry yeast

4 cups unbleached all-purpose flour

$^{1}/_{2}$ cup unbleached high-gluten bread flour such as Arrowhead or King Arthur (found at health food stores)

$^{1}/_{4}$ cup extra virgin olive oil

1 teaspoon salt

1$^{1}/_{2}$ cups lukewarm water (85°F to 95°F)

TO PREPARE THE DOUGH:
Put the yeast, flours, 2 tablespoons of the olive oil, and the salt into the bowl of a food processor. Pulse for a few seconds, add the water, and blend just until the dough pulls away from the sides of the bowl. Do not overmix, or the dough may heat up too much, which will kill the yeast. The dough will be barely tacky but not sticky to the touch.

Dip your fingers in a little olive oil, lift the dough from the bowl, and shape it into a ball. Put the dough in an oiled bowl and cover with plastic wrap. Or place in a large resealable plastic bag and refrigerate until needed. The dough will rise in a bowl in about an hour or in the refrigerator in about 3 hours or overnight and be ready for use.

TO MAKE THE PIZZA:
Preheat the oven to 525°F or as hot as your oven allows. Divide the dough between 2 oiled baking sheets for thin pizza, using one sheet for thick, flattening the dough with the palm of your hand. Let rest for 15 minutes. Begin stretching the dough gently toward the edges of the pan by pressing and pushing outward with the flat of your hands. Go slowly. Try not to tear the dough, but if you do, take a little piece of dough from the edge and use it to patch the hole. Stretch to $^{1}/_{4}$ inch thick (or $^{1}/_{2}$ inch thick on one pan if you are making a thicker pizza). Top and bake according to any of the following recipes.

Pizza con Mozzarella di Bufala e Pomodorini

. . . .

PIZZA WITH FRESH MOZZARELLA AND CHERRY TOMATOES

Makes 2 thin 13- by 17-inch pizze or 1 thick one

2 cups cherry tomatoes, sliced thin and drained through a strainer, or 2 cups tomato sauce from
Pasta al Pomodoro o al Sugo (page 100)
1 recipe Pizza (page 234)
$^{1}/_{4}$ cup extra virgin olive oil
2 cups chopped fresh mozzarella di bufala in water, drained, or other mozzarella in water
$^{2}/_{3}$ cup chopped fresh basil leaves

With the back of a large spoon, spread a thin layer of the drained tomatoes or tomato sauce to
cover the dough completely to the edges. Pour the olive oil in a thin stream over the pizza. Bake
the pizza for 6 to 7 minutes, remove from the oven, and sprinkle with the cheese and basil.
Continue to bake for 3 minutes or until the crust is brown.

Grissini

. . . .

BREADSTICKS

I am a terrible influence on children, living vicariously through and encouraging their antics, often giving in to the temptation of, say, having a whistling contest while munching breadsticks at a respectable trattoria.

Making grissini is as effective as worry beads or paper clips for calming the nerves, and shaping breadsticks will occupy a child (or a few) for a good half hour.

1 recipe Pizza (page 234), with 1 beaten egg white added to the dough (optional) and water reduced by 2 tablespoons

2 teaspoons extra virgin olive oil

2 tablespoons coarse sea salt

Place the dough in an oiled bowl, cover tightly with plastic wrap, and let rise until double. Preheat the oven to 400°F. Divide the dough into golf balls. Or roll out the dough to $^1/_2$-inch thickness and cut into $^1/_2$-inch strips. Roll the dough with the palms of your hands, exactly as you did with Play-Doh when you were a child to make "snakes," forming fantasy shapes at one end; leave the other end straight so that it fits into a container for the table (see illustration, page 229). Lay the breadsticks on an oiled baking sheet, brush with extra virgin olive oil, sprinkle with coarse sea salt, and bake for about 10 to 12 minutes, until golden brown. For crisper breadsticks, open the oven and leave the breadsticks inside to dry for 5 minutes more.

. . . .

To make poppy seeds or sesame seeds stick to grissini before baking, mix 1 cup water with 2 tablespoons rye flour. Transfer to a spray bottle and spritz the breadsticks with this mixture, then sprinkle with seeds.

Pizza con Funghi

. . . .

PIZZA WITH MUSHROOMS

Makes 2 thin 13- by 17-inch pizze *(or 1 thick one)*

Fresh or dried mushrooms may be used on this pizza, but dried ones must be soaked, then pressed quite dry and sautéed as usual before being used so as not to exude moisture into the dough.

2 cups sliced fresh mushrooms or I cup dried porcini
$^{I}/_{4}$ cup extra virgin olive oil
A few drops fresh lemon juice
2 cups tomato sauce from Pasta al Pomodoro o al Sugo (page 100)
I recipe Pizza (page 234)
$^{I}/_{2}$ cup grated Parmigiano-Reggiano

If using dried porcini, soak them in I$^{I}/_{2}$ cups hot water for 20 minutes to soften. Strain and cool the water and use it to make your pizza dough if you haven't already made it. If using fresh mushrooms, heat the olive oil in a skillet, add the mushrooms, and cook over medium heat until golden brown on all sides, 6 to 7 minutes. Sprinkle with lemon juice and cool. Spread the tomato sauce in a thin layer over the pizza dough. Sprinkle with the mushrooms and Parmigiano-Reggiano and bake for 8 to 10 minutes, until crisp around the edges.

Focaccia Croccante

. . . .

PLAIN CRISP FLATBREAD

Makes 2 thin 13- by 17-inch focacce (or 1 thick one)

This is really nothing more than an Italian tortilla, chapati, or matzoh with a minute amount of yeast added. Focaccia may be stored in a resealable plastic bag for a week or so or frozen indefinitely, and the yeast is optional. In trattorie, these are often brought to the table as soon as you sit down, sometimes brushed with oil, sometimes not.

3 cups unbleached all-purpose flour
$^1/_4$ cup extra virgin olive oil, plus 1 tablespoon for brushing the bread (optional)
$^1/_2$ teaspoon salt
$^1/_2$ teaspoon active dry yeast
1 $^1/_4$ cups lukewarm water (85°F to 95°F)
2 teaspoons coarse sea salt (optional)

Blend the flour with the $^1/_4$ cup oil and $^1/_2$ teaspoon salt in the bowl of a food processor. Add the yeast to the water, stirring to dissolve, then add the water to the flour mixture, pulsing until just blended and the dough pulls away from the sides of the bowl. Place in an oiled bowl, cover tightly with plastic wrap, and let sit for at least 30 minutes.

Divide the dough in two and roll or pat each part into a pancake. Preheat the oven to 425°F. Dust 2 baking sheets with a thin coating of flour (I use a tea strainer: just dip some flour from the sack and use the strainer to sprinkle it where you like), place each circle on a sheet, and with the palms of your hands, press the pancake out to the edges of the pan, forming a very thin focaccia, about $^1/_8$ inch thick. Brush with 1 tablespoon oil, if using, and sprinkle with coarse sea salt, if using, or simply dust with flour. Let rest for 20 minutes. Bake for 8 to 9 minutes, until golden and crackerlike.

Focaccia Croccante all'Olio di Tartufo:

Truffles smell strongly of skunk to me, a smell from my childhood that I have always loved, however perverse that might be. Both contain the chemical methyl mercaptan (a fact from chemistry class, which I, in my teens, dropped in conversation to attract smart boys). Truffle oil is as expensive as the fungus itself, and there are many brands in which truffles do not figure at all but are enhanced instead by chemicals. Read the label to check. Urbani is a reputable brand and readily available online or at most Italian markets.

To make a delicious truffle oil at home, invest in a small white truffle in season and cut off a $^1/_2$-inch piece (shave the rest over a plate of pasta). Place in a bottle of extra virgin olive oil. Use on focaccia croccante.

Pizza Napoletana

PIZZA WITH TOMATO, OREGANO, AND ANCHOVIES

Makes 2 thin 13- by 17-inch pizze or 1 thick one

There are two camps in Rome. One uses oregano on *pizza napoletana,* and one does not, but indisputably the anchovy prevails. When making *pizza napoletana* at home, I add far more anchovies than any trattoria would ever part with because of cost, but at home you can go bonkers. I am also more inclined to use basil, but a small quantity of fresh oregano is sometimes a nice change.

Follow the recipe for Pizza con Mozzarella di Bufala e Pomodorini (page 235), using tomato sauce in place of fresh tomatoes and substituting a few chopped fresh oregano sprigs for the basil. Arrange as many anchovies on the pizza as you like; I use a whole tin for the two *pizze.*

Pizza con la Rughetta

. . . .

PIZZA WITH ARUGULA

Makes 2 thin 13- by 17-inch pizze or 1 thick one

The Romans strew *rughetta* over many dishes, including pizza. This one is brought to the table as an appetizer in some trattorie.

1 recipe Pizza (page 234)
About $^1/_4$ cup extra virgin olive oil
1 tablespoon coarse sea salt
2 cups arugula leaves, chopped if large, left whole if small

Preheat the oven to 525°F. Oil two baking sheets, set half the dough on each, and let rest for 10 minutes. Stretch the dough with your palms, starting from the center and pressing the dough out to the very edges of the pan to make an extremely thin $^1/_8$-inch pizza. You may actually see the pan through the dough. Brush the pizza dough with $^1/_4$ cup olive oil, sprinkle with sea salt, and bake 7 to 8 minutes until golden brown. The pizza may be browner in some places than others and will get very crisp. Remove from the oven and immediately sprinkle with arugula and a few more drops of olive oil. Serve warm.

Pane Casereccio

. . . .

RUSTIC BREAD

Makes 2 medium loaves or 1 large one

My favorite Italian bread is a wonderfully holey, enormous, almost-burned-crust loaf brought to you by the same bakers from Genzano who work in their underwear. This rustic country bread is disappearing from Rome and many parts of Italy because bakers are aging, and the younger crowd has its eye on computer careers or running the family business, few of which are still bakeries, alas. Perhaps Buona Forchetta will find an outlet there!

I spent some time one afternoon with a delightful baker near the via Cola di Rienzo, with another near Piazza Mazzini, and yet a third, the youngest and hippest of the three, in Trastevere, near Piazza Trilussa, all of whom were still forming by hand and baking very nice pizza and some of their bread in wood ovens. Nothing came close to the loaves from Genzano, however.

This lovely *pagnotta,* which simply means "large bread," has the open texture of Rome's wood-oven bread with an expanded, nutty taste from the extraordinarily good high-gluten flour available here in the States.

You may use whey from ricotta making (page 252) as all or part of the liquid in this recipe (or any bread recipe) for a tangy flavor.

BIGA (SPONGE)
$^1/_2$ teaspoon active dry yeast
1 cup lukewarm water (85°F to 95°F)
$^1/_2$ cup unbleached high-gluten bread flour (found at health food stores)
$^1/_2$ cup rye flour

DOUGH
1 $^1/_2$ cups lukewarm water (85°F to 95°F)
2 teaspoons active dry yeast
4 to 4 $^1/_2$ cups unbleached high-gluten bread flour, plus $^1/_2$ cup for the baking sheet and loaves
2 teaspoons salt

To prepare the *biga,* whisk the $^1/_2$ teaspoon yeast, 1 cup water, $^1/_2$ cup bread flour, and the rye flour together in a glass bowl, cover with plastic wrap, and let ferment overnight or for up to 24 hours.

When ready to prepare the bread dough, sprinkle the 2 teaspoons yeast over the 1$^1/_2$ cups water in a large mixing bowl and stir until dissolved. Stir in the *biga*. Add the flour and salt and stir until the flour is thoroughly incorporated and the dough is smooth, with the consistency of very thick biscuit batter. It will be a rather sticky, soft dough. Cover the dough and let it stand in a warm place until doubled in volume, about 1 hour.

With a scraper or spatula, lift up the dough from underneath and turn it over on itself 2 or 3 times. Folding the dough gives the gluten a rest and activates the yeast by putting it into contact with more food.

Cover and let rise a second time for 40 to 45 minutes, until doubled in volume (the second rise takes less time), or cover and refrigerate until time to bake. If refrigerated, remove the dough and let it come to room temperature before forming. During this time it may rise slightly. It is then ready to shape and bake. The dough should be very soft and silky.

FORMING THE LOAVES:
Dust a baking sheet with a thin layer of flour. Carefully turn the dough out onto the baking sheet in one plop, being very careful to keep it as inflated as possible.

Let the loaf rise until doubled in volume, about 30 minutes. Preheat the oven to 500°F. Just before putting the bread in the oven, slip your hands under the loaf and flip it over softly onto the other side. Dust with flour and bake for 15 minutes. Reduce the temperature to 450°F. Bake for 15 to 20 minutes longer or until nicely browned.

Variation:
You can substitute 1 cup whole wheat or spelt flour for 1 cup unbleached flour and add a spoonful or two of bran to the dough. You can also add $^{1}/_{2}$ cup each toasted nuts and raisins when mixing the dough to make a bread that goes well with cheese.

· ·

At Pasqua (Easter), the top of a large loaf of **pane casereccio** *is cut off and the soft part is scooped out, then filled with hard-boiled eggs and salami. The top is replaced, and the pagnotta, as it is called, is put on a chair and draped with a cloth. The largest person in the family and then all the children take turns sitting on the loaf to compress it. The squished bread is then cut into slices and served.*

Uva bella e matura, tentazione sicura.—*Ripe grapes are a sure temptation.* • At a lunch some years ago, I placed a large tiramisù, made with fresh mascarpone and dusted with bitter chocolate, in front of ten or so of my stepchildren's teenaged friends, and every single one reached for the bowl of golden peaches, emerald Muscat grapes, and deep orange apricots before attacking the dessert. Romans enjoy the tiny wood strawberries (*fragoline*) from Lago di Nemi sprinkled with sugar and lemon instead of filling pastries, and cheese in place of cheesecake. Their ubiquitous *macedonia,* cut up seasonal fruits in a cup, is barely

dolci

sweetened (but is sometimes flavored with white wine!). There is a general view that obliterating the experience of a perfectly beautiful Roman meal with a large helping of sugar is not only uncomfortable for the *pancia* (stomach) but simply *pazzo,* crazy. • I love Gorgonzola and Parmigiano-Reggiano with pears, Taleggio with apples, and ricotta salata and pecorino Romano with grapes. There are so many cheeses to choose from nowadays that I leave it to you to pick those you love. • The kids eventually did polish off the tiramisù . . . • Sweets, along with sauces, are not as primary a part of the Italian menu as they are in other parts of Europe or

here. Of course, Italian cooks, living in the home of the world's best gelato, could stop right there and forget all other desserts. But a few dishes find their way onto almost every menu, and practically every household has a recipe passed down through generations for a *torta della nonna*, grandmother's tart, made with or without a crust and with some form of custard inside.

Italians prefer small portions of dessert after lunch and dinner because they tend to eat their sweets, such as a gelato or pastry, during the *passeggiata*, that languorous, sensual slide over the cobblestones that most of Rome enjoys daily in late afternoon. Eye meets eye, new styles are paraded and observed, and one of Rome's favorite pastimes, window shopping, is enjoyed. Take a few moments out of your afternoon to dip one of my Roman *cantucci*, yet another word for biscotti, in your syrupy little *caffè*.

Budino di Cioccolato

. . . .

CHOCOLATE PUDDING

Serves 4

Make this pudding with ladyfingers (called *savoiardi* in Italy) or chocolate wafers, and the texture
will be toothsome and substantial. You may also use a couple of slices of toasted rustic bread,
crusts removed, in place of cookies. Cut the bread into small cubes and increase the sugar to $3/4$
cup to transform this into a bread pudding.

2 tablespoons butter
2 cups heavy cream
6 ounces bittersweet chocolate, broken into pieces
1 teaspoon vanilla extract
6 ladyfingers or savoiardi or six 2-inch chocolate wafers, crushed
$1/2$ cup plus 1 tablespoon sugar
4 egg yolks
2 tablespoons Cognac or bourbon
3 egg whites

Butter an 8- or 9-inch soufflé dish and preheat the oven to 350°F. Melt the chocolate in the
cream in a saucepan over very low heat, stirring constantly. Add the vanilla and cookie or cake
crumbs and mix well. Beat the sugar with the egg yolks and Cognac or bourbon and stir into the
chocolate. Let cool. Beat the egg whites until stiff but not dry and gently fold into the chocolate
mixture. Pour into the soufflé dish and bake for 40 minutes, until the middle of the pudding is
set when jiggled or when a knife inserted in the middle comes out clean.

Crème Brûlée

. . . .

Serves 4

Crème brûlée, in one form or another, is a favorite found on most trattoria menus. I use only heavy cream, egg yolks, and sugar, although I have tasted some cut by milk, made with gelatin, or flavored with Amaretto or repellent liqueurs that have no place in this delicate custard. Chefs here use passion fruit, berries, and other additions to leave a distinguishing mark on this classic, which I can understand, but to me, plain and simple is best to start with.

6 egg yolks
^{2}/$_3$ cup sugar
2 cups heavy cream
One 2-inch piece vanilla bean or 1 ^{1}/$_2$ teaspoons vanilla extract

Preheat the oven to 325°F. Place ramekins or small individual baking dishes in a larger baking dish. Put the egg yolks and a generous ^{1}/$_2$ cup of the sugar in the bowl of a food processor and blend. Heat the cream (with the vanilla bean, split and scraped, if using one) just until tiny bubbles form around the edge. Add the vanilla extract or remove the vanilla bean and pour the cream into the egg mixture, pulsing until very smooth.

Strain into a pitcher or container that pours easily, then pour into the ramekins. Fill the larger baking dish with very hot water to reach halfway up the sides of the ramekins. Bake for about 30 minutes or until the custards move only slightly (under the "skin" that forms) when you nudge the pan.

Remove custards from their hot bath and cool to room temperature. Sprinkle the rest of the sugar evenly over the tops of the custards and place them close to the broiler, watching carefully so that the sugar caramelizes but does not burn. Or use a small handheld blowtorch, one of my favorite presents from my husband, and let your guests do their own.

Crème Caramel

. . . .

CARAMEL CREAM CUSTARD

Serves 4

This flan is found all over Rome and in most cooks' repertoires, possibly because it is one of the lighter custard desserts, which Romans prefer. Bake the flan just until set and the texture will be perfect.

2 $^{1}/_{4}$ cups sugar

3 eggs

3 egg yolks

A few grains of salt

2 cups heavy cream

1 cup milk

1 teaspoon vanilla extract

Preheat the oven to 350°F. Heat 1 cup of the sugar in a heavy saucepan until it melts, pushing down the bubbling sugar from the sides of the pan with a heatproof spatula. In 6 to 7 minutes or so, the sugar will take on a caramel color and be very smooth and liquid. Pour carefully into a ceramic 8- or 9-inch soufflé dish or individual ramekins, tilting the dish to cover the bottom and some of the sides. Let cool and harden.

Put the eggs, yolks, remaining sugar, and salt in the bowl of a food processor and blend. Heat the milk and cream in a saucepan until bubbles form around the edge. Add the vanilla, then pour into the egg mixture, pulsing until smooth. Strain the mixture into the soufflé dish, place the dish in a larger baking pan, and fill the larger pan with hot water to reach halfway up the side of the baking dish. Bake for 50 minutes to 1 hour for the soufflé dish or 35 to 45 minutes for the ramekins or until a knife inserted in the flan comes out clean. Remove flan dish from water bath, let cool, then run a knife along the edge of the flan, place a serving dish over the top, and invert, or serve in the ramekins.

Panna Cotta

. . . .

CREAM CUSTARD

Serves 6

I hope I do not lose friends in Rome when I say that not every trattoria knows how to make this smooth, elegant custard, but when it is good, it holds its own with crème brûlée, flan, or any other cream custard, and contrary to some opinions, panna cotta is always made with gelatin, albeit a very small amount.

Panna cotta (cooked cream) should be made with cream, not milk. The small amount of milk is intended only to dissolve the gelatin. According to the maestro of Italian cooking, Pellegrino Artusi, a gelatin made from sturgeon bladders called *isinglass* was used to stiffen the milk in the old days. *Grazie a dio* that we have gelatin in packages nowadays since fish bladders are hard to come by. I serve a fruit purée with panna cotta, but fresh fruit is just as good.

I teaspoon almond oil (found at health food stores and supermarkets) or soft butter to grease the
    custard cups
I $^1/_2$ teaspoons unflavored powdered gelatin
$^1/_4$ cup cold milk
3 cups heavy cream
Generous $^1/_2$ cup sugar
I teaspoon vanilla extract

FRUIT SAUCE
2 cups berries, peeled and pitted peaches, plums, nectarines, or any stone fruit or berries in season
$^1/_2$ cup sugar

Coat the inside of 6 custard cups with a little of the almond oil or butter or melt a few spoonfuls of the sugar in a heavy pan until it caramelizes (see Crème Caramel, page 249) and coat the insides of the cups. Set aside to cool.

Sprinkle the gelatin over the cold milk to soften. Mix the cream, sugar, and vanilla in a pan and heat (do not boil!) just until little bubbles form around the edge. Stir in the softened gelatin, whisking briskly to dissolve completely. Let cool for 15 minutes. Strain the custard and pour into cups. Refrigerate for 4 hours or overnight.

Serve plain or with a cold fruit sauce: Simmer the fruit and sugar in a saucepan for 5 minutes. Rub through a strainer, chill for 1 hour, and serve.

Variation:
Add $^{1}/_{2}$ cup very strong espresso or 6 ounces melted bittersweet chocolate to the cream for coffee or chocolate panna cotta.

Ricotta con Cioccolato

. . . .

FRESH RICOTTA WITH CHOCOLATE

Serves 4

A friendly, anonymous Italian gave me this recipe during a chat about cheese in a Roman supermarket. It is so easy that you'll have it on your to-do list often. The soft, creamy ricotta in Rome is made from the milk used for mozzarella di bufala or sheep's milk, and an even more refined one is made from the rich whey, a delicious by-product of cheese making. Save your separated whey for bread recipes (see Pane Casereccio, page 242) or for steaming vegetables. When the ricotta is ready, simply pile it in dessert dishes and sprinkle with a little sugar and unsweetened cocoa powder or grated bitter chocolate.

1 gallon whole cow's milk (milk from a goat, sheep, or water buffalo will work as well, but buffalo are pretty scarce around most cities)
$^1/_2$ cup strained fresh lemon juice
Very fine cheesecloth or an old clean cotton or linen pillowcase
$^2/_3$ cup unsweetened cocoa powder, mixed with 2 tablespoons sugar, or bitter chocolate, grated fine

Bring the milk slowly to a simmer (around 200°F) in a stainless-steel or enamel saucepan. Add the lemon juice and slowly bring it up to 200°F again, at which point you will see the separation between curds and whey beginning. Immediately remove from the heat, cover, and let sit for 20 minutes for the whey and curds to separate. Line a large colander or strainer with fine cheesecloth folded into 4 layers or a pillowcase and carefully pour the warm mixture into the container, gathering up the edges of the cloth and tying them off. Let the bag of curds and whey drip in the sink over a container in which to save the whey for about 2 hours or until the consistency of the ricotta is fairly firm but still creamy. I tie my cheese bag to the faucet or to a long kitchen utensil such as a barbecue fork laid across the sink. Turn the curds out into a bowl, add a little salt, and refrigerate for up to 5 days. Serve dusted with the cocoa mixture or chocolate.

Variation:
Fresh ricotta may be served with honey instead of chocolate.

Granita di Caffè

. . . .

COFFEE GRANITA

Serves 4

Granita is the warm-weather afternoon pick-me-up in Rome. Near the Pincio, where everyone goes at sunset to look out over rooftops and marvel at Rome's beauty, there is a tiny bar off to the left as you descend toward Piazza di Spagna, where excellent granita (and *tè freddo,* barely sweetened iced tea with ice removed, served in skinny, tall glasses) is made in various flavors. The best is at Yogurteria Santa Barbara in Largo dei Librari, as all are made from fresh fruit with little sugar. The owners are as sweet as the fruit. You can use any fruit juice, coffee, tea, even Champagne for granita. In summer I make extra espresso specifically for this purpose.

2 cups very strong espresso or any coffee you like
^{1}/$_4$ cup sugar, or to taste

Place the espresso and sugar in a metal bowl, stir to dissolve sugar, cover with foil, and freeze for 1 hour. Remove from the freezer and stir the mixture to break up the ice crystals, repeating one more time after 30 minutes. When the granita is the consistency of very fine crushed ice, serve it in tall glasses with a little cream poured over the top. Or freeze coffee and cream together and proceed as directed.

Granita di Frutta (Fruit Granita):
Mix 2 cups water with ^{1}/$_4$ cup sugar, or to taste, and 2 cups puréed fruit (berries, stone fruit, mango, and so on). Cool in the refrigerator for an hour. Freeze as directed.

. . . .

You can freeze any gelato, sorbetto, or granita in ice cube trays and use individual cubes when needed. These cubes can be crushed in a blender or pulsed in a food processor to make a quick granita.

Montebianco

. . . .

CHESTNUT MOUNTAIN

Serves 4

Chestnuts hold a special place in my olfactory memory. The irresistible smell of roasting chestnuts brings all of the autumns I have spent in Rome into focus. Seduced by their aroma for many years (before I knew what to do with them), I bought my cone of four or five, tasted one or two, and, finding them rather dry and hard to swallow, guiltily tossed out the rest.

I have since come to know the differences among vendors and which has the best nuts. I discovered that giving my roasted chestnuts another quick minute or two in my own oven, then dipping them in a little olive oil or melted butter with salt, produces one of autumn's great flavors. Grapes, too, are the perfect match for warm chestnuts and will help them slip down more easily.

Montebianco certainly shows chestnuts in a delectable light. Chestnuts are often the star in puddings and tarts, but I think they are best in this simple mountain of purée topped with *panna montata,* whipped cream. When available, buy roasted ones from a reliable street vendor, omit the boiling in water, and proceed with the recipe.

2 pounds fresh chestnuts (choose shiny, firm, dark brown ones that don't rattle)
Milk to cover
3/4 to I cup sugar (I use less to let the chestnut flavor shine through)
I teaspoon vanilla extract
2 teaspoons butter
2 cups heavy cream
Chopped toasted chestnuts for garnish (optional; see page 255)

Make a straight incision or an X in the rounded part of each chestnut. I do this by whacking the chestnut with a sharp knife without cutting through the whole nut. Boil the chestnuts in water to cover for 20 minutes. Peel and discard the outer shell and membrane.

Put the chestnuts in a pot, cover with milk, and add the butter, all but 2 tablespoons of the sugar, and the vanilla. Simmer over low heat for 15 to 20 minutes or until the chestnuts are soft. Save any remaining milk for other desserts, but you may not have much, because the chestnuts will absorb most of it.

Over a serving plate, push the chestnuts through a fairly large mesh strainer or put through a ricer to make the purée look like little noodles. Whip the cream with the remaining sugar. Form a crater in the purée and fill with the whipped cream, forming a little mountain peak. Sprinkle with chopped roasted chestnuts if desired.

. . . .

To roast your own chestnuts: Preheat the oven to 400°F. Make an incision in the chestnuts, spread them out on a baking sheet, and roast for 15 minutes. They will split, making them easy to peel. Serve with grapes, melted butter, or olive oil.

For garnish, reserve 3 or 4 chestnuts, chop, toss with melted butter, and roast for 4 to 5 minutes in a separate pan in the same oven. Set a timer so that they do not burn.

Gelati

· ·

BASIC RECIPES FOR ICE CREAM

Serves 4 to 6

The Romans, like all Italians, are crazy for gelati and sorbetti (ice creams and sorbets). One of the loveliest hours of a summer day is just after the daily *riposino,* a little snooze to settle one's lunch and avoid the heat. Later, the streets begin to fill with those taking the walk known as the *passeggiata,* an evening stroll to end the workday in a civilized manner. Popular ice cream shops such as Giolitti and Le Palme are buzzing with crowds lining up for square cones filled with such flavors as *fior di latte,* named after cow's milk mozzarella, *nocciola* (hazelnut), and the exotic *sorbetto di frangipane.* Discussion about ice cream can arouse as much passion as a soccer match, and everyone has his favorite gelateria.

Those who do not eat gelato are looked upon with mistrust and incredulity, so it is best to give up all Spartan thoughts of dieting or calorie counting and surrender to one (or several) of 30 to 40 flavors, including *peperoncino.* You'll be a better person for it.

This is a vanilla base for the gelato recipes that follow. You can make any gelato base the day before, cool and cover the container, and refrigerate overnight before freezing.

1 quart heavy cream
3 egg yolks, beaten
2/3 cup sugar
1 teaspoon vanilla extract

Heat the cream in a heavy saucepan. Stir in the egg yolks and sugar, whisking to keep the sauce smooth. Add the vanilla and keep whisking until the sauce begins to thicken. At this point you can add chocolate, if using, which will melt easily in the hot sauce. Strain, then add nuts, nut meal, or praline, if using. Cool before adding fresh fruit such as peaches, raspberries, and so on, and before freezing.

All ice creams and sorbets can be frozen easily in a refrigerator freezer. Place ice cream in a metal container, cover with foil, and freeze for 1 hour. Remove from the freezer and stir the mixture briskly with a whisk to break up and smooth out any ice crystals that have formed. Return to the freezer and freeze for another 3 to 4 hours. When not using an ice cream maker, I make my gelati and sorbetti in the afternoon, and the texture is perfect by dessert time. Take ice cream or sorbet out of the freezer a few minutes before serving and it will dip easily, or freeze in an ice-cream maker.

VAINIGLIA (vanilla):

Add 1 tablespoon vanilla extract or scrape 1 vanilla bean into the cream. Strain, cool in the refrigerator, and freeze in the freezer or an ice-cream maker.

CIOCCOLATO (chocolate):

Add $^1/_3$ cup more sugar to the cream. Break 10 ounces of bittersweet chocolate (70 percent cacao) into pieces and stir into the cream until smooth. Taste for sugar (you may need more, depending on the sweetness of the chocolate), strain, cool in the refrigerator, and freeze in the freezer or an ice-cream maker. I add 3 tablespoons of bourbon and 1 tablespoon of espresso for a really rich flavor.

FRAGOLA (strawberry):

Add 1 cup strawberries, crushed in a bowl with a wire whisk, $^1/_2$ cup puréed strawberries, and a squeeze of lemon to the cream. Cool in the refrigerator, then freeze in the freezer or ice-cream maker.

CAFFÈ (coffee):

Make 1 cup very strong espresso. Add the coffee to the cream and taste for strength. Add more coffee if necessary. Or, as you make the cream, add $^1/_2$ cup espresso beans, ground fine, and simmer until thick. Let sit for 30 minutes, then strain. Cool in the refrigerator, then freeze in the freezer or an ice-cream maker.

GELATO AFFOGATO DI WHISKEY (ice cream "drowned" in whiskey):

I had never seen whiskey poured over ice cream as a dessert until I traveled to Italy. Make your own delicious vanilla ice cream, put 2 scoops in a pretty dish, and drown it with 3 or 4 tablespoons of very good scotch. Bittersweet chocolate *cantucci* (page 275) go very well with this.

Sorbetto

· ·

BASIC RECIPES FOR SORBET

Serves 4

This is an easy sorbetto base, to which I add a little cream for body (optional) and which may be used as the start of any sorbetto made with stone fruit, berries, or citrus. I like to strain the purées of seeded berries, except for strawberries, because I don't like to bite down on seeds, but I do not strain citrus juices, because the pulp makes for an interesting texture. You can always put fruit purées or any ice cream base through a strainer for smoother results.

2 cups water
$3/4$ to I cup sugar, depending on sweetness of fruit
2 cups fruit, crushed in a bowl with a wire whisk (or I$^{1}/_{2}$ cups citrus juice for citrus sorbetto)
I tablespoon fresh lemon juice (or lime in some cases, such as for mango sorbet)
$^{1}/_{4}$ to $^{1}/_{2}$ cup heavy cream (optional)

Combine the water and sugar in a saucepan and boil for 5 minutes to make a syrup. Cool and then stir in the fruit or juice and lemon juice. If you like, stir in the cream and freeze. Take out of the freezer 10 minutes before serving to soften a little.

Sorbetto di Limone (Lemon Sorbet):
Use $^{3}/_{4}$ cup sugar for the syrup. Cool and add I$^{1}/_{2}$ cups fresh lemon juice and 2 tablespoons grated lemon zest to the basic recipe. If you are adding the cream, stir briskly so as not to curdle the mixture.

Sorbetto di Lamponi (Raspberry Sorbet):
Use $^{3}/_{4}$ cup sugar for the syrup. Cook 3 cups raspberries with 3 tablespoons sugar for 5 minutes. Cool, rub through a strainer, and add the purée to the basic recipe.

Sorbetto di Mango (Mango Sorbet):
Use $^3/_4$ cup sugar for the syrup. Peel 2 very ripe mangoes, slice the fruit, and place the slices, along with the seeds, in a saucepan. Add $^1/_2$ cup water and simmer for 5 minutes. Scrape the pulp off the seed (discard—or plant—the seed) and add it to the rest of the mango. Purée the mango, cool, add lime juice in place of lemon, and continue with the basic recipe.

Sorbetto di Pompelmo (Grapefruit Sorbet):
I use Ruby Red Texas grapefruit. Use $^3/_4$ cup sugar for the syrup. Cool and add $1^1/_2$ cups grapefruit juice to the basic recipe. Do not add cream. You can substitute any citrus for the grapefruit.

Sorbetto di Fragola (Strawberry Sorbet):
Use $^3/_4$ cup sugar for the syrup. Cool and add 2 cups strawberry purée to the basic recipe.

Sorbetto allo Champagne (Champagne Sorbet):
Use 1 cup sugar for the syrup. Cool and add $1^1/_2$ cups Champagne to the basic recipe. Do not add cream.

. . . .

Sgroppino is Rome's favorite summer dessert. It is made with sorbetto di limone, Limoncello (page 276), and vodka.

Whisk together $^1/_4$ cup vodka and $^1/_4$ cup limoncello with 2 cups sorbetto di limone in a metal bowl. Cover with plastic wrap and freeze just until firm, about 30 minutes. Place in a blender and pulse a few times, just until smooth. Serve in tall glasses.

Semifreddo di Fragola

. . . .

"HALF-FROZEN" STRAWBERRY ICE CREAM

Serves 4

3/4 cup heavy cream
1 teaspoon vanilla extract
1 1/2 cups sliced fresh strawberries
3 egg whites
2/3 cup sugar
Pinch of salt
1 teaspoon almond or apricot oil (found at health food stores or supermarkets) to grease the mold
Zabaione (page 262) for serving

Beat the cream with the vanilla until it holds soft, glossy peaks. Purée half the strawberries in a food processor and gently fold them into the cream. Refrigerate.

Place the egg whites, sugar, and salt in a bowl over a pan of hot water over low heat (or in a double boiler) and beat with a handheld mixer until double in volume, about 2 to 3 minutes. Remove the mixture from the heat and continue beating until glossy, thick, and cool, about 10 to 15 minutes. Fold a third of the egg white mixture into the remaining strawberries, then fold in the rest of the egg whites and the cold cream.

Oil individual molds or one large 1 1/2-quart metal mold with a bit of almond or apricot oil. Spoon the semifreddo into the mold, cover it with foil or plastic wrap, and freeze for 4 hours or more. Serve with zabaione.

Fragoline

Semifreddo di Nocciola con Salsa di Cioccolato o di Zabaione

. . . .

"HALF-FROZEN" HAZELNUT ICE CREAM WITH CHOCOLATE SAUCE OR MARSALA CUSTARD

Serves 4

This is exactly what it sounds like, a "half-cold" dessert that is neither ice cream nor a bombe. You can serve it with chocolate sauce or zabaione.

The beating of the meringue takes very little time, and you will impress your guests. I have yet to be served a true semifreddo at a dinner party, even in foodie Los Angeles.

1 cup heavy cream

1 teaspoon vanilla extract

1 cup toasted hazelnuts, pecans, or almonds

2 tablespoons softened butter

3 egg whites

$^1/_2$ cup sugar

Pinch of salt

1 teaspoon almond or apricot oil (found at health food stores or supermarkets) to grease the mold

FOR THE CHOCOLATE SAUCE

8 ounces bittersweet chocolate

$^1/_2$ cup heavy cream

Dash Cognac or strong coffee

FOR THE ZABAIONE

6 egg yolks

$^1/_2$ cup sugar

$^1/_3$ cup Marsala or Cognac

Beat the 1 cup cream with the vanilla until it holds soft, glossy peaks. Refrigerate. Grind the nuts very fine in a food processor with the butter and place in a large bowl.

Place the egg whites, $^1/_2$ cup sugar, and salt in a bowl over a pan of hot water over low heat (or in a double boiler) and beat with a handheld mixer until double in volume, 2 to 3 minutes. Remove the meringue from the heat and continue beating until glossy, thick, and cool, 10 to 15 minutes.

Fold a third of the egg white mixture into the nuts to lighten them, then fold in the rest of the egg whites and the chilled cream.

Oil individual molds the size of ramekins or one large metal 1 $^1/_2$-quart mold with a bit of almond or apricot oil. Spoon the semifreddo into the mold, cover with foil or plastic wrap, and freeze, no stirring needed, for 4 hours or more. Serve with warm bitter chocolate sauce or zabaione.

TO PREPARE THE CHOCOLATE SAUCE:
Melt the chocolate over very low heat with the $^1/_2$ cup cream and a dash of Cognac or coffee. Stir until very smooth but not grainy. If the sauce becomes grainy, stir in 1 tablespoon cold cream to rebind. Spoon over the semifreddo. (This can be made ahead and reheated.)

TO PREPARE THE ZABAIONE:
Whip the egg yolks in a bowl over hot water (or a double boiler) with the $^1/_2$ cup sugar. Add the Marsala or Cognac very slowly. Cook gently, beating all the while, until very light and foamy. Be careful not to let the eggs curdle. Spoon over semifreddo or eat as a custard with Cantucci, Tozzetti, o Mostaccioli (page 274).

Semifreddo di Cioccolato

. . . .

"HALF-FROZEN" CHOCOLATE ICE CREAM

Serves 4

3/4 cup heavy cream
1 teaspoon vanilla extract
3 egg whites
1/2 cup sugar
Pinch of salt
6 ounces bittersweet chocolate, melted
1 teaspoon almond or apricot oil (found at health food stores or supermarkets) to grease the mold
Chocolate Sauce (page 262)

Beat the cream with the vanilla until it holds soft, glossy peaks. Refrigerate.

Place the egg whites, sugar, and salt in a bowl over a pan of hot water over low heat (or in a double boiler) and beat with a handheld mixer until doubled in volume, 2 to 3 minutes. Remove the mixture from the heat and continue beating until glossy, thick, and cool, about 10 to 15 minutes.

Fold the melted chocolate into the egg white mixture, then fold in the cold cream.

Oil individual molds or one large 1 1/2-quart metal mold with a bit of almond or apricot oil. Spoon the semifreddo into the mold, cover with foil or plastic wrap, and freeze for 4 hours or more. Serve with Chocolate Sauce.

Crostata di Fichi

FIG TART

Serves 4 to 6

The fig holds a special place in Roman dialect, which I shall leave to your imagination. Unrelated to this fact (I think), Romans peel their figs, as they do most of their fruit, and so watch in horror as I eat the whole shebang, stem and all. The figs in Rome are large, blue-black succulent teardrops (*fichi Genovesi*) with brilliant crimson interiors, which is why, no doubt, their place in the vernacular is assured. The plump bright green figs are also extraordinarily sweet, and their trees are often found growing wild in a field.

My grandmother had fig trees, and after she shot the squirrels out of them with a .22 rifle, she cooked them in sugar syrup with lemon and served them cold. The figs, not the squirrels. The latter she served stewed.

PASTA FROLLA (SHORT PASTRY OR PÂTE BRISÉE)
$1^3/_4$ cups flour, sifted, plus 2 tablespoons
8 tablespoons (1 stick) very cold butter (I freeze mine, then cut it up into $^1/_2$-inch pieces before adding it to the flour)
$^1/_2$ teaspoon salt
2 tablespoons sugar, or to taste
Pinch of ground cinnamon (optional)
1 egg yolk
$^1/_2$ cup ice water

FILLING
2 pounds fresh figs or 1 pound dried, sliced
$^1/_2$ to $^2/_3$ cup sugar, to taste
Juice of 1 lemon
1 tablespoon grated lemon zest
Pinch of fennel seed
1 egg white
Whipped cream or mascarpone for serving

TO PREPARE THE PASTRY:

Put the flour, butter, salt, sugar, and cinnamon, if using, in the bowl of a food processor (or cut the butter into the flour with a pastry cutter or 2 knives). Pulse until the butter is the size of green peas. Add the egg yolk. Add the ice water, a little at a time, just until the dough is granular and moist but has *not* formed a ball. Turn the dough onto a floured board, piece of granite or marble, or other smooth surface, and with the heel of your hand, quickly distribute the butter throughout the dough in 2 or 3 movements. Form the dough into a flattened circle, wrap in wax paper, and put in a plastic bag in the refrigerator for 45 minutes to chill. The dough may be kept in the freezer for 6 weeks.

TO ASSEMBLE AND BAKE THE TART:

Put the fresh figs, sugar, lemon juice, zest, and fennel seed in a saucepan (if using dried figs, add 1 cup water as well) and cook over medium heat for 10 to 15 minutes, until most of the moisture has evaporated and the figs are shiny and syrupy. Let cool.

Preheat the oven to 425°F. On a lightly floured surface, roll out the dough to $^1/8$-inch thickness. Press the dough into a 9-inch tart pan, trim off the excess with a sharp knife, and prick the bottom all over with a fork. Line the dough with foil and fill with pie weights or dry beans.

Bake for 15 minutes, until the pie shell takes on a pale golden color. Remove from the oven and take out the pie weights. Brush the pie shell with egg white. Return to the oven and bake for another 5 minutes. Spread the cooled fig mixture evenly over the shell and bake for 20 to 30 minutes or until the crust is nicely browned. Cool and serve with whipped cream or mascarpone.

Crostata di Mela

. . . .

APPLE TART

Serves 4 to 6

Each trattoria serves its unique torta or crostata. In general, a crostata has a crust, below for sure and sometimes above in the form of a latticework, and a torta is considered a kind of cake, but a torta di ricotta, for example, might or might not have a crust. A torta might be made from toasted almonds, preserves, or jam, while some are simply a custard thick with candied fruits or nuts.

I like this simple apple crostata adapted from my tarte Tatin but eliminating labor-intensive puff pastry and adding fresh apricot purée to the tart apples. I freeze fresh Blenheim apricots in summer (if I can find them) so that I have them on hand for this tart, the Torta della Nonna o della Matrigna (page 270), or other recipes, such as a gelato (added to the basic gelato recipe, page 256), or simply to spoon over vanilla gelato.

I recipe Pasta Frolla (page 265)
I $^1/_2$ pounds fresh apricots, pitted, or I pound dried
$^3/_4$ cup plus I tablespoon sugar
4 tablespoons butter
4 large tart apples, peeled, cored, and sliced very thin (Granny Smith, Pippin, Fuji, or any tart
   apple, but not Delicious)
A few drops fresh lemon juice
Confectioners' sugar (optional)

Preheat the oven to 400°F. On a lightly floured surface, roll out the dough to $^1/8$-inch thickness. Press the dough into a 9-inch tart pan, trim off the excess with a sharp knife, and prick the bottom all over with a fork. Line the dough with foil and fill with pie weights or dry beans. Bake for 15 minutes, until the pie shell takes on a pale golden color. Remove from the oven and take out the pie weights. Return to the oven and bake for another 5 minutes, then remove and let cool.

Cook the fresh apricots in a saucepan with $^1/4$ cup of the sugar over medium heat until smooth and shiny, about 15 minutes. Push the mixture through a strainer or purée it in a food processor, let cool, and refrigerate for up to a week or so. If using dried apricots, barely cover the apricots with cold water. Stir in $^1/4$ cup sugar, bring to a simmer, and cook for 20 minutes. Let cool, then purée in a food processor. Refrigerate or freeze until needed.

Preheat the oven to 425°F. Melt the butter in a wide skillet over medium heat, add the apple slices, sprinkle with $^1/2$ cup of the remaining sugar, and cook until the apples begin to caramelize, 15 to 20 minutes. Cool. Spread the apples in the tart shell and spread a layer of the apricot purée over the apples. Sprinkle with lemon juice and the remaining tablespoon of sugar. Bake the tart for 10 minutes, then lower the heat to 350°F and continue baking for 25 to 30 minutes or until the apples and apricots are nicely caramelized and brown. Cool. If desired, dust with confectioners' sugar before serving.

Note: To make a simple apricot tart, spread the purée over a prebaked shell and bake again at 400°F for about 20 minutes.

Torta della Nonna o della Matrigna

. . . .

GRANDMOTHER'S OR STEPMOTHER'S TART

Serves 6

In typical Italian fashion, there are many recipes for this cake, although I've observed that pine nuts play a major part in most but not all. Some have two crusts, some do not; some are filled with pastry cream, some with custards; some use flour in the custards, and some do not.

Any dish named after the matriarch, in deference to the most hallowed position in the Italian family, requires the indisputable mark of each nonna on her torta, be it pine nuts, raisins or other fruit, custard with or without vanilla or flour, lemon or orange peel, or any other ingredient a sly grandmother (like mine) could surreptitiously slip into the mix and then innocently forget to mention when you ask for the recipe!

Being a special kind of nonna, I hold a place difficult to describe in the classic Italian family, but there appear to be more stepmothers than in earlier times, perhaps because even Italians have begun to change partners more frequently. In keeping with tradition, I have created my own *torta della matrigna* (not a nice word in Italian, but it's all I've got) to add to posterity.

1 recipe Pasta Frolla (page 265)
1 beaten egg white
1 cup almonds
A few grains of salt
4 tablespoons butter
$^2/_3$ cup sugar
1 teaspoon vanilla extract
1 tablespoon grated lemon, orange, or tangerine zest
4 eggs
$^1/_2$ cup apricot purée from Crostata di Mela (page 268)
$^1/_4$ cup pine nuts

Preheat the oven to 400°F. On a floured surface, roll out the dough to $^1/8$-inch thickness. Press the dough into a 9-inch tart pan, trim off the excess with a sharp knife, and prick the bottom all over with a fork. Line the dough with foil and fill with pie weights or dry beans. Bake for 15 minutes, until the pie shell takes on a pale golden color. Remove from the oven and take out the pie weights. Brush the pie shell with egg white. Brush the pie shell with egg white. Return to the oven and bake for another 5 minutes, then remove and let cool. Leave the oven on.

Place the almonds, salt, butter, $^1/2$ cup of the sugar, the vanilla, and the zest in the bowl of a food processor and grind to a paste. Transfer the paste to a mixing bowl and beat in the eggs one at a time by hand until the mixture is smooth.

Spread a thin layer of the apricot mixture over the bottom of the pie shell. Pour the custard into the pie shell and sprinkle the pine nuts and the remaining sugar over the top.

Bake the torta for 10 minutes. Lower the heat to 375°F and bake for 10 minutes more or until the custard is just set and the top is golden brown.

Variations:
For a lighter custard texture, but a little more work, separate the eggs. Combine the almonds, salt, sugar, vanilla, and zest, then add the egg yolks and mix well. In another bowl, beat the egg whites until stiff but not dry. Stir a little of the egg white mixture into the almond mixture to lighten it, then fold in the rest of the egg whites. Proceed as directed.

Add half the pine nuts to the almond and egg mixture, then use the rest for the top.

Tiramisù

· ·

Serves 4 to 6

Don't scoff at this familiar dessert, as it is one of the greats in Italian cooking even though its origin is still debated. (Some even think it originated here but Italians will contest this.) Tiramisù is often made incorrectly in restaurants—whipping cream is used in place of mascarpone or crème fraîche (a sacrilege), and too much Amaretto or other overpowering liqueur in place of a good Cognac. Tiramisù means "pick me up," and pick you up it does because of the coffee and chocolate.

1 package *savoiardi* (Italian ladyfingers) or, in a pinch, French champagne biscuits (practically the same thing)
$^1/_2$ cup very strong espresso
$^1/_4$ cup Cognac
4 large eggs, separated, whites beaten stiff but not dry
$^1/_2$ cup sugar
1 pound mascarpone or two 8-ounce cartons crème fraîche
$^1/_2$ cup unsweetened cocoa powder for dusting between the layers

Place one layer of ladyfingers in the bottom of an 8- to 10-inch glass dessert dish or bowl. Sprinkle the cookies with half the coffee and half the Cognac, wetting them evenly. They should not be entirely soaked.

With a wire whisk, beat the egg yolks and sugar until light yellow, add the mascarpone, and fold in the beaten egg whites, keeping as much air as possible in the mixture. Spread half of this over the ladyfingers, then dust liberally with cocoa. I use a kitchen saltshaker for my cocoa.

Add one more layer of ladyfingers, wet them well with coffee and Cognac (you may need a little more), then spread the rest of the mascarpone mixture over all. Dust again with cocoa, cover with plastic wrap, and refrigerate for at least 6 hours. This is good made in the morning and served at night.

· ·

To make crème fraîche: Stir $^1/_2$ cup buttermilk into 2 cups heavy cream. Let sit in a warm place overnight, covered, until thickened. Refrigerate.

Torta di Ricotta

. . . .

RICOTTA CAKE

Serves 6

This is another simple recipe from my husband's ex-wife, who got it from her cousin, who got it from her great grandmother. We always eat this at her special dinner parties, and she makes it for the children and grandchildren when they visit her, as I try to do in L.A. to make them feel at home. I like a small amount of lemon zest in most cheesecakes, but I have found that orange or tangerine zest is just as good and a lively change. Sour cream or crème fraîche (to make your own, see page 272) may be used in place of mascarpone.

$^2/_3$ cup sugar
5 eggs, separated
Pinch of salt
1 pound ricotta, or cottage cheese left out 8 hours or overnight to sour
2 tablespoons flour
$^1/_4$ **cup mascarpone or crème fraîche**
1 teaspoon baking powder
1 tablespoon grated lemon zest
Pinch of ground cinnamon
Confectioners' sugar for dusting

Preheat the oven to 350°F and butter a 9-inch springform pan.

Mix the sugar and egg yolks in a food processor. Add the salt, ricotta, flour, mascarpone, baking powder, lemon zest, and cinnamon and blend well. Whisk the egg whites until stiff but not dry and fold them gently into the cheese mixture. Turn the cheese mixture into the prepared pan and bake for 40 minutes or until golden brown and the center springs back when touched lightly. Let cool, turn out on a plate, dust with confectioners' sugar, and serve.

Cantucci, Tozzetti, o Mostaccioli

. . . .

BISCOTTI

Makes about 24 cookies

A biscotto is any cookie cooked twice, and there are so many varieties of biscotti in Italy that it's helpful to call regional ones by regional names. Hence the Roman version, *cantuccio,* which is also known as *tozzetto* or *mostacciolo,* the latter derived from the Latin *mustaceum,* a grape must (what is left after the juice has been extracted from the grapes in winemaking) from which the original dough was prepared.

My cantucci are rich with nuts, not hard or dry, and they won't break your teeth. They last for weeks in the freezer, and if they get a little soft, simply put them in a 350°F oven for a minute or two to crisp them up. Chances are this will not be your problem, because they disappear faster than you can make them. Crushed cantucci are also great beginnings for pie crust and budino fillings, not to mention sprinkled over any gelato.

8 tablespoons (1 stick) butter, softened

1 cup sugar

3 large eggs

$^1/_4$ cup fresh orange juice or sweet wine, such as a Malvasia or vin santo, plus a spoonful or two more
    if needed

1 teaspoon vanilla extract

3 cups unbleached all-purpose flour

2 teaspoons baking powder

$^1/_2$ teaspoon salt

1 cup chopped toasted almonds, walnuts, or pecans

1 tablespoon orange zest, chopped fine

Pinch of fennel or anise seed (optional)

Preheat the oven to 350°F. Butter a 13- by 17-inch baking sheet.

In the bowl of an electric mixer set on medium speed, cream the butter and sugar until light and fluffy. Add the eggs, one at a time, beating until blended. Add the orange juice or sweet wine and the vanilla and beat until smooth.

Sift together the flour, baking powder, and salt and add to the batter with the nuts, zest, and fennel seed, if using. Stir or beat on low speed until the dough is firm but malleable.

Divide the dough in half and transfer each half to the baking sheet. Shape each into a roll about 16 inches long and 3 inches wide. Flatten the rolls with the palm of your hand and then use 2 spatulas to square off the long sides to make each flattened roll about $3/4$ inch thick. Bake for 10 to 12 minutes or until slightly browned. Remove from the oven and cool on wire racks for about 15 minutes.

On a cutting surface, use a very sharp chef's knife (wide blade) to cut each roll into $1/2$-inch-wide slices. Lay the slices on the baking sheet, turning the cut side up. Bake for 7 to 9 minutes or until browned around the edges. Cool on wire racks. Serve immediately or store in an airtight container for up to 2 weeks. You may also wrap the cookies in foil and freeze for several months.

Variations:

Use orange juice, not wine, and add 4 ounces bittersweet chocolate, melted. Proceed as directed in recipe.

For a savory version, use only 1 teaspoon sugar and omit the orange juice. Add $2/3$ cup grated Gruyère, caciotta, or sharp Cheddar, $1/2$ teaspoon dry mustard, pecans instead of almonds, and a scant $1/2$ cup beer to make a stiff dough. Proceed as directed. This version is very good with drinks.

Use pistachios in place of other nuts and add $2/3$ cup dried, frozen, or cooked and drained fresh cranberries to the dough. These are especially pretty at holiday time.

Limoncello

LEMON LIQUEUR

Makes 2 liters

Often drunk after dinner as a digestive, limoncello became popular several years ago, and then suddenly every trattoria had its own version. It is normally too sweet for me, which is why I make my own.

The following recipe is from a good friend in Rome, who prefers to call her unique homemade brew by the lovely Sardinian name *limoncino*. Take off the zest with a Microplane or vegetable peeler and double this recipe, as limoncello makes great gifts. This recipe is also delicious and unusual when made with oranges or tangerines.

$2^{1}/_{2}$ pounds thick-skinned lemons, preferably Eureka
1 bottle 190-proof grain alcohol (Everclear, found through liquor dealers)
$1^{1}/_{3}$ cups sugar

Peel or grate the zest from all the lemons. Put the zest in a large glass container with a lid along with 3 cups Everclear. Close tightly and wait 1 month. Strain and remove the zest. Boil 4 cups water with the sugar, let cool, and add this mixture to the lemon mixture with the rest of the Everclear. Keep for 2 weeks before serving, then decant and store in the freezer or in the refrigerator indefinitely. Mine is used up fast! Good over vanilla ice cream or blended with lemon sorbetto to make *sgroppino* (page 259).

Variation:
If Everclear is not available in your area, two 750-milliliter bottles of 100-proof vodka can be substituted for the bottle of Everclear. Use only $1^{1}/_{4}$ cups of water to make the sugar syrup.

Limoncello

Restaurants, Bars, Food and Wine Shops, and Open Markets

RESTAURANTS

Al Gran Sasso *(closed Sat)*
Via Ripetta, 32 (Piazza del Popolo)
06.321.4883
A neighborhood place with no pretensions and gregarious owners. The daily specials are best.

Il Moro *(closed Sun)*
Vicolo delle Bollette, 13 (Trevi Fountain)
06.678.3495
It helps to be a regular here, but the cool atmosphere warms slightly when the very serious owner discovers your love of *la cucina romana.* Expensive and worth it. *Scampi alla Moro* and *spaghetti alla carbonara* are excellent.

Al Trentuno *(closed Sun)*
Via delle Carrozze, 31 (Piazza di Spagna)
06.678.6127
Our favorite trattoria for fresh mozzarella, pasta with artichokes, grilled lamb chops, and no-nonsense atmosphere. A very mixed crowd of local businesspeople and tourists.

Arancio d'Oro *(closed Mon)*
Via Monte d'Oro, 17 (Via Condotti)
06.686.5026
One of the three "orange" restaurants, as I have dubbed them, since all have *arancio* in their names (see Settimio all'Arancio and Piccolo Arancio). Lively atmosphere, excellent Roman fare with original menus at each, thanks to very attentive family members and three very talented and unusual chefs.

Checchino dal 1887 *(closed Mon)*
Via Monte Testaccio, 30
06.574.3816
One of Rome's oldest with classic Roman dishes: *saltimbocca, coda di bue alla vacinara, trippa alla romana,* and many others. Warm and welcoming, with boisterous waiters and attentive service.

Da Gino *(closed Sun)*
Vicolo Rosini, 4 (Parliament—Via di Campo Marzio)
06.687.3434
Gino, the owner, holds the honor of Cavaliere del Lavoro, similar to a knighthood, for being a successful businessman. The food will tell you why. Reservations a must. *Pasta e ceci* are memorable. Be sure to poke your head into the kitchen to thank the cook.

Dal Cordaro *(closed Sun and Mon)*
Piazzale Portuense, 4
06.583.6751
Giuliana, the cook, makes the best *coda di bue alla vacinara* and *cacio pepe* in Rome. An outdoor patio covered with grapes is lovely in spring and summer. A delight for lovers of *la cucina romana.*

Da Mario *(closed Sun)*
Via della Vite, 55 (Piazza di Spagna)
06.678.3818
Warm wooden-wainscoting interior, always filled with a lively crowd and many tourists as it is right in the center of Rome, like Nino down the street. Excellent game dishes. Priests and businessmen often eat here; therefore so do we, as they know the best!

Del Sostegno *(closed Mon)*
Via delle Colonnelle, 5 (Pantheon)
06.679.3842
A little jewel! Very small, reservations a must, an excellent cook, very good *vino sciolto,* and the sweetest people you will ever meet. Go for lunch, which is a bit less crowded.

Fiaschetteria Beltramme *(closed Sun)*
Via della Croce, 39 (Piazza di Spagna)
No phone, no reservations
Communal tables and reasonable prices make this tiny trattoria a good place to fraternize with strangers at table or eat quietly alone. Some days are better than others, but I wish we had more restaurants like this in L.A.

Gigetto al Portico d'Ottavia *(closed Mon)*
Via del Portico d'Ottavia, 21a (ghetto)
06.686.1105
Roman dishes at their best. Anyone who knows Rome knows Gigetto and takes friends and visitors for a not-to-be-missed Roman experience. Reservations a must.

Il Brillo Parlante *(closed Sun lunch)*
Via della Fontanella, 12 (Piazza del Popolo)
06.324.3334
I love the professional young couple who run this place (they had a good teacher—the young proprietor's father owns the Valadier, historically, first a convent, then a brothel, now a hotel, next door). It is our neighborhood trattoria with an eclectic crowd and extensive wine list. Downstairs the wood oven turns out excellent pizza. *Creativa* in a very good way and great for Sunday night pizza.

L'Ambasciata d'Abruzzo *(closed Sun)*
Via P. Tacchini, 26 (Parioli)
06.807.8256
A place to go with a group to taste all the wondrous dishes offered. Platters of antipasti come first—cheese, *salame,* prosciutto—then three or four *paste, secondi* of meat, chicken, or fish with *contorni,* if desired, and finally, trays of liqueurs with dessert and coffee. A long and rowdy evening you will love. Reservations a must.

La Campana *(closed Mon)*
Vicolo della Campana, 18 (Via della Scrofa)
06.686.7820
One of the oldest, most revered Roman trattorie for excellent pasta, the freshest fish, and the famous apple tart. The atmosphere is that of old Europe, when life was rich with time to spend enjoying courses and conversation. Engage the waiters (who have been there since the beginning) and learn something new about Roman food each visit.

Menu
Quello che se magna oggi

Rigatoni a ramatriciana
Tonnarelli ar Sarmone
Risotto ar gorgonzola
Bombolotti ar pomodoro e basilico
Ravioli ricotta e spinaci

Maiale ar forno
Vitello arrosto
Abbacchio ar scottadito
...etti con ...ghetta

Una trattoria Romana

Lucifero *(open 7 days—evening only)*
Via dei Cappellari, 28 (Campo de' Fiori)
06.688.05536
An engaging engineer runs this tiny, delightful *taverna,* as he calls it. I found the best pasta stuffed with artichokes I had ever tasted, and all the other dishes are equally extraordinary.

Nino *(closed Sun)*
Via Borgognona, 11 (Piazza di Spagna)
06.679.5676
One of the best. Excellent *pasta e ceci,* unusual pasta dishes, and the freshest of fish. Many tourists and regulars, such as Gore Vidal and friends, all mixed together. Go for the food, service, and convivial crowd.

Otello alla Concordia *(closed Sun)*
Via della Croce, 81 (Piazza di Spagna)
06.679.1178
The waiters and antipasto are worth the trip. Engaging, boisterous, and knowledgeable, the waiters run the show and have a piece of the action, which may be why they work so hard. The back room on Wednesdays is filled with show biz diners. Plain, simple food. No frills. Reservations needed for outside, but Romans sit inside.

Piccolo Arancio *(closed Sun)*
Via Scanderbeg, 112 (Trevi Fountain)
06.678.0766
Excellent, tiny trattoria near the Trevi Fountain. *Spaghetti all'aragosta* is easily enough for two, and the *vino sciolto* is one of the best in Rome, served from huge casks at the rear of the restaurant. Very welcoming owners and waiters.

Settimio all'Arancio *(closed Sun)*
Via dell'Arancio, 50 (Via Condotti)
06.687.6119
Another of our favorites for groups of people as the room for parties is relatively quiet. Prosciutto cut by hand by the owner, excellent mozzarella at all times, and original dishes such as *risotto al radicchio* and *farfalle ai fiori di zucchine.* These change daily with the whim of the cook.

Tullio *(closed Sun)*
Via San Nicola da Tolentino, 26 (Via Veneto)
06.481.8654
One of the old greats, frequented by businessmen (always a good sign) and regulars. Possibly the best mozzarella and prosciutto in town, along with extraordinary fish and shellfish, a very good house wine, and the famous Napoleon dessert, portions of which people reserve as they walk in!

BARS

Bar d'Angelo *(open Sun)*
Via della Croce, 30 (Piazza di Spagna)
06.678.2556
This *tavola calda* draws a crowd of neighbors, charming little old ladies on a shopping spree, and those who wish a quick meal: at least one pasta and risotto, tongue with green sauce, roast chicken, veal, or pork with potatoes, all sorts of vegetables, and of course, great gelato. The baristi are some of the most attractive in town, working nonstop all day, faster than an espresso machine!

Canova

Piazza del Popolo, 16
06.361.2231
On Piazza del Popolo, this lively, welcoming bar is my choice, as opposed to Rosati across the piazza, where the beautiful jet set hangs out. I love Canova because it was Fellini's favorite for his after-dinner coffee. People watching is at its best here.

Notegen

Via del Babuino, 159 (Piazza del Popolo—Piazza di Spagna)
06.320.0855
An informal and dependable neighborhood bar near the Piazza del Popolo where, as you sip your late-night espresso or Cognac, little whiffs of marijuana perfume the air, coming no doubt from the poetry readings frequently held downstairs.

Bar Scapi

Via della Croce, 80 (Piazza di Spagna)
06.678.3209
My tiny breakfast bar with a smiling barista and excellent rosette and tramezzini. A good place for a lesson in mayonnaise! Attentive, courtly owners from another era.

WINE SHOPS

Buccone

Via Ripetta, 19 (Piazza del Popolo)
06.362.2154
A large selection of wines and daily specials from everywhere. Succulent little plates of tapalike morsels at lunchtime, and a favorite for a taste of wine in the evening, served with nuts and little hors d'oeuvres by a very-serious-wine-buff manager.

Enoteca al Parlamento

Via dei Prefetti, 15
06.687.3446
An elegant wine shop. Wine may be tasted at a small counter with little tidbits to eat. A grand chocolate and candy section along with many specialty baskets and novelties for St. Valentine's, Christmas, and Easter.

FOOD SHOPS

Carilli (*the best mozzarella di bufala in Rome—fresh Mon, Wed, Fri, but call first*)
Via Torre Argentina, 11 (Largo Argentina, Pantheon)
06.6880.3789
Taste this mozzarella and you will know what to look for when you buy fresh mozzarella. Almost as fresh as at the farm. Beautiful handmade sausages and cured meats along with many cheeses, but a neighborhood place, very modest.

Castroni
Via Cola di Rienzo, 196 (Piazza Risorgimento, Vatican)
06.6830.1600
This is a gastronome's delight! Coffees, teas, grains, sweets, truffle oils, smoked salmon, exotic spices, even tortillas and Mexican specialties (which are not easy to come by in Rome), these are Castroni's best. And hundreds of items I had never encountered elsewhere in Italy.

Fabbi
Via della Croce, 27 (Piazza di Spagna)
06.679.0612
A small, perfect deli near our apartment that caters to those who live in the center and have been shopping there for eons. Tourists are received coolly by the owner (at the cashier), but he doesn't mind taking their money for excellent cured meats and cheeses, great pasta sauces to go, and myriad little specialty items such as tuna, capers, olives, and several hundred things one could take back as souvenirs for friends.

Franchi (*next door to Castroni*)
Via Cola di Rienzo, 204 (Piazza Risorgimento, Vatican)
06.6880.5869
A marvelous deli with take-out that sometimes equals any good trattoria, certainly as good as the best *tavola calda*. Eat here at tall tables for a quick lunch to break up a day of adding to your wardrobe on Rome's best shopping street. Then pick up vacuum-packed bottarga, guanciale, Parmesan, or a perfect picnic for the flight back home.

Rampicante

Olive oil Lemon Parmigino — Reggiano

SOURCES AND SEEDS

www.agferrari-foods.com Italian wines, oils, most products. Bay area stores.

www.chefshop.com Seattle based. I use this site often; very sophisticated, with an emphasis on Italy and France.

www.growitalian.com The website of the U.S. distributor for Franchi Sementi of Bergamo, Italy, which has been selling seeds to Italians since 1783; a tremendous selection of vegetable seeds, volume discounts, and a money-back guarantee.

www.italcont.com/ingegnoli/firstcat.htm An Italian website with a vast assortment of Italian vegetable seeds. You will have to trust the Italian mail, so buyer beware.

www.italianmade.com "The official site of the foods and wines of Italy."

www.kingarthurflour.com I love King Arthur flour, ingredients, and equipment.

www.nimanranch.com All pork products, including guanciale, lardo, casings for making sausage, great bacon, and suckling pigs.

www.shepherdseeds.com, now combined with **www.whiteflowerfarms.com.** Most of my vegetables and fruits, including fragoline, basil, Rampicante, and tomatoes, are grown from these seeds. Very dependable, fresh seeds.

www.surlatable.com I often teach at the sumptuous Santa Monica store. Enter at your own risk, with credit card handy.

www.vinegarman.com The guru of vinegar making.

Supermarkets in southern California: **www.gelsons.com; www.bristolfarms.com.** Nationwide: **www.wholefoods.com; www.wildoats.com; www.centralmarket.com.** As always, a Google search (www.google.com) on "Italian specialty foods" will turn up hundreds of entries. Most or all offer web commerce, and some may have stores in your area.

INDEX